ABDEL BARI ATWAN is a Palestinian writer and journalist. The former editor-in-chief of the London-based daily *al-Quds al-Arabi* for twenty-five years, he now edits the Rai al-Youm news website – the Arab world's first Huffington Post-style outlet. He is a frequent guest on radio and television, often appearing on the BBC's *Dateline London*. Atwan interviewed Osama bin Laden twice in the late 1990s and has cultivated uniquely well-placed sources from within the various branches of al-Qa'ida and other jihadi groups, including IS, over the last twenty years. His other books include *The Secret History of al-Qa'ida* and *After bin Laden: al-Qa'ida, the Next Generation*, as well as a memoir, *A Country of Words: A Palestinian Journey from the Refugee Camp to the Front Page*.

www.bariatwan.com

ALSO BY ABDEL BARI ATWAN

The Secret History of al-Qaʻida

After bin Laden: Al-Qaʻida, the Next Generation

A Country of Words: A Palestinian Journey
from the Refugee Camp to the Front Page

ISLAMIC STATE

THE DIGITAL CALIPHATE

ABDEL BARI ATWAN

SAQI

First published in 2015 by Saqi Books
This paperback edition published 2015

Copyright © Abdel Bari Atwan 2015

Abdel Bari Atwan has asserted his right under the Copyright, Designs
and Patents Act, 1988, to be identified as the author of this work.

ISBN 978-0-86356-134-4
eISBN 978-0-86356-101-6

A full CIP record for this book is available from the British Library.

Printed and bound by CPI Group (UK) Ltd, Croydon, CRO 4YY

Saqi Books
26 Westbourne Grove
London W2 5RH
www.saqibooks.co.uk

I dedicate this book to the souls of my parents, Zarifa and Mohamed Abu Atwan. It is my hope and belief that they would be very proud of this work if they were alive – though they never received the education that would have allowed them to read it.

CONTENTS

PREFACE

As this book goes into a new edition, I would like to offer the reader a few updates to set what follows in context.

First of all, despite a vigorous air campaign by a US-led coalition, Islamic State has continued to expand its territories and influence. In response, the international community has placed the destruction of Islamic State (IS) at the top of its security agenda and erstwhile enemies – the West, Russia, Iran and the rogue Syrian regime of Bashar al-Assad – seek to join forces to combat this most pernicious danger in the heart of the Middle East. This is a major development and comes as result of simultaneous diplomatic thrusts from Washington (which brought Iran back into the international community with the Nuclear Agreement and lifting of sanctions set for January 2016[1]) and Russia. London and Washington now accept Moscow's position that Assad has to be part of the solution to the IS problem, whereas before they were adamant he should go.

Western military interventions to date have been lamentable failures. Much mooted plans to recapture Mosul in spring/summer 2015 did not materialise and Washington's efforts to transform thousands of 'moderate' rebel fighters into crack troops to combat IS produced just 52 soldiers at a cost of $500 million. By September 2015, just four of these remained in action, the rest having surrendered their expensive vehicles and arms to the al-Nusra Front (an al-Qaʿida-linked offshoot of IS) to obtain safe passage.[2]

In June 2015, the US announced that its air strikes had killed 10,000 IS fighters in just nine months,[3] yet the group's capabilities remained undiminished. This strongly suggests it is more numerous than previously thought and several different sources indicate that it has at least 300,000 fighters.

In May 2015, the group overran the ancient Syrian city of Palmyra and Ramadi in Iraq. In September 2015, it captured Jazal, the last remaining Syrian oil field not under IS control. The Syrian regime controlled just one-sixth of the country by September 2015 while almost half of Iraq is now held by IS.[4]

Colleagues who have returned from visits to Syria and Iraq report that its territories are regarded as islands of relative stability – in that they are more likely to have electricity, clean water, affordable food and rudimentary (albeit draconian) law and order – amid region-wide turmoil. Some Syrian and Iraqi refugees have even sought shelter in IS controlled zones and inward-bound migration continues apace; a new phenomenon of entire families 'migrating' to IS from European countries has emerged with a French family of eleven, a family of twelve from Luton in the UK and three sisters and their nine children from Bradford all hitting the headlines in recent months. The population in the areas under IS control has increased from 8 million when I first wrote this book to between 10 to 12 million.[5]

It is now clear that the *modus operandi* whereby IS consolidates territory is by establishing *wilayats* (governates) in areas it has overrun or where it has sympathisers. These *wilayats* are semi-autonomous; they run their own local economies and have a strong military presence enabling IS to fight on many fronts at once. A system of local government is also more likely to win hearts and minds as opposed to a remote, centralised seat of power. The *wilayats* are used as 'lily pads', the eventual aim being to form contiguous swathes of land controlled by the group. IS has used this tactic effectively in Iraq and Syria; by September 2015 it maintained one or more *wilayats* in Libya, Algeria, Nigeria, Afghanistan, Yemen, Egypt, Turkey and Saudi Arabia.[6]

IS has continued to attack beyond its own territories and to strike European targets. In June 2015, to mark the first anniversary of the declaration of the caliphate, it launched simultaneous atrocities on three continents with a suicide bombing at a Shi'i mosque in Kuwait which killed 27, the massacre of 38 (mostly British) tourists on the beach in Sousse, Tunisia, and an attack by a lone wolf assailant on a gas factory near Lyon, France.

IS would like to make the holy cities of Mecca and Medina (in Saudi Arabia) the centrepiece of their 'caliphate'. The group has established a presence inside the Kingdom and has been able to breach its security: during the summer 2015 IS sleeper cells carried out several suicide bombings in Shi'i mosques in Saudi Arabia killing dozens of worshippers.[7]

The continued unrest in neighbouring Yemen, where Saudi Arabia (supported by the US and UK) first began bombing rebel Houthi targets in March 2015, presents a parallel threat to the Kingdom's safety. The Houthis are backed by Riyadh's foremost regional rival, Iran, and the air strikes have caused at least 7,000 civilian casualties, creating a virulent anti-Saudi movement on the ground.[8]

IS has been quick to exploit the opportunities offered by the absence of an effective central government in Sanaa. Yemen is already home to the most active remaining branch of al-Qa'ida which has pledged allegiance to Islamic State leader, Abu Bakr al-Baghdadi. Situated on the Arabian Peninsula, Yemen is of great strategic importance since whoever controls the impoverished country can threaten much of the world's oil traffic which passes through the Bab el-Mandeb Strait to the Red Sea and the Suez Canal.

Rather than seeking to collaborate with other powerful Jihadi-Salafist entities, IS has mounted direct challenges to al-Qa'ida and the Taliban. Potential IS rival al-Qa'ida has continued to diminish in size and importance with large numbers of fighters defecting to IS and leader Ayman al-Zawahiri looking increasingly irrelevant. Under pressure from IS leaders, the Taliban admitted in July 2015 that its leader, Mullah Omar, had been dead for more than two years. Several divisions within the Taliban then shifted allegiance to Baghdadi and IS now has a solid presence in Afghanistan.

As in Iraq, where former generals from Saddam Hussein's army and intelligence services joined forces with IS, sources confirm that IS is putting down strong roots in Libya with the help of military men who gained the knowledge and experience they are now sharing with the extremists under the command of the late Colonel Gaddafi.

IS continues to commit headline-grabbing atrocities. The destruction of ancient shrines and temples in the world heritage site at Palmyra and the beheading of its devoted 82 year-old custodian, archaeologist Khaled al-Asaad, drew collective gasps from around the world. In June 2015, following on from the graphically-filmed burning alive of Jordanian pilot Muath al-Kaseasbeh came the drowning of caged prisoners in a Mosul swimming pool with underwater cameras recording their death-throes. In August 2015, four Syrian prisoners were simultaneously roasted alive over log fires and the resulting video posted across jihadist social media platforms.

IS leader Baghdadi has kept a low profile, avoiding self-promotion or becoming the kind of figurehead whose demise would precipitate the implosion of the organisation – as was the case, in retrospect, with Osama bin Laden. There are rumours that he was seriously injured but even if he resigned or died, the core structure of IS is now well-established: Baghdadi has three deputies who are seasoned and experienced in the role and who could feasibly take over command of the group.

Well into its second year of existence, IS has turned Middle Eastern politics upside down. The former paradigm, whereby Saudi Arabia and the Sunni bloc maintained the balance of power against the Shi'i bloc headed by Iran, is no longer tenable. The refugee crisis which has seen 4.5 million Syrians flee their country – half heading for Europe – has increased the pressure on external powers to intervene.

Russia began a serious military build-up inside Syria in September 2015 with tank-landing ships arriving in Tartus (Moscow's only Mediterranean naval base) while an air base at Latakia now houses Russian fighter jets and anti-aircraft missiles. The latter are of little use against IS which has no air capability and suggest the Russians are intent on shoring up the Assad regime as well as confronting IS.

The danger now is that, rather than act in concert with the West against IS, Russia will attempt to exploit regional instability to extend its own influence (as it did in the Crimea). Such a scenario is reminiscent of the Soviet invasion of Afghanistan in 1979 which saw the West join forces with the mujahideen to oust it. While it is unlikely that London and Washington would work with IS it is not entirely impossible and reliable sources inform me that Washington has already opened communication channels with some jihadist groups in Syria, including al-Nusra. Nothing is certain in the Middle East these days.

London, September 2015

INTRODUCTION

On 1 July 2014, a twenty-minute audio recording by Islamic State's leader, Abu Bakr al-Baghdadi, was released across extremist websites and social media platforms. He declared a new caliphate and announced he would be its caliph.[1] In the speech, 'Caliph Ibrahim' outlined his vision for Islamic State, urging Muslims from around the world to migrate (make *hijra*) and to join it, 'because *hijra* to the land of Islam is obligatory'. He painted the embryonic state in rosy colours: 'where the Arab and non-Arab, the white man and black man, the easterner and westerner are all brothers... Their blood mixes and becomes one, under a single flag and goal.' Finally he announced plans for global expansion: 'This is my advice to you. If you hold to it, you will conquer Rome and own the world, if Allah wills.'[2]

Without digital technology it is highly unlikely that Islamic State would ever have come into existence, let alone been able to survive and expand. This is why I choose to describe the new entity as a 'digital caliphate'. Islamic State has been able to encompass a territory the size of Great Britain as a result of a perfect storm of political, historical, cultural and technological circumstances. From recruitment and propaganda, to directing simultaneous military actions at great distances apart and consolidating allegiances with like-minded groups, IS has used the internet and digital communications with great skill and inventiveness, competently fending off threats from global intelligence bodies and military opponents.

In January 2015, Islamic State declared 'cyber war' on the US government, with its 'Cyber Caliphate' division hacking into the

Pentagon's Central Command data and taking over its Twitter and YouTube accounts.[3] CentCom is the Pentagon division responsible for Middle East strategy and operations and the jihadists triumphantly disseminated sensitive information, including the names and addresses of military personnel. Soon, IS released further lists from hacked military databases in May and September 2015. 'Cloud' links to CentCom files were shared, quickly going viral across jihadist social media platforms where they were downloaded and archived. In June 2015, James Comey, the head of the FBI, admitted that 'we cannot restrain IS' online.[4]

It is paradoxical, of course, that a group whose expressed aim is to take the world back to the days of the 'Righteous Caliphs' (the first generations of Muslims) should be so dependent on the most sophisticated and modern technology; but in war people use every weapon at their disposal. Besides, its leaders and foot soldiers are twenty-first-century men – even the grey-bearded 'Caliph Ibrahim' himself was born in 1971. Most have never known a world without the internet and have been brought up with computers, mobile phones and social networking platforms as part of their natural environment.

Other extremist Islamist groups are apprised of Islamic State's 'successes' by digital means, and most have transferred their allegiance to Baghdadi. Where possible, allegiance is given in person, or via an intermediary, but, increasingly – for security reasons – electronically. In terms of audience, such groups can address hundreds of thousands, if not millions. Not only that, they acquire their own select audience; only those who are already interested for one reason or another will 'like' a Facebook Page, join a group on Ask.fm or 'follow' on Twitter. Conformity of message and a shared religious zeal are essential ingredients for expanding a caliphate, or indeed any state institution predicated on ideology. The internet allows millions of Muslims to stay 'on message' and hear the same sermons, view the same video messages, witness the same punishments, simultaneously.

Islamic State is the latest, most deadly, incarnation of the global jihad movement established by Osama bin Laden and Ayman al-Zawahiri in 1998. Yet the 'digital caliphate' is no mere virtual reality. It has a very real geographical, territorial presence. In traditional terms of politics and boundaries, can a 'state' be established in just a few months? German journalist Jürgen Todenhöfer, who spent ten days in the Islamic State in both Iraq and Syria, is categoric in his assessment that, 'We have to understand that ISIS is a country now.'[5]

What is a state?

Under International Law the criteria for statehood are relatively simple. The 1933 Montevideo Convention on the Rights and Duties of States concluded that there are two types of statehood: the 'declaratory' and the 'constitutive'. The former requires that, in order to declare itself a state, the entity must have a clearly defined territory, a permanent population and a government capable of exercising authority over the population, its territories and its resources. Montevideo also determined that declaratory statehood is independent of recognition by other states. Constitutive statehood, by contrast, requires recognition by existing states; but this has proved untenable, since there is no official international body with the authority to recognise states on behalf of the entire world community of states (the UN cannot do this). The authority exercised by government is generally accepted to include a judicial system and the capacity to engage in international relations with foreign states. The political or ideological tenets of a state are not prescribed, and at the moment our planet boasts democratic and theocratic states, dictatorships and kingdoms.

In September 2015, the Institute for the Study of War released new maps showing the extent of territory controlled by Islamic State. Despite ongoing bombardments by the US-led Alliance, it had continued to expand and now controlled more than one half of Syria and at least one third of Iraq.[6] It is difficult to quantify exactly its territory, because much of the area between the major towns and cities under its control is completely uninhabited. Nevertheless, even taking the most modest estimates, with Iraq's total territory at 437,000 square kilometres and Syria's at 186,500 square kilometres, Islamic State occupies well over 200,000 square kilometres. By way of comparison, the whole of the UK (including Northern Ireland) is only 40,000 square kilometres bigger. The population under Islamic State control currently numbers at least six million – larger than many European countries, including Denmark and Finland. Colleagues on the ground have recently reported an increase in 'reverse migration', whereby Syrians fleeing the regime have taken refuge inside Islamic State territories and this has boosted the number of citizens.

The Islamic State has its own army and sophisticated weapons, seized from regime stockpiles in both Iraq and Syria. It has in all probability used mustard gas in Syria, according to several reports.[7] In October 2014, Islamic State announced online that it had struck its own coinage, reviving the silver and golden dinars of the First Caliphate, and that this is now the official currency of the 'state'. In January 2015, it opened its own bank in Mosul, offering Islamic loans (it is *haram*, sinful, to charge interest) and a facility for exchanging damaged notes. It also has its own car number plates, police force with brand new, freshly painted police cars and its own uniform, and flag.

Although it may at some point in the future seek international recognition (as did the Taliban) Islamic State is unlikely to be particularly concerned with the demands and principles of international law, believing that its moment has come. The Salafists (who adhere to the earliest versions of Islam) have a vision of history that sees a period of ignorance (*Jahiliyyah*) followed by an Islamic stage. They believe that the world has been in a state of ignorance from which it can only emerge through three steps: faith (Salafist Islam); *hijra* (the migration of Muslims from 'infidel' countries to communities of the faithful); and jihad (struggle to establish an Islamic state for the *ummah*, or nation). All Islamic State propaganda focuses on these three stages. The migration of large numbers of foreign fighters to join its cause is a crucial aspect of its online PR and recruitment material. Online videos often show joyful new arrivals burning their passports. The jihad stage has been under way for the best part of two decades, and Baghdadi and his followers are clearly convinced that the momentum for re-establishing the caliphate is now unstoppable. This is why they have confidently declared an Islamic State (although rival organisations such as al-Qa'ida believed the declaration was premature).

The term 'Islamic State' will be used in this book (unless persons quoted or interviewed have used a different one) because it is the name by which the group identifies itself.

Opposition and support

As Osama bin Laden did before him, Islamic State's leader, Abu Bakr al-Baghdadi, is actively, mockingly, inviting the West to intervene. Sixty nations have joined the US in a nominal Alliance against the Islamic State, but none dares to put troops on the ground. This leaves Kurdish militias to battle IS alone in oil-rich northern Iraq while, in Syria, both the regime and the moderate opposition are battling the extremists. Ongoing air strikes have had limited impact and they risk killing more civilians than jihadists, potentially escalating recruitment to Islamic State.

The nightmare scenario for the West is that diverse global jihadist groups in the Middle East, Africa and Asia web up and act together under the IS banner. Blowback from battle-hardened jihadists returning to their adopted Western homelands after training and fighting for IS is another security concern as foreigners flood, in unprecedented numbers, to join Islamic State and produce its next generation.

With most of the world's media carrying an agenda with regard to IS – whether the conservative Arab nations' campaign against it or Islamic State's own increasingly slick proselytising – it is difficult to get any sort of true picture of public opinion. Four surveys that were carried out in the Middle East between October 2014 and March 2015 suggested that as many as 42 million Muslims supported – or at least did not oppose – IS.[8] In recent travels throughout the Middle East, I have talked to hundreds of people, from 'ordinary' men on the street to government officials and top politicians. I have also engaged in online conversations with everyone from key players to 'ordinary' residents within Islamic State. Arab governments are, without exception, entirely opposed to Islamic State, from whom they have much to fear. Among the people, however, my impression is that opinion is polarised. The liberal middle classes are violently opposed to a fundamentalist group that seeks to restrict their freedoms and impose the burqa on their women; for the first time there is widespread support among this class for a Western military intervention to prevent the further expansion, and ultimately destroy, Islamic State (many I spoke to had previously demonstrated against Western actions in Afghanistan, Iraq and Libya). Where there is sympathy, on the other hand, it is characterised by vigorous enthusiasm and appears to be more widespread than support for al-Qa'ida, even in its heyday. The fact that Islamic State has taken territory and declared a caliphate reawakens the common Arab dream of a return to the 'Golden Age' and the unity of the *ummah* (worldwide Muslim nation). Members of a third group are more guarded about their opinions but, one surmises, secretly celebrate the 'achievements' of Islamic State. If it were it to come to a town near them, I deduce they would not oppose it – this category I call the 'ideological sleeper cell'.

My own study of Islamic State, and of the circumstances that gave rise to it, goes back many years. In 1996 I spent seventy-two hours in the company of Osama bin Laden in his Tora Bora cave complex. The experience prompted me to investigate and observe the jihadist phenomenon in depth. I was editor-in-chief of the London-based pan-Arab independent newspaper *al-Quds al-Arabi* for twenty-five years. I now run an independent online newspaper, Rai al-Youm, which aims to supply objective news. Articles about Islamic State attract up to ten times the readership of any others – particularly from the Gulf States – and generate hundreds of comments, most of them expressing positive views of Islamic State. Through this experience, and as a result of regular travels throughout the Middle East, I believe I have developed an unusually strong, if not unique, network of contacts, sources and correspondents. Many are extremely close to the leadership of al-Qa'ida and Islamic State. I have drawn on these extensively in the writing of this book. I ask the reader to be understanding if in the course of it I prove unwilling to give names or even precise dates or places. This is entirely to protect these people from very real danger.

ONE

MASTERS OF THE DIGITAL UNIVERSE

Islamic State could never have achieved its territorial ambitions, nor could it have recruited such a large army in so short a time, without its mastery of the internet.

Al-Qa'ida was the first major jihadist network to sense the potential of the worldwide web, using its darker recesses in a covert manner to share ideology, information, plans and correspondence. Its younger operatives also launched early cyber attacks on 'enemy' websites, presaging the emergence of the 'cyber jihad' that is raging today.

Today, Islamic State and its supporters use the internet and social networking platforms in a brazen, overt way, marketing their 'brand' and disseminating their material via mainstream networks such as Twitter. For those already in the territories of Islamic State, as much as for potential recruits on their laptops in a thousand bedrooms across the globe, concealing identity and location remains a priority. But there are myriad ways this can be done. Advice on the wide range of 'anonymity products' available online is freely available for those who seek it – much of this advice is produced by Islamic State recruiters for the would-be jihadist. Those who fail to ensure their online anonymity are those we see detained and prosecuted. Sadly, this is only a tiny minority.

Most Islamic State commanders and recruits are tech-savvy; coding (writing software programs, inputting information in html) is as familiar to them as their mother tongue. Most of the digital caliphate's business is conducted online, from recruitment and propaganda to battlefield strategy and instruction. What the jihadists lack in the way of sophisticated weaponry they more than make up for with their online expertise.

The range, quality and availability of today's digital equipment, such as HD cameras, editing software, special effects libraries and so on, enable Islamic State's professional media teams to produce the slick and gruesome high-definition videos and 'glossy' online magazines for which they have become infamous.

The digital generation

Most people who participate in, or are attracted to, Islamic State are in their late teens and early twenties. Researchers have shown that, among this age range in the developed world, 89 per cent are active online, 70 per cent use social networks daily and each spends an average 19.2 hours a week on the internet.[1] The jihadists are no exception and may spend even more time on their laptops, tablets and smart phones, since their output across social media platforms is vital to maintaining the digital health of their project.

The paradoxical clash between advanced twenty-first-century technology and the Salafist-jihadist interpretation of Islam, which espouses the values of life in the seventh century, ceased to be a topic for heated debate among extremist ideologues and clerics when the potential of the internet was fully realised. The Taliban smashed televisions in the 1990s, but al-Qa'ida led the way online with email lists being used to disseminate information as early as 1995. Encrypted communications were used to orchestrate all al-Qa'ida's major attacks from the 1998 embassy bombings in Nairobi and Dar-es-Salaam on, and Osama bin Laden's organisation had its first website up and running by 2000. The Taliban followed suit soon after. By 2003, 'cyber jihad' was cited as one of al-Qa'ida's widely circulated 'Thirty-nine Principles of Jihad'.

Al-Qa'ida attempted to free itself from its dependence on mainstream media exposure by starting its own online news service, 'The Voice of the Caliphate', in 2005. At that time, however, there was no obvious way to disseminate its content, apart from among a small pool of subscribers. It continued to rely on television channels such as Al Jazeera for the wide exposure it sought for videos featuring bin Laden's increasingly empty threats, and for the ultra-violent Abu Musab al-Zarqawi, who would become al-Qa'ida's *emir* in Iraq. Zarqawi pioneered the tactic of recording every successful attack on Coalition targets in Iraq on digital video, complete with cries of 'Allahu Akbar' ('God is Great') and a soundtrack of the rather beautiful, stirring *Nasheeds*. (These Islamic hymns are specifically written for the purpose of praise, adoration or prayer, and are typically addressed to a deity or to a prominent figure.) YouTube, which was launched in 2005, provided the perfect forum for these videos, as well as for the filmed posthumous 'wills and testaments' of suicide bombers, which could be uploaded anonymously.

The problem of dissemination remained, however. Even on YouTube, the potential viewer would need either to have been informed about a video's existence, or to have conducted an almost intuitive search. Anwar al-Awlaki, a US-born, youthful cleric prominent in al-Qa'ida-offshoot AQAP (al-Qa'ida in the Arabian Peninsula), was the first to suggest exploiting social networking platforms to spread jihadist material more widely and reach new recruitment pools. The so-called 'bin Laden of the Internet' created his own blog, Facebook page and YouTube channel, and used them to distribute the online magazine *Inspire*, which included recipes for bomb-making and increasingly sophisticated films. Awlaki's over-confident use of social media platforms almost certainly led to his death from a US drone attack in Yemen in September 2011. Facebook use in particular was very easy to track at that time, as it did not accommodate anonymous operating systems such as TOR (see below).

Islamic State's internet strategy has taken Awlaki's innovations one step further. In the past, the leadership would produce and release material; now, every jihadist is his or her own media outlet, reporting live from the frontline in tweets, offering enticing visions of domestic bliss via short films and images posted to JustPaste. it and Instagram, entering into friendly conversations via Skype, messaging on anonymous Android platforms, and posting links to the group's propaganda material and its infamous catalogue of videos. All of this output is systematically retweeted and, by clever use of hashtags, generates a huge audience.

Islamic State has made a point of recruiting IT specialists and those with online marketing experience. As a result, its social media activists are well versed in the most effective 'brand sharing' strategies – except its brand is death. One very effective method is to hijack 'Twitter storms': the activists include high-trending hashtags in their own tweets, which then include a link to Islamic State material hosted on an anonymous, unpoliced platform such as JustPaste.it. In August 2014, for example, IS activists included Scottish Independence hashtags, such as #VoteNo and #VoteYes, in their tweets during the run-up to the referendum. Trending celebrity stories are also exploited in this manner. People searching for #LewisHamiltonGrandPrix in November 2014 received, instead, a link to an Islamic State video showing child soldiers training with Kalashnikovs. Activists realise that material has to be widely distributed in as short a time as possible, and uploaded to 'safe' archiving platforms, before YouTube, Facebook and Twitter administrators are alerted and remove both material and their accounts.

Islamic State's recruitment machine is largely online. In the course of researching this book we communicated in a variety of ways with young men and women who had either joined, or were considering joining, Islamic State. In Islamic countries, initial approaches were more often made via an intermediary or recruiter but, in the West, most said they had either direct messaged someone via Twitter or Facebook, or had been contacted by a friend, relative or acquaintance already inside Islamic State, to initiate their own 'migration' and to receive practical advice and logistical instructions. After the initial contact has been made, anonymous smart phone instant messaging platforms such as Kik and WhatsApp are used to deepen the contact. These are completely unpoliced and unregulated. The former, with 14 million users, appears to be largely used for pornography and drug dealing – it is easy for jihadists to hide here. Skype, the internet telephone system, is another favourite means of communication, allowing 'real time' reporting by jihadists, and dialogue between recruiters and potential recruits. It is encrypted and can be used in conjunction with so-called 'dark internet' service providers and anonymous operating systems, of which more below. Secret discussions, via messaging or telephone applications, conducted via a laptop or smart phone in a teenager's bedroom, are extremely difficult for parents and the authorities to police, which makes these digital devices perfect recruiting instruments.

Twitter and Facebook profiles are also used to 'cyber stalk' and to identify and locate 'enemies'. Military personnel, politicians and journalists are particularly at risk; many have not taken even the most basic security precautions to conceal their work and home addresses, their daily schedule, where their children go to school and so on.

The jihadists have their own community of web developers who pool their knowledge and developments, producing online resources such as 'Technical Mujahid Magazine', a training manual for jihadists released every two months. Extremists have developed their own, closely guarded version of Facebook – Muslimbook – and Islamic State recently launched a mobile phone app: 'Dawn of Glad Tidings' updates users on IS's news and uses their Twitter accounts to automatically disseminate information and reach potential funders.[2]

Islamic State has also produced its own video game, hijacking and modifying the extremely popular 'Grand Theft Auto', which it has re-named 'Salil al-Sawarem' (Clashing of Swords). The game takes place in terrain resembling that of northern Iraq; players can ambush and kill American soldiers, or plant improvised explosive devices (IEDs) which blow up military vehicles transporting groups of Western soldiers to shouts of 'Allahu Akbar' ('God is Great').

Information hub

IS realises that it has to keep pace with the internet generation in order to remain relevant. Thousands of Twitter accounts, RSS feeds (a form of automatic digital distribution) and messaging networks provide a constant stream of battle reports and news about life in Islamic State. Thus they keep potential recruits and supporters engaged, and counteract the propaganda efforts of the enemy and 'bad news' such as the loss of Kobani in early February 2015. Although most online material is still in Arabic, English is fast catching up and a lot of Arabic material that is considered important is subtitled in English. Much material is also available in many other languages, including Russian, Urdu and Chinese. After all, the jihadist network is now more or less global.

The relentless stream of information from the extremists is also used to build up the image of Islamic State as an emotionally attractive place where people 'belong', where everyone is a 'brother' or 'sister'. A kind of slang, melding adaptations or shortenings of Islamic terms with street language, is evolving among the English-language fraternity on social media platforms in an attempt to create a 'jihadi cool'. A jolly home life is portrayed via Instagram images where fighters play with fluffy kittens and jihadist 'poster-girls' proudly display the dishes they have created. These 'Muslimas' also tweet about domestic concerns or the absence of decent clothing: 'Honestly we need some professional dressmakers for sister in Islamic State' tweeted one young woman, @UmmMariAndaluciya.

The jihadists' social media output also works hard to maintain a consistency of message, reminding the network that the enemy is the apostate and *kufr* (denier) who must convert or die. The menace is often embellished with a quote from the Qur'an. A recurrent thread upholds a mindset where the desire for martyrdom is normalised and death is sought and celebrated. This is the jihadists' most potent weapon. A soldier who does not fear death is an invincible enemy, and close-up photos of dead fighters' smiling faces are frequently posted across all platforms. The Islamic State 'salute' – the index finger of the right hand pointing heavenward – reflects this ideology. The female jihadist holder of one Twitter account I investigated had posted a shocking photograph as 'wallpaper': two little boys, presumably her own, aged around four and six are dressed in black and masked; they are dwarfed by the Kalashnikov rifles supported by their left hands while their right hand index fingers point to the sky. On 3 February 2015, one female resident of Islamic State, Al-Britaniya (British), shared 'glad tidings' via Twitter: 'My husband Rahimuh Allah has done the best transaction you can make his soul [sic] and in return Jenna [heaven] may Allah accept you yaa shaheed [martyr].' Five hours earlier she had posted a picture of a bowl of cream desert with bits of Toblerone chocolate stuck on top.

The head of the Islamic State's media department is Ahmed Abousamra, a Syrian who was born in 1981 in France and then brought up in Massachusetts where his father is a well-known endocrinologist. He obtained a degree in IT and worked in telecommunications before becoming self-radicalised; he encountered no obstacles in relocating to Aleppo in 2011 thanks to his dual Syrian-American nationality. Under Abousamra's direction are several media organisations with full-time staff, the main ones being al-Hayat, al-Furqan and al-Itisam. These are solely for the purposes of propaganda. Al-Hayat was formed in May 2104 and its operations offices are based in Syria. Iraqi al-Furqan, originally the media mouthpiece of the Islamic State of Iraq (ISI), has been going since 2006. Al-Itisam is a film production unit, based in Syria and responsible for most of the slick, high-production-value videos al-Hayat disseminates.

It employs professional journalists, film-makers, photographers and editors (who must swear allegiance to Caliph Ibrahim as part of their contract) and has brought in cutting-edge technology and qualified operators. As a result, its film output is of a quality more usually associated with national broadcasters or even Hollywood. A slick recruitment video titled 'What are you waiting for?' features attractive youths with dramatic long black hair, including a Frenchman with blue eyes. Al-Hayat releases regular short, snappy films called 'MujaTweets' which show scenes of daily life among the mujahideen. One, shot during Ramadan in a large canteen where a cook ladles stew into bowls, shows fighters breaking their fast with local children, laughing and joking; another shows fighters helping an old Kurdish lady, abandoned by her family, on to the back of a moped to be taken to other relatives; a seventy-year-old white-haired fighter is interviewed in another, 'Why Did You Come to Jihad, Uncle?', which has become a great hit on YouTube.

Al-Furqan has produced whole television series glorifying Islamic State's achievements and deeds, including 'Messages from the Land of Epic Battles' and 'Flames of War'. They feature IS fighters, many of them foreign, in the midst of fierce battles. Its most infamous productions show increasingly barbaric executions designed to terrify enemies and the world at large with horrifying, unforgettable images: a small young boy personally executes adult hostages; a fighter holds up two severed heads; a woman is stoned to death; an old man alleged to be a paedophile is tipped off a white plastic chair from the top of a high building; and in February 2015 came the repellent, high production-value video of a captured Jordanian pilot, Moaz al-Kasasbeh, being burned alive in a cage.

The latter was disseminated within seconds of being released, enabling me to trace the method by which it reached hundreds of thousands of people and all the media outlets. First, operatives tweeted that something was going to happen and recommended followers set up several duplicate accounts in case of suspension. Next came links to copies of the film on JustPaste.it (this anonymous message board, run by a twenty-six-year-old Pole, has become an integral part of Islamic State's media machine) and its Arabic equivalents Nasher.me and Manbar.me, among many other anonymous platforms. These were tweeted with messages urging followers to retweet widely and for 'people with hi-speed connections' to download and 'archive' the film either on anonymous 'clouds' or 'mirrored' websites (whereby the content of a known jihadist website is reproduced, or mirrored, on hundreds of others under different names and identities). However fast the authorities removed Twitter accounts and sites that were hosting the film it remained, and remains, available. The same is true of the files the group 'Cyber Caliphate' managed to download when it hacked the US Army's Central Command accounts in January 2015, of which more below.

The murder of al-Kasasbeh immediately divided the followers of Twitter accounts I was monitoring. Some expressed horror and sadness and said this had nothing to do with Islam; others revelled in the cruelty, with one account holder, Faris al-Britani, chillingly tweeting 'Burn baby Burn!!! Starring "best scream" award winner Moaz al Kassasbeh.'

Islamic State also runs its own radio station, al-Bayan, which is based in Mosul, and a satellite TV station, Tawheed, based in Libya. In January 2015 a trailer announced the imminent arrival of a twenty-four-hour internet television channel, The Islamic Caliphate Broadcast, to be hosted on one of the group's websites, KalifaLive.info. The channel will host a series of videos by John Cantlie, the British photojournalist kidnapped by ISIS in November 2012, along with James Foley who was subsequently executed. Cantlie has appeared in eight Islamic State propaganda videos to date, a cause of much debate and speculation.[3]

The group's websites also contain or link to a huge archive of ideological treatises, monthly reports, sermons, Qur'anic interpretations, *fatwas*, magazines, training manuals, and guidance on issues such as how to treat 'slaves' or life for women in the Islamic State.

Security matters

'You are engaging in war tactics so that you can spread the true *dawaa* and discuss matters of jihad, to uncover news about your mujahid brothers, to dismiss lies. You are entering into a sort of psychological warfare with them, they do not take it lightly, and we do not take it lightly. Therefore, we can trick them and it is

totally permissible...' So begins the welcome on a website called
alkalifat.com that aims to keep cyber-jihadists up to date with
security developments.

Islamic State's activists are able to be brazen online because they
understand security issues and keep one step ahead of government
agencies and service providers seeking to close them down. I have
been able to put together the following overview of how the
more canny activists and fighters navigate and exploit the internet
without fear of detection.

Key to anonymity are the 'virtual private networks' (VPN) that
conceal the user's IP address and instead create a false location in
another country, usually in the middle of nowhere. Ghost VPN
is one such program and is particularly effective when used in
conjunction with an anonymous browser such as Third Party
Onion Routing (TOR), which was initially developed for US Navy
intelligence and remains the most effective product. TOR conceals
the user's location by sending his or her internet signal through
nodes in dozens of different countries; it also enables the user to
access the so-called 'dark internet', the anonymous zone of criminals
and child pornographers. The recommended combination for
maximum security, according to alkalifat.com, is Ghost VPN with
an operating system called The Amnesic Incognito Live System
(TAILS), which boots from an exterior source – a CD or flash-
drive for example – and therefore leaves no trace of activity on
the computer hard drive. TAILS has TOR pre-installed, enables
multiple desktops, and can be switched off instantly if the user fears
detection. TAILS also has a suite of cryptographic tools for files,
email and instant messaging. With these security features in place,
and provided the user does not make a basic mistake and betray
his or her real identity voluntarily (by checking personal email or
Facebook, for example), it is possible to remain entirely anonymous
and conduct a false, untraceable, online life with a series of aliases
inhabiting social media platforms. Twitter is TOR compatible and
Facebook recently enabled it too.

Once equipped with VPN/TAILS, the cyber-jihadist can

subscribe to a (free) encrypted email service via bitmessage.ch; this system sends an email that is encrypted (turned into an unintelligible code which can only be unlocked by someone with the key) to the intended recipient, who is given the key – but also to hundreds of other random accounts, which do not have the key and so are unable to read the email. Anyone spying on the sender would never be able to deduce which was the real, intended, recipient. The bitmessage email account is also used to establish and maintain social media accounts under aliases and enables anonymous communication, via direct messaging, from Twitter and Facebook. This is how jihadists are able to conduct their social media networking, overtly communicating the most extremist material with impunity. Jihadists do use open-source, decentralised, software-based networking platforms such as Diaspora and Friendica, but these are not useful for 'outreach' to the pool of potential recruits surfing the public information highways.

When operators are alerted to extremist accounts and material they take it down. In the US, the State Department's intelligence unit oversaw the removal of 45,000 items in 2014, while a specialist department within Britain's Metropolitan Police takes measures to delete around 1,100 items a week. Speaking to the *Guardian* newspaper, 'Hamid', an online cheerleader for Islamic State, admitted that having a well-established Twitter account with thousands of followers removed is 'a disaster... but we have to be patient'. 'Hamid' warned his followers not to give up, and tweeted 'Be ashamed if you worry about your account being deleted when there are other people willing to sacrifice themselves for their religion.'

Like criminal gangs, jihadists need to be able to send and receive funds without security services being tipped off or spotting online transfers. They use 'cryptocurrency': bitcoins and dogecoins, internet money 'mining' systems that are popular with the underworld because they are bought in complete anonymity and their movements are untraceable. Recently available 'stored value credit cards' are another godsend to the underworld, forming part of another anonymous, untraceable, method of transferring funds.

It works like this: the sender loads the amount they wish to transfer on a stored value card; next he or she buys a prepaid, unregistered, disposable mobile phone with cash; next they register online with a mobile-payment service provider, using an anonymous, free email account, the number of the disposable mobile phone and the money on the stored value credit card. Using the mobile phone, they log on to the 'm-payment' account and give the number of the mobile phone to which funds are to be transferred. This will also be a disposable, non-registered phone. The recipient then requests the transfer of funds to his or her own, anonymous and untraceable stored value card and that can, in turn, be used to withdraw cash from an ATM, after which both phones and cards are thrown away.

Mobile phones are an important part of the required communications arsenal, but until recently were notoriously easy to pinpoint when in use. Disposable phones become traceable after time if they become part of a communications network that is under surveillance. A new Android phone, nicknamed the 'Snowden Phone' (after Edward Snowden, the IT professional and whistle-blower who leaked classified information from the US National Security Agency to the media in 2013) is proving popular in the Islamic State, sent in from the West by jihadists' friends and contacts. The phone can change numbers on demand and uses 128-bit encryption, VPN and cryptocurrency to conceal all mobile footprints; it can be used for Skype, messaging, social media and all other internet activities with minimum risk of its user being traced. TOR has also developed a system that can be used with mobile phones in conjunction with TAILS; the phone's memory is automatically erased as soon as the user removes the external booting device so no trace of activity remains. ChatSecure is the instant messaging platform of choice for the anonymous phone user. It runs through TOR and messages are encrypted.

Cyber jihad

In January 2015, Islamic State dominated world headlines yet again through a group of 'black hat' (i.e., maliciously destructive) hackers calling themselves the 'Cyber Caliphate'. They took control of the social media platforms run by the US government's Central Command (CentCom), which oversees military operations in Iraq and Syria. The authorities were quick to say that no harm had been done, but immediately rendered this claim implausible by offering the explanation that the hackers had simply 'guessed the password' – the preceding section on the many available layers of encryption and other security precautions should make the unlikelihood of this obvious. On CentCom's YouTube platform, the hackers discovered files that contained personal details of hundreds of US military personnel who were either veterans of, or currently deployed in, the Middle East. Clearly this greatly compromised their personal safety and that of their families. The files were swiftly disseminated and duplicated on to 'mirror sites' and stored in anonymous archive clouds. It *could* have been worse – the hackers did not manage to get into the main information handling system or the organisation's websites – but it was a declaration of 'cyber jihad' with the American military.

The Cyber Caliphate had built up a solid presence on Twitter in the run-up to the attack, with 110,000 followers – a very large amount for extremist accounts, which are usually shut down before they achieve such numbers. The account featured as wallpaper and 'gravatar' (a kind of trademark image) a man's head entirely masked by a black-and-white keffiyeh (headscarf). At the time of writing (February 2015) the account had been deleted and there was no active account for group. That is not to say that they have ceased their activities; they have simply changed identity in the anonymous world of cyber space.

In February 2015, the French Minister of the Interior, Bernard Cazeneuve, revealed that, since the previous month's *Charlie Hebdo* atrocities, the country had been hit by 25,000 cyber attacks by at least twenty-seven hacker groups claiming allegiance to Islamic State. French cyber defence chief Admiral Arnaud Coustillière told a press conference that this was 'the first time that a country has been faced with such a large wave'.[4] Most of the attacks, on targets ranging from tourism pages to military defence websites, resulted in denial of service (DoS), which clogs a site with traffic and renders it unusable. There are no reports that any of the attacks resulted in data theft, but viruses may have been left and nearly all affected sites were left displaying pro-Islamic State messages on their homepages. Many of the hacker groups were based in North Africa and the Sahel, and warned that another, more devastating wave of attacks would follow, targeting higher-level organisations.

There is some speculation that another, very active, group of black hat hackers calling themselves The Lizard Squad are linked to Islamic State. On 25 January they hijacked the website of ill-fated Malaysia Airlines, who lost one plane and had another crash in 2014. For several hours the homepage displayed the words 'ISIS Will prevail' and '404 – Plane Not Found: Hacked by Cyber Caliphate' over an image of a Malaysia Airlines plane in flight.

Islamic State's most likely 'cyber *emir*' – and almost certainly the man behind the CentCom hack – is a UK citizen, twenty-one-year-old Junaid Hussain (aka Abu Hussain al-Britani) from Birmingham. Hussain spent six months in jail in 2012 for hacking into the personal Gmail account of former British Prime Minister Tony Blair's special advisor Katy Kay. He obtained the emails and phone numbers of the Blair family members and of various MPs and House of Lords members, then posted them on various social media platforms across the internet. Hussain led a gang of teenage hackers called 'Team Poison' which also blocked a police anti-terror hotline by bombarding it with more than 100 prank calls. Undergraduate Hussain was on bail following separate allegations regarding a violent disorder offence when he evaded surveillance and fled to Syria, where he joined ISIS in 2013.

Apart from crashing websites, experienced and inventive hackers like Hussain can use their skills to intercept real-time battle information, giving Islamic State's fighters and commanders an obvious advantage and opportunities for ambush. Less tech-savvy fighters in rival opposition groups, militias (such as the Kurdish PKK) and even Iraqi and Syrian state forces, rely on digital, hackable, means to communicate battle plans, the location of protected supply routes, ammunition requirements and strategy. In addition, phones, screens and laptops not using TAILS will also reveal records of previous emails, messaging and Skype calls.

Islamic State hackers have also taken to laying cunning cyber traps for their opponents away from the battlefield. In Raqqa, one of the group's Syrian strongholds, a grass-roots organisation called 'Raqqa is Being Slaughtered Silently' (RSS) set up a website to highlight human rights abuses perpetrated by Islamic State and to document the hardships of daily life under their interpretation of Sharia. Posing as a group of Syrians in exile in Canada, Islamic State hackers sent RSS an email expressing support and thanks 'for your efforts to deliver a true picture of the reality of life in Raqqa'. They told RSS that they were sending them the first draft of a news report they were preparing in order for them to comment and amend if necessary. The document contained images and, being a large file, was stored on a file-sharing site: links were provided in the email. On opening the link, RSS activists found the report and some satellite images of Raqqa, but while they were viewing the files malware files were secretly downloading into their system with one very simple purpose: to obtain the IP addresses of members of the network. Anybody who had worked on or visited the site would be vulnerable because their IP address, stored in the system, can often reveal the actual location of the computer being used. As a result of this 'sting', members of RSS were attacked by Islamic State 'police'; houses were raided, two were kidnapped and tortured and at least one was murdered.

A similar ruse sees the extremists setting up fake websites purporting to be against them in order to identify their enemies. When the visitor to the site clicks on a link, malware is downloaded to their system and their IP address obtained.

Hacking can be a useful source of funds, too. Without a fraud squad to bother them, cybernauts in Islamic State are having a field day hacking unsuspecting retail sites in the West from which they can extract thousands of credit card details. These can then be used to charge pre-paid, anonymous credit cards (discussed above) enabling the hackers to withdraw large sums in cash from ATMs. Although other systems can be hacked, hackers are aware that Windows XP's security protocol has not been updated because it is now obsolete – yet this is the operating system many retailers are still using. Despite showing the locked padlock symbol indicating that a Secure Socket Layer (SSL) is in place, the system can be infected with malware that can initiate a Random Access Memory (RAM) scraper attack that downloads all the data in the targeted system to the hacker's computer.

Islamic State's friends abroad are also exploiting the opportunities the internet affords them. The 'Tunisian Cyber Army' and al-Qa'ida's 'Electronic Army' have both launched successful cyber raids on US targets including Customs and Border Protection and the Office of Personnel Management. Boko Haram produced a hacker who obtained from the Nigerian Secret Service's digital records the personal details of sixty spies, which were then published online.[5]

Governments appear relatively powerless to confront these attacks. Most social media platforms will voluntarily delete obviously extremist content and many have a fast-track system for government agencies reporting it (Twitter, apparently, does not);[6] but there are political sensibilities around issues of free speech and privacy, and, crucially, very real technical obstacles.

To date, the most effective cyber-retaliation on Islamic State for the murderous January 2015 Paris attacks (on satirical magazine *Charlie Hebdo* and a kosher supermarket) has come from an unlikely source – the veteran anarchist hacking collective Anonymous. Anonymous declared war on IS in January 2015 by means of a dramatic video[7] and swiftly followed with the destruction by DoS attack of an extremist website, ansar-alhaqq.com. Anonymous also started a Twitter campaign #OpCharlie; paradoxically, the group reports that Twitter administrators have twice deleted their burgeoning following on @OpCharlie handles. #OpCharlie has leaked a list of Islamic State recruiters and go-betweens the group uncovered on JustPaste.it and it has acquired more than 900 links to IS-linked accounts, websites and assorted online material, which it then hacks or denounces to service providers.

In October 2013 a group of countries opposing Islamic State formed an informal US-led 'technical' coalition to combat its cyber activities. The coalition includes Britain, France, Egypt, Saudi Arabia and the UAE, but has little to show for its efforts. International cooperation is impeded by legislation, bureaucracy and, quite simply, lack of knowledge and experience. The serious curtailment of internet usage proposed by more draconian regimes does not sit well with the more liberal Western countries and, as many security analysts have pointed out, much of what they actually know about extremist groups has been gleaned from online sources.

The digital caliphate's young warriors are certainly working on, and may soon discover, ways to compromise the military superiority its opponents enjoy – if they learn how to hack the control systems of drones, for example, or jam communications between the Alliance's commanders and pilots. The battle in cyber-space is not going the way of governments. It is one that Islamic State, and other outlaw agencies, can continue to dominate, so long as the world's most tech-savvy youth – who hold the key to the codes required for effective cyber-warfare – do not want to fight in the same trench as the authorities.

TWO

THE ORIGINS – PART ONE: IRAQ

In April 2003 the newspaper I was editing, *al-Quds al-Arabi*, received a fax from Saddam Hussein, who was then in hiding. The US believed that the Second Gulf War was over. Saddam knew that the real war would be one of insurgency, and that it was about to begin. He urged the Iraqi people to rise up against the American occupiers. But something else struck me as very significant at the time – this faxed message (and others we received until the beginning of June) was full of Qur'anic quotations and references as well as jihadist rhetoric. Saddam's intuition had told him that political, radical Islam would provide the cohesion necessary for the insurgency to be effective.

At this moment the seed that would eventually produce Islamic State was planted. Its germination, however, had begun years before.

Until 1990, Saddam Hussein's Iraq had enjoyed a robust economy that provided its people with education and health care systems that were envied throughout the region. It was no democracy, however, and the dictator and the ruling Ba'ath party had ruthless ways of maintaining control. Even so, Kurds, Shi'i and Sunnis lived relatively harmoniously, side by side; mixed marriages were commonplace.

When Iraq invaded Kuwait in August 1990, America tried to engineer a regime change. Saddam was not ousted by an indigenous uprising or coup, as the West had expected, and the international community – led by the US – proceeded to inflict what was, in effect, collective punishment on the whole nation. During the 1991 First Gulf War, 200,000 Iraqis lost their lives. Then, in April

1991, UN Resolution 687 imposed an almost total embargo on goods entering or leaving the country. These measures were to prove the most severe of the twentieth century. As Luiz Martinez points out in *The Violence of Petro-Dollar Regimes,* 'Not even the Treaty of Versailles went as far. Certainly, the victors of World War 1 amputated German territory, forced the vanquished to pay reparations, bridled its military power, but nothing prevented Germany from re-establishing normal trade relations and rebuilding its infrastructure.'

The embargo included materials necessary to provide clean water and electricity; the UN insisted that even basic medication and foodstuffs should be blocked, on the basis that they could be used to manufacture chemical weapons. Half a million children under the age of five were among the 1.7 million Iraqis who lost their lives as a direct result of sanctions, which endured, in one form or another, until the US-led invasion of 2003, which would itself claim a further 1.4 million Iraqi lives. In addition, the US and UK continued to bomb Iraq between 1999 and 2001, in response to violations of air space and anti-aircraft fire from Saddam Hussein's forces.[1]

Saddam Hussein himself, hitherto a defiantly secular leader, realised that Islam could become a rallying cry against the West. At the height of sanctions he launched a 'Faith Campaign' supervised by his deputy, Izzat al-Douri. Reversing his former stance, this made Islam not only part of the national identity (and his own personality cult) but also firmly linked it to international politics, the region's rising tide of anti-Western sentiment and, crucially, military prowess.

In 2001, Saddam inaugurated the astonishing 'Mother of All Battles' mosque, the latest in a string of enormous religious edifices. It boasted eight minarets, all of them in the shape of weapons: four represented the barrels of AK-47 assault rifles, the remainder, Scud missiles. The mosque also housed a dramatic and alarming artefact: the Qur'an written out by hand in three pints of Saddam's own blood, which had been extracted by his doctor over a period of two years.

Political Islam was not new. It had existed in Iraq since the 1940s. In that decade, a branch of the Muslim Brotherhood called 'the Islamic Brotherhood Society' was formed under the leadership of Sheikh Mohammad Mahmoud al-Sawwaf and Sheikh Amjad al-Zahawi. Its members became engaged mostly in social welfare work and outreach. In 1960, the more overtly political Iraqi Islamic Party (IIP) was established. In 1968 the Ba'ath party seized power, with Saddam Hussein at its head, imposing a mixture of Arab-centred socialism and Arab nationalism. Muslim Brotherhood and IIP members were persecuted; those who did not flee the country were arrested and, in some cases, executed.

At the beginning of the twenty-first century Saddam's viewpoint changed. He realised that, with the decline of pan-Arabism, political Islam was emerging as a new, radical, unifying force across the region. As the threat of a further US invasion loomed, Saddam saw in Islam a key to the formation of a cohesive resistance. Clerics went on the public payroll; he ordered his army commanders to become practising Muslims.

Now Saddam tolerated the presence of a small jihadist enclave near the border with Iran. Controlled by the movement Ansar al-Islam ('Helpers of Islam'), it imposed Sharia law on towns and villages under its control. Unbeknown to Saddam, al-Qa'ida had sent some of its own operatives into this enclave. They were instructed to make valuable connections with the newly Islamised army commanders from Saddam's brigades. Following Saddam's fall from power, these regular Iraqi Army personnel would become absolutely crucial to the success of the insurgency and, later, the Islamic State. They brought to the table real experience of the front line (having fought a bitter, seven-year war with Iran, followed three years later by the First Gulf War). They also offered practical and strategic expertise that would later be exported to other al-Qa'ida branches, first in Afghanistan and then in Syria.

Saddam Hussein's Iraq

Until the end of the 1980s, Washington had maintained largely cordial relations with Baghdad. The two countries were united in their concerns about the burgeoning strength of the Islamic Republic that had taken power in Iran following the 1979 revolution that ousted the Shah. In September 1980, the US backed Saddam in all-out war against Iran. The war would last nearly eight years, cost a million Iraqi lives and put the country $100 billion in debt.

Saddam was undeniably a ruthless dictator. His worst atrocities were committed in the 1980s; they included the murder of more than 180,000 Kurds in a campaign code-named *al-Arfal*. Saddam used chemical weapons in his attacks on forty Kurdish towns and villages, including an infamous attack on Halabja in 1988 – but neither the US nor the UK took him to task for these genocidal crimes against humanity. Instead, the US doubled its financial aid to the country that year and the UK's Export Credits Guarantee Department underwrote a loan worth $300 million in today's money. Saddam was an indispensable ally in the region's balance of power, particularly in relation to Iran.

When the war with Iran ended in August 1988, Iraq was financially and physically ruined. Paradoxically, Saddam and his army had become stronger, more experienced and finely tuned. The US started to reflect that a highly militarised Iraq under the unpredictable Saddam could threaten America's regional interests. While not yet confronting him, Washington was recalibrating its perception of Saddam, finding in him not an ally but a monster of its own creation, in possession of chemical weapons and harbouring nuclear ambitions. This posed an enormous threat to the security and regional military supremacy of Israel.

Following the devastating war with Iran, Iraq desperately needed its oil revenues to repair its infrastructure and facilitate economic recovery. Iraq possesses the third largest oil reserves in the Middle East (after Saudi Arabia and Iran) with 300 billion barrels. Oil prices, however, were tumbling owing to over-supply from Saudi

Arabia and neighbouring Kuwait (it is possible to infer a conspiracy here, since the US were intent on weakening Saddam's Iraq). The final straw came when Iraq suspected Kuwait of using new slant-drilling technology to take oil from Iraqi oil fields. Considering Kuwait to be historically part of Iraq (the British had artificially divided the two in 1922) and requiring easy access to the sea for shipping, Saddam began to weigh up the possibility of annexing the tiny kingdom. At this point he decided to consult his 'allies', sending a diplomatic delegation to meet the US Ambassador in Baghdad, April Glasbie. Glasbie informed them that the US would 'take no position' on border disputes. Saddam took this as a green light and invaded in August 1990.

The arrival of half a million US troops in Saudi Arabia just weeks later therefore came as somewhat of a surprise. US President George Bush, urged on by British Prime Minister Margaret Thatcher, rebuffed all calls for a diplomatic solution – from Congress, from the international community and from Iraq itself – and launched Operation Desert Storm on 16 January 1991. Right at the beginning a ferocious aerial bombardment destroyed what was left of Iraq's infrastructure; this was followed by a ground war in late February, forcing a humiliating Iraqi retreat from Kuwait and sowing the seeds of enduring hatred for America in many Iraqi hearts. That hatred was intensified by the introduction of devastating sanctions for the next twelve years, the impact of which is recorded above.

Despite the virtual destruction of Iraq, Saddam remained firmly in control. There was no hoped-for coup or revolution. The US and UK were more determined than ever to effect regime change in Baghdad. Saddam had crossed red lines where Israel was concerned, launching missiles in its direction during the First Gulf War and agitating on the international stage in support of the Palestinians during the Second Intifada, which erupted in September 2000. He backed up this verbal support with action, giving $1 billion in food and medical aid to Palestine and $10,000 to the families of each martyr. He also (somewhat hyperbolically) threatened to organise and train a seven-million-strong 'Jerusalem Liberation Army' to fight alongside the Palestinians.

Perhaps what finally tipped the balance and galvanised the West into an invasion was Saddam's use of oil as a potent political weapon against Israel. In April 2002 he announced that Iraq would cease all oil exports, 'for a period of thirty days or until the Zionist entity's armed forces have unconditionally withdrawn'. At that time, despite the enmity that ensued following the First Gulf War, 40 per cent of Iraq's two million barrels per day was being exported to the US.

The removal of Saddam Hussein

In the period leading up to the Second Gulf War, fantastic claims were made that Saddam Hussein was encouraging al-Qa'ida to enter the country to help him fight the Americans. The speculation was based on Saddam's 'Faith Campaign', his politicisation of Islam and the fact he tolerated the emirate run by Ansar al-Islam in Northern Iraq. Some even suggested that he was in cahoots with bin Laden. Nothing could have been further from the truth. In separate interviews in 1996 and 2000, bin Laden and Saddam Hussein both told me how vigorously they disliked each other. While it is true that there were some al-Qa'ida operatives in Iraq from 2001 onwards, they were there without Saddam's knowledge.

Yet the Allies had two cards they could play to gain international assent for an invasion: Saddam's alleged arsenal of Weapons of Mass Destruction (WMDs) and his supposed involvement with al-Qa'ida (especially in the aftermath of 9/11).

As we now know, there were no WMDs; they had all been destroyed or degraded after the First Gulf War or during the sanctions era. Successive visits through the 1990s by the specially constituted UNSCOM – which the Security Council charged with locating and dismantling Saddam's biological and chemical weapons – were unable to find anything. The International Atomic Energy

Agency (IAEA) also dispatched inspections teams throughout the decade, with a similar lack of results. Nevertheless, the UN's chief weapons inspector, Hans Blix, headed several teams searching for Iraq's elusive WMDs in the run-up to the invasion in March 2003. Hans Blix told the UK's Iraq Enquiry in 2010 that it was his 'firm view' that the war against Iraq was unfounded and 'illegal'.[2]

In 2004, I shared a debating platform in Europe with a former high-ranking US general, who had been directly involved in strategic planning for the Second Gulf War. He told me that there had been two schools of thought within the Bush administration: one wanted to allow the UN weapons inspectors to be allowed to finish their job, the other wanted to go for an immediate, all-out invasion. The former had lost, the general informed me, because if it were proved (and it looked increasingly likely that it would be) that Saddam had no WMDs, sanctions would have to be lifted immediately and Saddam would emerge from the whole experience as a great hero of the Arab world.

Having discarded a plan whereby troops would swiftly occupy Baghdad while a team of commandos would locate and assassinate Saddam and his immediate entourage, the US strategists decided instead to occupy Iraq, dismantle its army and state institutions and let it start from scratch – according to the American model of democracy and with a new constitution. Naturally, any new regime would also have to be willing to share the nation's oil with its Western 'partners' after 'liberation'.

The required number of votes in favour of a military intervention was not achieved in the UN Security Council (only Spain and Bulgaria voted with the UK and US). Regardless of that fact, Washington decided to go ahead and invade. London agreed.

The Second Gulf War opened with 'Operation Shock and Awe' on 19 March 2003. This was a third attempt at regime change in oil-rich Iraq and, once again, the entire country was to pay for it.

As before, a devastating air strike was followed by a ground invasion and the 'Coalition of the Willing' troops met with surprisingly little resistance – final proof of just how little threat

Saddam Hussein really did present to the world. Baghdad fell on 9 April and, on 1 May, George W. Bush (son of George Bush senior, who had presided over the first assault on Iraq) declared the 'end of major hostilities'.

All the elements that would later form the insurgency lay low to begin with. They knew that taking on the world's most sophisticated and powerful military power was a non-starter. The largest contingents would be Ba'ath party members, officers and troops from Saddam's defeated armies, Salafi-jihadists, including Kurdish groups in the north and, increasingly, al-Qa'ida.

Saddam had already made plans for an insurgency. In the months before the invasion he had sent messengers to buy small parcels of land from Sunni farmers. Under cover of darkness, soldiers would bury arms and money for later use by the resistance.

Foreign Salafi-jihadists enter Iraq

Saddam Hussein had stamped out the Muslim Brotherhood early on in his regime. Since the 1980s there had been several Sunni jihadist groups in Iraq, but these were based inside semi-autonomous Kurdistan in the north of the country, near the borders with Iran and Turkey. They were opposed to Saddam and the Ba'ath regime; Ansar al-Islam emerged from these isolated groups in 2001, headed by Mullah Krikar. When I met him in Norway in 2005, he told me that he had met Osama bin Laden, but denied that the al-Qa'ida boss had helped them in any way.[3]

Ansar al-Islam imposed a strict Salafi lifestyle on the ten villages it had in its enclave – that is, a return to the practices of the earliest Muslim generations. The independent organisation Human Rights Watch (HRW) reported that 'On September 8, 2001, one week after it came into being, Jund al-Islam issued decrees, including: the obligatory closure of offices and businesses during prayer time and enforced attendance by workers and proprietors at the mosque during those times; the veiling of women by wearing the traditional 'abaya; obligatory beards for men; segregation of the sexes; barring women from education and employment; the removal of any photographs of women on packaged goods brought into the region; the confiscation of musical instruments and the banning of music both in public and private; and the banning of satellite receivers and televisions'.[4]

In December 2001 the US bombed al-Qaʿidaʾs mountain stronghold in Tora Bora, Afghanistan, in retribution for 9 /11. As a consequence, hundreds of al-Qaʿida men, and 'Afghan-Arabs' who had fought with the Taliban, made the long trip across Iran to find a refuge with Ansar al-Islam; in addition, al-Qaʿida had earlier sent a small advance party of 300 fighters (according to the London-based Saudi Islamic scholar Saad al-Faqih) which established itself in the Sunni triangle between Baghdad and Mosul. 'Migration' (hijra) continued for the next eighteen months and, in the run-up to the Coalition invasion, thousands of jihadists from different countries arrived in Iraq, mainly locating themselves in the Ansar al-Islam enclave. In a pattern that had now become familiar in jihadist strategy, the new arrivals were careful to remain inconspicuous, patiently awaiting their hour.

In 2002, a very significant figure had arrived in the Ansar al-Islam mini emirate, quickly starting to establish his own camp. The Jordanian jihadist Abu Musab al-Zarqawi had been lying low in Iran after the 2001 Tora Bora bombardment, but he was expelled from that country in April or May 2002 after a sleeper cell linked to him was discovered in Germany. Zarqawi would later become the emir of al-Qaʿida in Iraq, but at this time he was acting independently of Osama bin Ladenʾs organisation.

His independent streak had first asserted itself in Afghanistan where he set up his own camp, with the Talibanʾs blessing, in Herat in the west of Afghanistan – this was as far away from al-Qaʿidaʾs operations in Jalalabad and Kandahar as he could manage. The reason Zarqawi chose Herat is of significance to the evolution of the Islamic State: he was facilitating the entry of foreign recruits via Iran. His camp accommodated just 100 fighters, mostly Syrians,

Palestinians and Jordanians who had been living in Europe. He named his group al-Tawhid wal Jihad ('Monotheism and Jihad') and, when they migrated to Iraq, it would become synonymous with the first headline-grabbing suicide attacks in that country.

Certain that an American invasion was imminent, Zarqawi started to construct local support networks within the Sunni triangle. Al-Qa'ida's advance party had adopted the same tactic, which suggests either that they were working in tandem or that Zarqawi was intuitively on the same wavelength as the al-Qa'ida leadership.

Another factor is of great relevance to the rise of the Islamic State: Zarqawi travelled widely, determining the best entry points for jihadists arriving from abroad, and deciding on the Syrian border as the most 'porous'. Al-Tawhid wal Jihad quickly became the 'go to' organisation for fighters seeking to join the imminent jihad. Zarqawi's group had already established contacts and a logistical infrastructure. The group also had a well-developed intelligence gathering capability, enabling co-ordinated attacks on 'high value' targets – something that would prove invaluable once the insurgency got under way.

As the US invasion began, Zarqawi met with 'Mohammad Ibrahim Makkawi' (one of Saif al-Adel's many aliases), al-Qa'ida's military strategist, agreeing to help al-Qa'ida recruits enter Iraq via Syria. By the autumn of 2003 Zarqawi had already established himself as the *emir* of foreign jihadists in Iraq, but he remained independent of al-Qa'ida for another year.

Breeding resentment

In terms of public relations in Iraq, the Americans were their own worst enemy. Partly because of the US President's rhetoric, many Muslims, and not necessarily extremists, saw what was happening in religious terms: the Christian 'Crusaders' invading Muslim lands. The conventional war lasted less than six weeks. There was little resistance as tons of explosives, cluster bombs and even napalm laid waste to Baghdad, Basra, Kirkuk and Mosul. American television sanitised its broadcasts, emphasising the political narrative whereby the despotic Saddam was being replaced by democracy and freedom, and ignoring the blood and guts reality of the 'Shock and Awe' bombardment. Modest estimates put Iraqi civilian deaths at around 7,400, with 45,000 Iraqi soldiers killed or injured. American casualties were just 141.

Having successfully deposed Saddam Hussein, the US-led Coalition was unable to usher in the new era of freedom and democracy it had promised. From the outset the political process was dominated by the Shi'i majority, with Sunnis increasingly marginalised. A US-brokered Government of Unity, led by Nouri al-Maliki (who had been at the helm since 2006), fell apart in December 2011. The day after the US withdrew all its troops from Iraq and left it to its fate, Tariq al-Hashemi, a leading Sunni politician, was arrested on trumped-up 'terrorism' charges. The Sunni bloc immediately announced a boycott of parliament and the cabinet. With the Arab Spring raging across the region, mass demonstrations erupted across the Sunni regions, and in the capital, Baghdad. A Sunni anti-government protest camp in Hawija, near oil-rich Kirkuk (now in the hands of the Kurds) was attacked by government troops in April 2013, killing fifty and wounding hundreds. By July 2013, the country was in the grip of a bitter sectarian war.

Al-Maliki's government set the wrecking ball in motion. Notoriously self-interested and corrupt, his regime saw the nation's wealth, and the foreign aid it received, squandered and abused by a small elite. Since 2010, the anti-corruption campaigning organisation Transparency International has been ranking countries by 'their perceived level of corruption', where corruption is defined as 'the misuse of public power for private benefit'. In 2010, Iraq was rated the fourth most corrupt government in the world (out of 177 countries); in 2011 and 2012, it was the eighth and, in 2013, seventh.

These, then, are the roots of the chaos and sectarianism that are pulling Iraq apart. IS is provided with fertile territory as a disgruntled Sunni minority grasps for any hand that offers salvation.

In the so-called 'blueprint' for post-war Iraq, drawn up by the US and Britain and adopted by UN Resolution 1483 on 22 May 2003, the allies described themselves as 'occupying powers', a term that was an anathema to the proud Iraqi people. To add insult to injury, they also took over all administration of Iraq's oil industry and revenues. The rationale was that these billions would be needed to restore Iraq's infrastructure (that the allies had destroyed); the reality was that Western companies largely benefitted from these lucrative contracts, while the multinational oil conglomerates were already prowling around such tantalising prey.

There is another aspect to the intended privatisation of the Iraqi oil industry: the West believed that if the third largest reserves in the Middle East were managed outside OPEC, it would break the power of the cartel and the stranglehold they had on the West in terms of pricing and supply of oil. As we have seen, Saddam had already used the state-run oil industry to create pressure on the West over Palestine when he stopped exporting oil for a month in 2002 in support of the Intifada.

The US sent a pro-consul to Iraq to administer the formation of an interim governing entity and oversee the establishment of a democratic infrastructure and constitution. The first incumbent of the euphemistically titled post Director of the Office for Reconstruction and Humanitarian Assistance was General Jay Garner, who was removed from office in May 2003 for doing exactly what he was meant to be doing: prioritising elections and self-rule. The US was not ready to relinquish the reins of power just yet, labouring under the illusion that a strong, popular and pro-US leader would be identified and promoted. Garner was replaced by the aggressive and ill-mannered Paul Bremer, and the post redesignated with the more honest (if colonial) moniker 'Governor of Iraq'. Bremer told the BBC's David Frost in June 2003, 'We dominate the scene and we will continue to impose our will on this country.'[5] Osama bin Laden famously offered '10,000 grams of gold to whoever manages to kill the occupier, Bremer'.[6]

Meanwhile, in a July 2003 press conference, the man who had been appointed Deputy Prime Minister, Ahmad Chalabi, thanked the Americans 'on behalf of the Iraqi people... for helping us liberate ourselves from the scourge of Saddam Hussein'.[7] Chalabi had been living in London where he chaired the Iraqi National Congress, a 'government in exile' that received $97 million in funds from Washington. Chalabi has been accused of grand corruption, including allegedly receiving a payment of $1 million for 'information' about Saddam's WMDs – information that was presented as justification for the invasion of Iraq. Chalabi was also once sentenced to twenty-two years in jail for his role in a $200 million banking scandal in Jordan.[8]

The interim administration, headed by Bremer, enshrined in law the privatisation of all Iraq's state-owned industries, including the petroleum industry.[9] At the same time, a law prohibiting unionisation, imposed by Saddam, was retained on the statute books, preventing possible trouble from the newly revived Iraqi Oil Workers' Union.

The Pentagon took advice from Israel on how to manage its new Occupied Territories. The results were remarkably similar to the collective punishments and brutal treatment of the Palestinians regularly meted out by the Israel Defence Forces (IDF). In the aftermath of insurgency operations Iraqi villagers found their orchards uprooted, while civilian homes were raided and bulldozed by US troops. Paradoxically, the occupying forces were behaving exactly in the manner they had castigated the former dictator for adopting.

Evidence of the humiliation and mistreatment of Iraq prisoners in US and British-run jails – particularly in the notorious Abu Ghraib facility – first began to appear in May 2003. Graphic pictures of hooded victims being given electric shocks, naked prisoners being hounded by barking dogs, and first-hand accounts of rape and sexual humiliation were posted online.[10] The British were no better. Baha Mousa, a hotel receptionist, was ruled to have been killed as a result of 'inhumane treatment' by UK soldiers in September 2003; another was allegedly kicked to death in an RAF helicopter; and two others died after being held for questioning.

In 2010, the *Guardian* newspaper revealed that even several years after the death of Mousa, which caused world-wide public outrage, the British continued training interrogators in abusive, humiliating techniques that breach the Geneva Conventions. The UK ran its own version of Abu Ghraib in a shadowy facility near Basra run by the 'Joint Forces Interrogation Team'. In a joint court action in 2010, 200 ex-detainees described how they were starved, sexually humiliated by women soldiers, given electric shocks, forced to kneel in stressful positions for days and deprived of sleep. In December 2014, a Senate report confirmed the very worst excesses of the CIA torture machine in graphic detail with descriptions of 'rectal re-hydration' (anal rape with a water hose, causing prolapse and lasting internal damage) and water-boarding among many other horrors.[11]

With the rise of social media, these images and reports – first published in the Western media – were widely shared throughout the Arab world, stoking rage and hatred towards the West in general and the US and UK in particular.

All of this feeds into the mass psyche in Iraq. The Iraqis are extremely proud people; as if the occupation of their country were not enough, they now had to contend with the murder, torture, abuse and humiliation of their jailed compatriots, who had been imprisoned without charges or the prospect of a fair trial. When the US ended combat operations in September 2010, they handed over 10,000 Iraqi prisoners to the Iraqi authorities.

The Maliki regime, which lasted 2006–2014, was as corrupt as any Middle Eastern dictatorship; pro-Iran, and openly prejudiced against the Sunni minority, it not only reopened sectarian wounds but allowed them to fester.

In retrospect, I believe that Washington and London had a game plan for post-invasion Iraq that was being prepared well

before 2003. Neo-conservative Defence Department strategists
Paul Wolfowitz and Douglas Feith were communicating their
vision for the future to selected individuals in Iraq as well as to Iraqi
exiles. This focused on determining sectarian and ethnic identities
and promoting the advantages of a loosely federal system. Perhaps
there was a deliberate plan to disarm and fragment Iraq in order to
eliminate the threat such a large, oil-rich country could offer both
Israel and US regional hegemony. Now Iraq has an army that runs
away at the first sign of trouble. And when its politicians talk openly
of the tragic, imminent division of their country into three distinct
parts, no dissenting voices are heard from Washington or London.

The insurgency

The first act of violence marking the beginning of the insurgency
occurred on 1 May 2003 – the same day that George W. Bush
announced the end of 'major combat' – when seven US soldiers
were injured in a hand-grenade attack on their base in Fallujah.[12]

Al-Qa'ida chief Osama bin Laden had been anticipating new
opportunities for al-Qa'ida in the inevitable chaos that would
follow the US invasion, and he was swift to mobilise his men. Al-
Qa'ida at this time was much diminished. Those who survived the
US attack on its Tora Bora hideout had fled to different countries
and al-Qa'ida central was virtually non-existent. However, by 8
April 2003, Osama bin Laden was urging jihadists already in Iraq
to start a campaign of suicide bombings: 'Do not be afraid of their
tanks,' he urged them. 'These are artificial things. If you start suicide
attacks, you will see the fear of the Americans all over the world.'[13]

From the outset, the insurgency was composed of several
completely different groups. There were the indigenous, secular
rebels: up to 50,000 Ba'athists, ex-Iraqi Army officers and men, ex-
members of Saddam's security forces, and citizens. Then there were
seven major Sunni Islamist groups, with Zarqawi's al-Tahwid wal
Jihad dominating proceedings.

Initially there were five Shi'i resistance groups. However, all but the leading group, Moqtada al-Sadr's Mahdi Army, swapped their guns for jobs and influence once the new, Shi'i-dominated government was installed in Baghdad. In a rare example of Sunni-Shi'i military co-operation, the Mahdi Army fought alongside the Islamists against the US in the 2004 Battle of Fallujah, and thousands of Sunni and Shi'i fighters celebrated their victory with joint prayers. This brief moment of secular unity was not to last.

Five months after the occupation of Iraq, all the Islamist groups with the exception of Zarqawi's al-Tahwid wal Jihad merged under an umbrella initially called Jaish Ansar al-Sunna (Army of the Followers of the Teachings – JAS). JAS espoused similar aims to Zarqawi's group which, in turn, was increasingly in line with al-Qa'ida ideology and world vision. From the outset, all these groups – from which ISIS/IS would emerge – expressed the intention of establishing an Islamic state in Iraq once the invaders had been expelled.

In December 2004, Zarqawi officially allied his group with al-Qa'ida and began a campaign with several aims, some of which continue to inform IS's strategy. To prevent Iraqis from co-operating with the government, and to destabilise the national security forces, there has been a decade-long campaign of infiltration and attacks on recruitment centres for the military and police.

Iraq was rapidly becoming the perfect training ground for jihadists. Recruitment to the insurgency inside Iraq flourished and a steady flow of foreign fighters began to enter the country, mostly via the border with Syria. The pan-Arab mujahideen had last congregated in significant numbers in 1980s' Afghanistan; Iraq was in many ways an easier, more attractive environment for its members to navigate, being Arab-speaking and culturally familiar. 'Afghan-Arabs' had reported language and cultural difficulties with their Pashtun comrades in the war against the Soviets and the civil war that followed.

The extremely violent and ruthless military approach espoused by Zarqawi marks a turning point in the history of global jihad. It acted as a magnet for foreign recruits who witnessed his brigades' acts of war via the internet in pioneering short videos with a backing track of harmonious *Nasheeds*, Islamic vocal music. Though they did not take root and flourish in Zarqawi's lifetime, the seeds of Islamic State were planted at this time.

Just as the Taliban would prove sympathetic hosts to al-Qa'ida after bin Laden relocated there from Sudan in 1996, Iraq's Sunni civilians at first offered Zarqawi's men safe passage through their tribal lands, shelter in their homes, money and military hardware. Zarqawi's strategy from the outset was not merely to fight the American occupation. Along with al-Qa'ida's most extremist strategists, he believed that fomenting sectarian violence between the minority Sunnis and the ruling Shi'i would allow the group to expand its influence, both among the indigenous Sunni population and by bringing Sunni fighters from neighbouring countries to help them. Sunnis are in the majority in Syria, Turkey and Jordan.

Zarqawi led the way with the kind of extreme, gruesome, violence now openly embraced by Islamic State. Like Islamic State, Zarqawi understood the psychological warfare value of videos depicting ruthless, cold-blooded murder. In May 2004, Zarqawi personally beheaded twenty-six-year-old American businessman Nick Berg and posed with his head on camera – an abhorrent image, ensuring wall-to-wall global media coverage, that has frequently been replicated by members of IS. In August 2014, an image of a seven-year-old boy, the 'son of a mujahid' holding up a severed head, ensured maximum publicity for Islamic State as it seeped through Iraq and Syria.

In its online literature and YouTube videos, first ISIS and now Islamic State celebrate Zarqawi as the icon of their generation and their first *emir*. Like Zarqawi, Islamic State enforces the prescribed punishment system under Sharia Law, *Tazeer* and *Hudd*. While the former consists of 'naming and shaming' with a view to reforming the individual's bad behaviour, the latter – usually applied for 'intentional' crimes such as murder, theft and adultery – includes beheading, amputation of limbs and stoning to death. Shocking videos demonstrate that such punishments are regularly carried out in Islamic State's catchment.

Islamic State's extreme violence is not only about upholding the 'law', it is also a deliberate strategy to instil fear in both its enemies and the people it seeks to subjugate. As we will see in subsequent chapters, it is by no means unique in this. Throughout history, empires have been ushered in on a sea of blood and we should not forget that Islamic State does indeed seek to re-establish the caliphate (read 'empire') in its entirety.

Zarqawi's 'branch' of al-Qa'ida briefly flourished until his extremism incurred the disaffection of, and ultimately betrayal by, ordinary Sunni Iraqis and tribespeople. The key to this period of success – familial and tribal interconnectedness – remains relevant in seeking to understand how ISIS managed to move so quickly to establish itself on an area the size of the UK on both sides of the Syria-Iraq border.

Through fomenting sectarian and ethnic violence, Zarqawi led the way for Islamic State. I believe his intention was to drag the Shi'i into a civil war.[14] In a June 2004 letter to bin Laden he accuses the Shi'i of colluding with the Americans in order to consolidate power for their own people, and adds that 'this lurking serpent... has been a sect of treachery and betrayal through all history and all ages.'

Zarqawi instigated an early campaign against Shi'i targets, including the March 2004 Ashura massacre of 185 Shi'i pilgrims by suicide and car bombs in Baghdad and Karbala. He also claimed the August 2003 assassination of Shi'i leader Ayatollah Mohammad Baqr al-Hakim. By 2014, the fire of sectarian conflict ignited by Zarqawi a decade earlier had engulfed most of the country.

Osama bin Laden and the current leader of al-Qa'ida 'central', Ayman al-Zawahiri, initially opposed Zarqawi's sectarian agenda. But they must have accepted it by the time Zarqawi pledged his *bayat* (allegiance) to bin Laden and renamed his group 'al-Qa'ida in the Land of the Two Rivers' on 28 December 2004. From that point on, sectarian murders escalated. Like Islamic State, Zarqawi did not worry about the loss of innocent civilians' lives in the course of jihad, saying that such 'collateral' killing was justified under *dharura* (overriding necessity).

Having Zarqawi on board revived al-Qa'ida's fortunes. Newly radicalised recruits from around the Arab and Muslim world poured into Iraq to fight their main enemy – America. However, Islamic State's commanders are indigenous, ensuring that the group's operations are facilitated by social and tribal networks on both sides of the border. Its leader, Abu Bakr al-Baghdadi, has two native Iraqi deputies: Abu Ali al-Anbari was a major general in the army and hails from Mosul; Abu Muslim al-Turkmani was a lieutenant colonel in Saddam Hussein's military intelligence.

Two 2006 studies, one by the Saudi government and one by an Israeli think tank, found that most foreign fighters were not jihadists before the 2003 invasion of Iraq but had been radicalised by the American occupation. Although Iraq had little history of radicalism, 'sanctions generation' Iraqis began to join Zarqawi's group. The first indigenous suicide bombers emerged, as evidenced by leaflets dropped in the aftermath of attacks which gave each 'martyr' a *kunya* (*nom de guerre*). Among jihadists, the *kunya* traditionally references the mujahid's birthplace – for example, 'al-Baghdadi' – and an increasing number of those willing to die for their extremist beliefs were to come from Iraq itself.

Zarqawi's personal star began to wane in November 2005 when he ordered a triple suicide bombing in his native Jordan. Of the sixty people who died in Amman, more than half were Jordanians and Palestinians celebrating a wedding. It is interesting to note that Zarqawi, like Abu Bakr al-Baghdadi, had his eye on a wider prize than Iraq alone, bringing terror to neighbouring countries. At the time, however, it was too much and too senseless even for the al-Qa'ida leadership: Ayman al-Zawahiri, yet to succeed bin Laden, chastised Zarqawi for jeopardising the 'circles of support, assistance and co-operation' essential for the jihadists' survival and the expansion of their aims.

Increasingly criticised for autocratic arrogance and hot-headedness, Zarqawi was rapidly losing support in al-Qa'ida circles. At the same time he was making al-Qa'ida unpopular within the insurgency by imposing his wider agenda on what was still, essentially, a civil conflict. In 2006 Zarqawi attempted to build bridges by creating an umbrella group of Sunni insurgent groups, offering a higher profile to indigenous groups. The organisation was initially named the Mujahideen Shura Council and its leader was Abdullah Rashid al-Baghdadi; the elevation of a native Iraqi was designed to ease concerns that the insurgency had been hijacked by a foreigner. Osama bin Laden was not convinced by the younger man's strategy, and Zarqawi was demoted from the leadership of al-Qa'ida in the Land of the Two Rivers (Iraq) in April 2006. By June Zarqawi had been tracked down and killed by the Americans.

In October 2006, the name of the umbrella organisation was changed to the Islamic State of Iraq (ISI). Again, it was headed by a man with an Iraqi moniker, Abu Omar al-Baghdadi, although most commentators agree that the actual leader of al-Qa'ida's 'branch' at the time was an Egyptian, Abu Ayyub al-Masri.

Significantly, in terms of the present narrative, ISI announced that its intention was now to establish an Islamic emirate in Iraq by military means. It appointed a cabinet and imposed Sharia law in the areas where it had become the dominant force: parts of Baghdad, Samarra, Mosul, Anbar, Kirkuk and its 'capital', Baqubah. This forebear of Islamic State began to flourish. Iraq became the international jihadist destination of choice, to the growing alarm of Iraq's prime minister Nouri al-Maliki and his Western sponsors.

In autumn 2006, the US embarked on the so-called 'Awakening' campaign, which aimed to harness growing discontent with ISI extremism among Sunni tribes in Anbar province. Led by wealthy businessman and tribal leader Sheikh Abdul Sattar Abu Risha, Sunni tribesmen were encouraged to co-operate with the US military and sign up to a new, anti-al-Qa'ida militia, the Sons of Iraq. Paid $300 a month by the US military, the movement spread to other areas of the country and by 2007 had as many as 100,000 armed members. At the same time, George W. Bush committed an additional 21,500 troops to Iraq for a military 'surge'. The Awakening campaign, the US troops and the Sons of Iraq militia together made a lot of ground against al-Qa'ida through 2007.

Despite the success of the new American strategy (formulated by General Petraeus) ISI remained extremely dangerous and committed to its sectarian agenda. On 14 August 2007 it launched four simultaneous attacks that would have echoes in August 2014, targeting the Yazidi minority in two Kurdish towns. The attacks killed 796 people and wounded 1,562. The Yazidi have lived in this area for 2,000 years but their idiosyncratic, peaceful religion has seen them branded 'heretics' by the hardline Salafists.

On 13 September 2007, ISI assassinated 'Awakening' leader Sheikh Abdul Sattar Abu Risha; but the US-led campaign had achieved its aims. Ordinary Sunnis had turned against ISI because of its extremism and because they still believed a fair, democratic and representative new regime would emerge.

Without support at Sunni grass-roots level, ISI was significantly weakened. From spring 2008 there was a steady migration of fighters and key figures from Iraq, travelling to other battles or, sometimes, home.

Political instability provides new opportunities

The new Iraqi government and the US administration were so confident that they had beaten the insurgency that on 27 November 2008 the Iraqi parliament passed the Status of Forces Agreement (SOFA). Under its terms US troops would withdraw from Iraq's cities by 30 June 2009 and from the entire country by 31 December 2011.

In late 2008 the US had handed over control of the Sons of Iraq to the Shi'i-dominated Maliki government, which made a catastrophic mistake in its dealings with these, by now, highly trained fighters. The Americans had promised them that they would be retained by the new Iraqi government on salaried positions either in administrative roles or within the security forces. Instead, they were dismissed without compensation and for overtly sectarian reasons. These disaffected Sunni fighters would come back with a vengeance. Many were absorbed back into the insurgency, on condition that they repented their 'collaboration' with Maliki and the Americans. In 2014 they then became the backbone of Islamic State's army. Having been trained by American personnel and having fought alongside them, they had invaluable insight into the *modus operandi* of the 'enemy'.

As the US commenced its staged withdrawal from Iraq, ISI's presence returned concomitantly. In January 2009, as part of a 'normalisation' process, the US handed over supervision and control of Baghdad's Green Zone – where all the most sensitive governmental buildings are housed – to Iraqi security forces. When US troops withdrew from Iraqi cities in line with SOFA, the Iraqi government removed blast walls and other defences around and within the Green Zone. This optimistic gesture was greeted with a series of devastating attacks in the very heart of government on 19 August 2009, actions that would be claimed by ISI. As Prime Minister al-Maliki prepared to give a speech at a hotel inside the Green Zone, two massive truck bombs hit the Ministries of Foreign Affairs and Finance and several mortar rounds were fired, killing 122.

In spring 2010, US and Iraqi troops made a renewed effort to eliminate the insurgency, announcing that they had killed up to 75 per cent of al-Qaeda leaders in the country. But political instability following January's inconclusive parliamentary election results created a political vacuum, which gave the insurgency new room to manoeuvre. On 10 May 2010 ISI carried out a series of bomb and sniper attacks in several major cities.

In 2009 al-Maliki had formed a new political alliance called the 'State of Law' alliance. With great historical irony, given the state of Iraqi politics today, he had promised to build strong state institutions, public educational and health services, and to root out corruption. In keeping with the much-vaunted march towards democracy, another significant political entity was created, purportedly to establish the infrastructure for a stable, harmonious state: the Iraqiya alliance.

I remember meeting Iraqi friends at this time, Shi'i, Sunni and Kurds alike, political exiles based in London and elsewhere. Although they had a few grumbles I was struck by how positive and optimistic they were about the future of their country. At that time, Iraq could have progressed into the regional beacon of democracy the Americans hoped it would become. However, al-Maliki embarked on a series of self-interested, ill-considered blunders that would result in total chaos, fragmentation and a failed state.

Having obtained a second term in 2010 (in questionable elections), al-Maliki's personal hunger for power saw him behaving in an increasingly autocratic manner, inviting comparison with Saddam Hussein himself. The cabinet was not announced until nine months later, with al-Maliki appointing himself Minister of Defence and Minister of the Interior and National Security. He started referring to himself as 'commander in chief of the armed forces'. In breach of the new constitution, al-Maliki did not bother to seek parliamentary approval for top army and security appointments and took to making them himself. In addition, al-Maliki ran his own militias, including the Baghdad Operations Command. Next, al-Maliki's government passed a series of 'de-Ba'athification' laws intended to obstruct members of the former regime from the corridors of power. A witch-hunt ensued and the laws were used against anyone who had been in the Ba'ath party, regardless of whether they had been for or against Saddam Hussein.

At the time, Iraq was benefitting from $100 billion in foreign aid to help it rebuild its infrastructure and vital services; it was left largely untrammelled by the need for accountability. Back in 2006, Transparency International warned that this could produce 'The biggest corruption scandal in history'. In fact that scandal was already under way. Al-Maliki's budget for security (funded by foreign aid) was larger than the combined budgets of the departments of education, health and the environment, yet it was subject to little scrutiny. Friends and colleagues in Iraq related how soldiers would be enrolled and paid salaries, but no one knew if they reported for duty or not. The public no longer felt protected – terror attacks and episodes of sectarian violence occurred with increasing frequency, but they were rarely investigated. The insurgency developed a second wind and was quick to exploit the weaknesses and corruptibility of the army and security services, which had also been infiltrated by insurgent sympathisers.

By summer 2010, civil leaders were warning that al-Qaʿida was resurgent in the country and that 'Awakening' leaders were becoming disaffected in the absence of the power-sharing opportunities they had been led to expect. Little heed was taken, and the last US troops withdrew in December 2011, leaving Iraq to its fate. No care was taken to help inexperienced politicians form a truly representative parliament and establish a working democracy. Instead, American policy seemed to be to shoo-in anybody they believed would be friendly to US interests both geo-political and economic. Naively, or arrogantly, Washington considered Nouri al-Maliki to be their man. In fact he was much closer to America's regional nemesis, the Shiʿi Republic of Iran, having spent eight years of his exile (1982–1990) in Tehran. The US invasion had succeeded only in handing Iraq to Iran on a golden platter.

The US withdrawal, in December 2011, opened the floodgates for a renewed, deeply sectarian insurgency, headed by ISI. In 2012, there were 4,594 violent deaths of Iraqi citizens (4,153 more than in 2011) and in 2013 this nearly doubled to 8,000.

The sectarian conflict was fomented by al-Qaʿida and its successor ISI, but equally by the exclusionist policies of al-Maliki's successive governments. Fear and hatred has bitten deep into the fabric of Iraqi society; even Baghdad has divided into enclaves dominated by Sunni and Shiʿi militias. Sunni discontent escalated through 2013 but any protest was met with Saddam-style brutality.

Young men who complained about government corruption, who criticised the regime, who went to the mosque too often, would be taken from their homes at night, either never to return, or to be sent back tortured beyond recognition. A Sunni protest camp in Hawija, near Kirkuk, was attacked by Iraqi government troops in April 2013, killing fifty. By June 2014, Hawija had become a jewel in the Islamic State's crown, having been overrun not only by Islamic State's fighters but, crucially, by local, Sunni, tribesmen too.

By July 2013, Iraq was subsumed by sectarian civil war, and ISI was transforming into an even more deadly force, having merged with Syria's jihadist rebel brigades in al-Nusra Front in April 2013. The new jihadist juggernaut rebranded itself the Islamic State of Iraq and al-Sham (ISIS).

The *emir* of ISIS, who would declare himself Caliph Ibrahim in Mosul's Grand Mosque in July 2014, was ISI leader Abu Bakr al-Husseini al-Quraishi al-Baghdadi. Baghdadi launched the new group with spectacularly daring raids on two of Iraq's main prisons – Abu Ghraib and Taji – where hundreds of convicted al-Qa'ida fighters languished. Months in the planning, the 22 July 2013 attacks saw mortar shells fired at the buildings, while car bombs and suicide bombers blasted the gates open. More than 500 al-Qa'ida commanders and fighters escaped from Abu Ghraib, whose security guards had been infiltrated by ISIS sympathisers.[15] Not only had ISIS demonstrated its power and gained a psychological victory over the foundering al-Maliki government, but its ranks were boosted by hundreds of experienced, angry and pent-up fighters.

ISIS was to expand its range of targets in 2013. While the campaign against the Shi'i remained ongoing, the process would culminate in the overtly sectarian massacres of minorities including Christians, Kurds and Yazidis. The Kurdish capital, Arbil, was targeted for strategic reasons, for its lucrative oil fields, and also as revenge because Kurdish fighters had taken up arms against ISIS and affiliated jihadists in Syria.

As ISIS strengthened its grip on Iraq, the country sank still further into chaos and instability caused by the abject failures of the al-Maliki government and, most importantly, its army. The army would prove incapable of, or more likely, uninterested in fighting Islamic State when it made its definitive push on Mosul in summer 2014. Under al-Maliki, commissions and positions of power were bought rather than earned, which meant that many good officers were either pushed out or passed over. The phenomenon of 'ghost soldiers' – whereby men were paid but did not actually attend their jobs – mushroomed. As a result, the US-trained troops lacked belief. Why would they risk life and limb for a corrupt, disastrous regime? They also lacked loyalty, morale and leadership. The police were equally ineffectual, corrupt and lacking commitment. There are many tales of officers racing for cover back at the police station at the first sign of any serious resistance.

Al-Maliki became increasingly isolated. He alienated first the Kurds, who were essential to his grip on parliamentary power, then the US and, finally and fatally, Tehran, on whose support he believed he could always count. Al-Maliki had no understanding, ultimately, of politics and the political game. For many, al-Maliki had become a Shi'i version of Saddam Hussein – as bad a dictator, if not worse, because he coupled his autocratic, repressive rule with incompetence.

The political crisis in Iraq that escalated through 2013–14 offered ISIS a second shot at gaining widespread Sunni support for its ambitious drive to establish a caliphate in the heart of the Middle East. Unlike Zarqawi, Islamic State's Iraqi leaders had been able to establish lasting alliances with other, local, Sunni groups and tribes. In its assault on Mosul in June 2014, ISIS was careful to join forces with local Ba'athists and tribal groups, recruiting from among the city's own youth as well. Izzat al-Douri, Saddam Hussein's former vice president, was among the high-profile former regime members who turned up in Mosul, and the city's new administrative body features several members of the *ancien régime*.

After eleven years of chaos, lawlessness, and persecution by the Baghdad regime, the majority Sunni population in the region welcomed some semblance of law and order, even in the most extreme manifestation proposed by Islamic State. When ISIS brigades entered Mosul in a convoy of vehicles they were welcomed by cheering crowds.

In May 2014 al-Maliki secured re-election. But by August he had been removed from office by President Faoud Massoum. This was certainly with the encouragement of the Obama administration, who had belatedly realised that the absence of an effective central government in Baghdad had facilitated the unprecedented advance of Islamic State by creating a security vacuum. Not only that, the increasingly disaffected Sunni minority was now in no mood to confront the jihadists and, in some towns and villages, welcomed their arrival with enthusiasm. The situation is very similar to the way in which the Taliban brought law and order in Afghanistan in the aftermath of the war against the Soviets and the subsequent civil war, and thus were initially welcomed by the populace. It will take years for faith in the democratic project to be restored. Even if future Iraqi leaders create a genuine government of national unity, it may prove to be a case of shutting the gate after the horse has bolted. Having fomented the break-up of Iraq, the West now wants to put the genie back in the bottle.

THREE

THE ORIGINS – PART TWO: THE TALIBAN, AL-QA'IDA AND IS

When Abu Bakr al-Baghdadi declared himself caliph and *Emir al-Muminin* (commander of the faithful) on 1 July 2014, many commentators overlooked one important fact: the position is already occupied by Mullah Omar, the leader of the Afghan Taliban, who declared himself the caliph back in 1996, famously wrappng himself in the Prophet Muhammad's cloak in a Kandahar mosque. This 'battle of the caliphs' is at the heart of current jihadist politics. Mullah Omar has been remarkably cautious on the subject of Islamic State, limiting his response to Baghdadi's declaration to this advice: Muslims should 'avoid extremism in religion, and judging others without evidence, and distrusting one another. Muslims should avoid conflict.'[1]

Ayman al-Zawahiri (the current leader of al-Qa'ida) and Osama bin Laden had given Mullah Omar their *bayat* in the late 1990s, accepting his authority over them (and, by association, al-Qa'ida).[2] In 2008, in a rather bungled 'Town Hall' style Q&A session (it took four months for the second lot of answers to appear online!), al-Zawahiri had announced to the jihadist community that he and bin Laden were Mullah Omar's 'soldiers'.[3] He responded to Baghdadi's declaration by reaffirming his personal fealty to Mullah Omar, and to al-Qa'ida as an organisation. In mid-July 2014, he used the first edition of a new online newsletter, *Al-Nafir*, to 'renew the pledge of allegiance to the commander of the faithful, Mullah Mohammad Omar Mujahid, may Allah preserve him, and confirm that al-Qa'ida and all its branches are soldiers among his soldiers'.

Mullah Omar has been somewhat forgotten by the chroniclers

of modern Islamist history. However, the Taliban will no doubt
welcome the opportunity to re-establish the Islamic Emirate of
Afghanistan, which it governed until the US invasion of 2001 –
it already controls about 54 per cent of the country in any case.[4]
In autumn 2014 the Taliban unleashed a new, ongoing wave of
violence that has claimed hundreds of lives at the time of writing
(March 2015). The US and NATO formally ended their combat
mission in Afghanistan in 2014 and the US withdrew most of
its 100,000 troops, leaving just 10,600 at the beginning of 2015.
President Obama has reiterated that he is committed to a final
withdrawal of remaining US troops from Afghanistan by the end
of 2016: as we have seen in the previous chapter, the withdrawal of
US troops from Iraq in December 2011 facilitated the emergence
of ISIS, followed by Islamic State. Most commentators will agree
with US Senator John McCain that it is likely 'you'll see the same
movie again in Afghanistan.'

Suggesting that negotiations with the Taliban are no longer
unthinkable, the organisation was encouraged to open a quasi
'embassy', or at least an office staffed by envoys, in Qatar in 2013.
In July 2014 Mullah Omar commented that, 'Many entities that
used to oppose us now have come around to accept the Islamic
Emirate as a reality' and he hailed the (Qatar-based) diplomacy
that secured the release of five high-ranking Taliban prisoners from
Guantanamo as a 'spectacular achievement'.[5]

In order to convince the international community – and the
Afghan people – that it is ready for another run at power, the
Taliban has been trying to present a more 'moderate' face. The more
radical 'global jihadists' complain that the Taliban is interested in
establishing an Islamic emirate only in Afghanistan. Yet in July
2014 Mullah Omar called on the *ummah* to move against Israel and
protect the Palestinians during the Gaza onslaught, demonstrating
that his concerns are not entirely local.

Disagreements and damaging disputes could contain the seeds
of the radical Islamist movement's destruction. On the other hand,
if the three main groups – the al-Qa'ida network, the Taliban (both

Afghan and Pakistani) and Islamic State – were to overcome their differences and create a united front, it would present a devastating force that would dominate the political landscape of the Middle East for decades to come.

The Zarqawi factor

As the lines are drawn in the sand, it is clear that the ideological battle between al-Qa'ida's old guard and IS matters just as much as the military conflicts on the ground. As Islamic State seeks to extend its influence throughout the region, it needs the support and assistance of the existing jihadist network which is (or has been) largely affiliated to al-Qa'ida. Following Baghdadi's refusal to leave fighting in Syria to al-Qa'ida's 'official' affiliate al-Nusra, Zawahiri formally dissociated al-Qa'ida from ISIS in February 2014.[6] But much has changed since then, as we will see.

We can trace the roots of this ideological conflict back to the stand-off between Abu Musab al-Zarqawi, al-Qa'ida's *emir* in Iraq until 2006, and the 'old guard', Osama bin Laden and Zawahiri. Zarqawi was younger (born in 1966 as against Zawahiri's 1951), a worldly, tattooed, Jordanian street-thug-turned-jihadist. He brought an even more extremist and violent element into the al-Qa'ida firmament, as well as a Rambo-style obsession with physique (in jail he worked out with rocks). For the younger generation that populates the Islamic State, Zarqawi is a hero and online material refers to him as their 'first *emir*'.

The scholarly higher echelons of al-Qa'ida believed that the Muslim world's problems would be solved by the removal of foreign interference and apostate Arab regimes; the aggressive Zarqawi and his followers held to the *takfir* doctrine espoused by IS that, in order for the *ummah* to reign supreme, the true faith (as they see it) must be purged of *murtad* (unbelievers, deviants). This unleashed the bloody campaign of sectarian violence and 'religious cleansing', which began in earnest under Zarqawi in Iraq, and which informs

Islamic State's activities to date.

Zarqawi was zealous in enforcing his interpretation of Sharia law. Public executions, stoning and floggings were commonplace in areas under his control and even petty crimes received the harshest punishment – smokers had their fingers amputated, for example. Al-Qa'ida's older generation fretted that Zarqawi's 'extremism' (as even they framed it) would alienate the public and lose the group the grass-roots and tribal support it had initially enjoyed. They were right.

Zarqawi believed that psychological terror was as important a weapon in the jihadist arsenal as the Kalashnikov. He also understood the value of engaging (or horrifying) the media: his statement, 'Remember, more than half this battle is taking place in the battlefield of the media' could have been written by Islamic State's strategists. It is a sentiment echoed by another al-Qa'ida man who has posthumously become an IS hero, Anwar al-Awlaki.

In 2013 Zawahiri released a document titled 'General Guidelines for the Work of a Jihadi', re-examining the concerns he had voiced in regard to Zarqawi back in 2005, but now clearly aimed at ISIS. Zawahiri urged jihadists not to attack other sects and faiths either militarily or verbally, but instead tell them about 'true' Islam and offer them the chance to come into it. He also stated that attacks on marketplaces and public places are unacceptable because these kill and maim Muslims. He urged respect for leaders (maybe out of fear for his own position) and said that they should 'neither be fought nor killed except if they commit a military act against the Muslims or the mujahideen'.

Zarqawi's assassination in June 2006 at the hands of an American fighter plane was an indirect result of his own arrogance. Whereas bin Laden and al-Zawahiri always diligently ensured that the background setting of their to-camera video speeches would never betray their location, Zarqawi's last video shows him 'Rambo'-style, striding about and blasting a machine gun (with a bit of help from a friend after he left the safety catch on by mistake) in a clearly identifiable landscape, enabling US surveillance to pinpoint his location shortly afterwards.

In October 2006 Zarqawi's successor, Abu Hamza al-Muhajir, brought his group under the leadership of Abu Omar al-Baghdadi, and the umbrella Islamic State of Iraq was announced. Here is an interesting technicality that may prove significant: a *bayat* can only be pledged by an individual to an individual. In effect – since neither Abu Hamza nor Baghdadi pledged allegiance to either Osama bin Laden or his successor, Ayman al-Zawahiri – ISI was no longer subordinate to al-Qa'ida. Technically, ISI and its heirs (ISIS and Islamic State) have been independent of al-Qa'ida for the past eight years, and may wish to remain so for political reasons.

Osama bin Laden had already expressed concern that the al-Qa'ida 'brand' had become tarnished in PR terms, not only by Zarqawi's excesses, but because, post-9/11 and the subsequent attacks in Madrid (2004) and London (2005), the organisation's name was associated entirely with terrorism and extremism. In 2011, by way of an experiment, al-Qa'ida in the Arabian Peninsula (AQAP) formed a parallel group called Ansar al-Sharia (Partisans of Islamic Law). It found the name was received more sympathetically by the wider population and increased recruitment locally. Papers found at the Abbottabad, Pakistan, compound where bin Laden was killed contain notes and letters concerning name changes. The ideas he came up with lacked the ring of al-Qa'ida and were cumbersome and overly explanatory; but they demonstrate bin Laden's concerns and the ideological direction he wanted the group to take: Taifat al-Tawhed wal Jihad, meaning Monotheism and Jihad Group; Jama'at wahdat al-Muslimin (Muslim Unity Group); Hizb tawhid al-Umma al-Islamiya (Islamic Nation Unification Party); Jama'at tahrir al-Aqsa (Jerusalem Liberation Group); or Jama'at I'Adat al-Khilafat al-Rashida (Restoration of the Caliphate Group).

Following the success of the 'Awakening' campaign and the military surge, violence in Iraq subsided; the Islamic State of Iraq (ISI) retreated and, in accord with the tradition of *hijra* (migration), removed themselves from unwinnable battles and travelled to another fight. Now, many of the key ISI jihadists, including bin Laden's son Saad, and right-hand man Saif al-Adel, started appearing in Afghanistan, renewing their comradeship with the Taliban. Their presence was demonstrated by the appearance, in autumn 2008, of sophisticated IEDs (improvised explosive devices) which the ISI fighters had learned to manufacture from former members of Saddam Hussein's Republican Guard. The point is this: at this stage, with Baghdadi to all intents and purposes the deputy leader of ISI, his group, the Taliban and al-Qa'ida were on the same path.

Indeed, in April 2008, Zawahiri had overtly championed ISI, which was under immense pressure, urging: 'Providing assistance to the mujahideen in Iraq – and at their head, ISI – is one of the Islamic *ummah*'s most pressing duties at this point in time.'[7] Always an intelligent commentator, Zawahiri predicted the chaos that would engulf Iraq and open the window of opportunity to the jihadists. In an interview released by al-Qa'ida's official media outlet As-Sahab in November 2008, he said of the 'Awakening' campaign, 'This was only possible through huge American support for the Iraqi army and police, whom the Americans will in turn abandon to face their fate at the hands of the mujahideen after the Americans depart.'

The generational division begins

Even during the downturn in ISI's fortunes, when relations with al-Qa'ida Central were relatively harmonious, ideological cracks were still apparent. Osama bin Laden was increasingly out on a limb. Unlike al-Zawahiri and unlike the leaders of ISI, bin Laden began giving statements that focused on the Palestinian cause. He even linked the situation in Iraq to this, writing in March 2008, 'the best way for Muslims to help the Palestinians is to support the Iraqi insurgency.'[8] In 2010 he started to voice concerns about climate change and the plight of disaster-hit Muslims in Africa and Pakistan. This was all very much out of touch with the younger generation, who were more concerned with what would happen when the US ended its 'combat mission' in Iraq on 31 August 2010. They sensed that with this withdrawal their moment would come – a leader who could 'seize the day' was required. The two elderly men, Zawahiri and bin Laden, constrained by their own fugitive status, were losing touch and relevance.

Meanwhile, ISI had revived its military campaign in Iraq. Summer 2009 saw a resurgence in bombings of government buildings, Shi'i targets, embassies and hotels. The sectarianism that would achieve the chaos and fragmentation the ISI project required took greater hold. People started to move according to the demographics of towns and regions. The south became predominantly Shi'i; the centre, Sunni (except for Baghdad, the seat of the Shi'i-dominated government); and the north, Kurdish.

At the same time, the failures of the democratic process had produced only corrupt, Tehran-backed, exclusionist and self-interested governments; food was scarce, inflation rampant; and electricity, even in the boiling furnace of summer, was limited to two hours' supply a day. The lack of credible government and infrastructure led to a new conservatism whereby religious identity and cultural traditions became a form of rebellion. Democracy and liberalism had been 'tainted' by association with the occupation forces. As the years went on, Islamic extremism became a more acceptable alternative – a phenomenon that would benefit ISIS when it rampaged across Iraq in 2014.

For bin Laden and Zawahiri, woefully disengaged from events on the ground in Iraq, ISI's strategy – to plunge Iraq into chaos, enabling it to come to power and establish an Islamic State – was at odds with the al-Qa'ida leadership's ideological focus, which was still on 'international jihad'.

The global jihadist movement was thus beginning to polarise along generational lines. In 2009 a new wave of youthful and more extremist jihadist groups emerged who would appeal to a catchment of recruits (mostly online) for whom 9/11 was ancient history. Islamic State is born of this new wave. At the other extreme were the increasingly ponderous 'Afghan-Arab veterans', who nevertheless retained the leadership of al-Qa'ida and its affiliates, as well as the respect and loyalty of its cadres. As we will see, the new groups all sought affiliation with al-Qa'ida, but most would shift allegiance to Islamic State when the chance came.

The new wave of violent extremism

Among the new generation of al-Qa'ida affiliates was AQAP, based in Yemen, which announced its foundation in January 2009 and would soon become the most powerful of the 'branches'. It was headed by the then thirty-two-year-old Nasir al-Wuhayshi, who had served as Osama bin Laden's private secretary in Afghanistan and was also close to Ayman al-Zawahiri. AQAP hit the ground running and quickly took over vast swathes of Yemen, buoyed by tribal loyalties and a general sympathy for al-Qa'ida in the land of bin Laden's fathers.

AQAP had a highly effective weapon for international radicalisation and recruitment in the form of Anwar al-Awlaki, an American-Yemeni who was bilingual, well educated and charismatic. Then thirty-six years old, Awlaki set about harnessing the potential of the internet. He released fiery sermons and engaged potential radicals in English-speaking countries in lengthy email conversations, before persuading them to carry out 'lone wolf' attacks. His protégés include Major Nidal Malik Hasan, who in November 2009 would open fire on his military colleagues at US base Fort Hood in Texas, killing thirteen; on Christmas Day 2009, the so-called 'underwear bomber', twenty-three-year-old Umar Farouk Abdulmutallab, attempted to detonate explosives on board Northwest Airlines Flight 253; in the UK, twenty-one-year-old student Roshonara Choudhry attempted to murder British MP Stephen Timms, with whom she had gained an interview in May 2010. Awlaki was also behind some imaginative attempts to plant explosives on international flights, including the plot of October

2010 that saw innocuous-looking print cartridges packed with explosives loaded on to a cargo plane, with a timer set to detonate them over the US. The cartridges were discovered only after a tip-off from Saudi intelligence; they had evaded detection by X-ray, chemical swabs and sniffer-dogs at the UK's East Midlands Airport.

Awlaki, like Zarqawi before him, was 'worldly' before his conversion to Islam and had a criminal record for soliciting prostitutes in 1996 and 1997. Far from alienating these men from the youths they sought to recruit, the leaders' backgrounds (and their repentance) served to help them find common ground and establish trust and empathy with troubled, disaffected youths both in Arab lands and in the West.

Awlaki pioneered the exploitation of social networking platforms (which Islamic State would take to another level). He had a Facebook page with thousands of 'likes', which Osama bin Laden and al-Zawahiri did not. Awlaki launched – and co-wrote – *Inspire*, a glossy English language online magazine that taught 'self-radicalised' young people how to make bombs 'in the kitchen of your mom': just such bombs, packed into pressure cookers, were used in the 2013 Boston Marathon attacks. We know that Osama bin Laden did not approve of all of *Inspire*'s content: one of his notebooks seized in the Abbottabad compound criticised the outlandish idea mooted in one issue which proposed fitting a tractor with blades on its wheels to become a sort of mowing-down-of-humans-machine, creating havoc and terror on Western streets. Bin Laden noted that 'indiscriminate killing' was not something al-Qa'ida approves of; yet by late 2014 a rash of deliberate, indiscriminate, running-over incidents took place in the West and were claimed, and applauded, by Islamic State. One senses that the older man was already losing control of the group he had established in the late 1980s and was increasingly unfamiliar with the world outside his voluntary prison.

Meanwhile the extremist new wave had also swept into Africa. In Somalia, al-Shabaab had overrun all of southern Somalia by 2009, including the capital, Mogadishu. Al-Shabaab (The Youth) had emerged from the Islamic Courts Union, a coalition of Sharia courts that had come together to oppose the Transitional Federal Government. It was as fierce, violent and extremist as they come. In December 2008 it hit world headlines with the public stoning to death of rape victim Aisha Ibrahim Duhulow for 'adultery' – her father asserted that she was only thirteen years old. Anwar al-Awlaki sent al-Shabaab a congratulatory message, thanking them for showing Muslims 'the correct path'. As IS has discovered, extremism is the fastest way to generate global publicity. Thereafter, al-Shabaab was constantly in the news, whether for the extraction of gold teeth as 'un-Islamic' or for its collaboration with Somali pirates. Al-Shabaab demonstrated that its reach was not only local when two of its members carried out the horrific murder of British soldier Lee Rigby on the streets of Woolwich, south-east London in May 2013. They also dominated the world's news when they laid siege to the Westgate Mall in Nairobi, massacring at least sixty-two people in September the same year.

Despite its remote location, al-Shabaab, like AQAP, attracted significant numbers of recruits from abroad – including Western converts – entirely online, mostly using social media platforms. High-profile members include the Briton Samantha Lewthwaite and the American Omar Hammami.

Far from the impassioned (and, one suspects, often boring) religious sermonising that was the hallmark of bin Laden and Zawahiri, al-Shabaab's spokespeople by turn menaced and joked in videos posted on YouTube and their own satellite television station, Al-Kataib, introducing slogans and gangster-type slang to the jihadist lexicon. Appealing to the Western ghetto and street, al-Shabaab's Twitter account brazenly ridiculed the authorities and referenced ordinary things that would have resonance with their Western followers – one post stated a longing for a 'caramel cappuccino' coffee. Al-Shabaab produced rap videos, with Omar Hammami punctuating the rhythmic words with plenty of spit and vitriol (although without music, as Salafists believe music is *haram*). This shift towards the mentality of the gang, the brotherhood of the street, the black and white, 'us against them', is very much part of Islamic State's current appeal. Clever use of the internet creates a self-sustaining following.

Al-Shabaab became an official branch of al-Qa'ida in February 2012. Membership of al-Qa'ida still confers kudos, prestige and credibility in the international jihadist scene. Meanwhile Boko Haram (whose official name is Jama'atu Ahlis Sunna Lidda'awati wal Jihad) also emerged in 2009 in Northern Nigeria and quickly gained a reputation for the most vicious and random violence; it has scarcely been out of the headlines since. This group flies the ubiquitous black flag of global jihad, but has a more local agenda. In November 2011, Boko Haram's spokesman, Abu Qaqa, announced: 'We are one with al-Qa'ida, they help us in our struggle,' and leader Abubakar Shekau gave his *bayat* (allegiance) to Ayman al-Zawahiri. As we will see, however, they were to take great interest in Baghdadi's Islamic State, with which they have so much in common.

The Arab revolutions

The beginning of 2011 brought the Arab Spring, a series of revolutions that unseated the 'apostate' rulers Islamic extremists had for decades longed to depose. The events took the jihadist groups by surprise. Many commentators suggested that the Arab Spring heralded the end of al-Qa'ida and its affiliates; their dissident purpose had been usurped by a more palatable, liberal, all-purpose, popular movement which had achieved its aims through non-violent protest, discrediting the jihadists' assertion that violence was necessary. Certainly the West must have hoped that this would prove to be the case, and immediately it championed the revolutionaries. Al-Qa'ida was more cautious and at first said nothing.

It is interesting to note how divergent the different groups' responses were – another indication of the deepening gulf between the old guard and the new wave extremists. On 8 February 2011 the increasingly hardline ISI had issued a vitriolic statement through its 'Ministry of War', attacking the ongoing struggle in Egypt (arguably the crucible of extremism). It warned against 'un-Islamic ideologies, such as filthy and evil secularism, infidel democracy, the putrid ideology of patriotism and nationalism'. ISI stood against the tsunami of Arab revolutions and warned, 'do not replace better with worse.'

For the older generation, Mullah Omar, the *emir* of the Faithful, took the opposite stance completely and issued a congratulatory statement on 14 February: 'The Islamic Emirate of Afghanistan prays to Almighty Allah to grant further success to the Egyptian people to follow on from the victory of the historical uprising which they have already attained.' Mullah Omar urged the Egyptians to 'establish a real, independent and Islamic government and foil conspiracies of the foreign enemies'. For Mullah Omar, the revolution created opportunities for the Islamists; and indeed, initially, it did.

Bin Laden and Zawahiri remained silent through the Tunisian revolution. Even the fall of Egypt's Hosni Mubarak on 11 February 2011 failed to provoke a reaction – even though the Egyptian Zawahiri had worked against the 'apostate' dictator for decades, and had masterminded a failed assassination attempt on him in Addis Ababa in 1995. Zawahiri finally issued a statement a week after Mubarak's fall, on 'Victory Friday' when a million people were celebrating in Tahrir Square. It was a long-winded and boring half-hour history lecture about the roots of Egypt's problems (even going into Bonaparte's 1798 expedition to the country). While its avowed purpose was to deliver 'a message of hope and glad tidings to our people in Egypt' it was clear that it was days old – and out of date, since it did not even refer to Mubarak's resignation. The problems al-Qaʻida Central was having with delivering messages and posting on the internet (due to security considerations) were becoming seriously debilitating. We now know that messengers were dispatched with messages on memory sticks to internet cafes in towns and cities. Bin Laden's situation was even more challenging.

He was in hiding on the outskirts of Abbottabad in a walled-in compound with no communications facilities because of the huge security risk they would pose. The impression was compounded of an inactive, remote leadership, lacking relevance to the digital generation brought up on 'instant' texting, Twitter and Instagram.

These diametrically opposed responses to the Arab Spring revolutions epitomise the ongoing polarisation within the jihadist movement. The hardline ISI will not support rebels who are not part of the jihadist movement, and seek to violently eliminate them from the battle – even when they are fellow Sunni Muslims. Al-Qa'ida, and its (official) branch in Syria, al-Nusra, took a more pragmatic and revolutionary stance, believing that the people could be won over to the 'true faith' over time and when the battle was done, regardless of their creed. Islamic State brands all those who do not follow its strict interpretation of Sharia as apostates and believes it is legitimate to murder them.

It gets personal

In May 2011, the jihadist community was dealt a seismic blow when US SEAL commandos assassinated Osama bin Laden in his Abbottabad compound. If loyalty to the figurehead, bin Laden, had held the diverse affiliates together, what would happen now? Zawahiri, as deputy and second-in-command, should have been a shoo-in; but sources suggest that the succession was fiercely debated within al-Qa'ida's central Shura (counsellors) and it would be six weeks before the group issued a press release announcing him as the new *emir*.[9]

Osama bin Laden was revered by the jihadist community, regardless of ideological disputes and differences. This was not to be the case with his successor, the severe and 'difficult' Ayman al-Zawahiri, who had always been acutely aware of, and consistently warned against, the dangers of in-fighting within the jihadist movement. Now, ironically, the controversy around his own leadership threatened to divide the community. Bin Laden's personal bodyguard, Nasser al-Bahri, who spent seven years in the heart of the al-Qa'ida leadership, was certain that 'he does not possess the personal qualities required to run the organisation.'[10] He predicted that, 'Many members of al-Qa'ida will refuse to accept Zawahiri's leadership... Sometimes his ideas were rejected by other leaders and I doubt he can command the necessary authority for the post, even though he is known for his authoritarian and controlling attitude.'[11] Zawahiri's lack of charisma cleared the way for the younger, more extremist, element to establish a viable alternative to the organisation he had co-founded.

It was not until August 2011, after heated argument and debate, that ISI commented on the new *emir*. Its statement, delivered by spokesman Abu Muhammed al-Adnani, was rather lukewarm: 'I send sincere greetings to the honourable Sheikh, the reputable instructor, the experienced, wise, leader of the *Ummah* Sheikh Dr Ayman al-Zawahiri. We beseech Allah to bless him and his recent accession to the leadership.' Later, as we will see, Adnani would turn against Zawahiri and accuse him of losing his way along the path, which ISIS now framed as being shared by bin Laden, effectively isolating Zawahiri.

The ISIS/al-Nusra split

In summer 2011, with the Syrian uprising in full swing in Syria, Abu Bakr al-Baghdadi, the *emir* of ISI, sent a senior member of his group, Abu Mohammad al-Jolani, to establish a jihadist group in Syria. The result, Jahbat al-Nusra, officially announced itself in late January.

Baghdadi's strategic decision had been taken in consultation with al-Qa'ida leader Ayman al-Zawahiri (before a rift between the two men had emerged). Initially the association between al-Nusra and ISI was deliberately obscured because of the historic al-Qa'ida connection, which would alienate some potential recruits as well as the other rebel groups fighting the regime. By the end of 2012, al-Nusra was one of the most effective fighting groups and it was also fulfilling socio-judicial functions, arbitrating in local disputes and challenging corrupt practices. In April 2013 Baghdadi unilaterally announced the merger of ISI and al-Nusra, forming what would now be known as the Islamic State of Iraq and al-Sham (ISIS). Jolani refused, on the basis of the ideological differences outlined above, and instead pledged his allegiance to Ayman al-Zawahiri. Al-Nusra now became the 'official' branch of al-Qa'ida in Syria. But some of its fighters – particularly foreign jihadists – switched allegiance, joining ISIS, which retained this moniker despite Jolani's rejection of the merger.

Now Baghdadi posed a personal challenge to Zawahiri's claim to be the *emir* of the global jihad movement. He was moving swiftly towards its ultimate goal: the re-establishment of the caliphate. Zawahiri attempted to pull rank on the younger man, ordering him to withdraw his forces from Syria and limit his activities to Iraq; this was when Baghdadi responded with the icily sardonic observation that he did not recognise the artificial border between the two countries created by the 'infidel' Sykes-Picot agreement of 1916.

ISIS became as extreme as Zarqawi – if not more so – in its sectarian intolerance, its violence and its implementation of Sharia punishments. It also began to seize territory, equipment and provisions from other rebel groups in Syria. At the end of 2013 all the other resistance groups, including al-Nusra, declared war on ISIS and managed to temporarily dismiss its fighters from Idlib, Aleppo and Deir al-Zour.

By early 2014 ISIS once more dominated the Syrian opposition, prompting Zawahiri to disown the group in a February 2014 statement: 'ISIS is not a branch of al-Qa'ida, we have no organisational relationship with it and we are not responsible for its actions,' he gruffly proclaimed.[12]

ISI spokesman Abu Muhammad al-Adnani responded aggressively and with a clear challenge: 'If God decrees that you would ever set foot in the land of the Islamic State, you must pledge allegiance to, and be a foot soldier of, its *emir* [Baghdadi].' The comment contained an additional, hidden, barb: Zawahiri will never 'set foot' in the Islamic State because he is a fugitive. The younger generation were no longer willing to take orders from older men who had not seen military action since the 1980s in Afghanistan.

Ayman al-Zawahiri now sought to heal the rift between al-Nusra and ISIS. He arranged for trusted figures on the ground to act as mediators, including Saudi cleric Abdullah bin Muhammad al-Muhaysini; the late Abu Khalid al-Suri, a leader in the indigenous Salafist group Ahrar al-Sham; and, as al-Nusra's Sharia advisor, the Australian national Abu Sulayman al-Muhajir. Reconciliation proved impossible, not least because ISIS was increasingly turning against Zawahiri, contesting his claim to the leadership of al-Qa'ida and to be bin Laden's heir. On 17 April 2014, ISIS spokesman Adnani issued a definitive statement: 'Al-Qa'ida today is no longer the seat of true jihad; its leadership has become an axe, trying to destroy the project of the Islamic State and the coming caliphate... its leaders have deviated from the true path... al-Qa'ida now panders to the majority, believing it to be the *ummah* and seeks its approval, thereby compromising the religion.'[13]

Now, ISIS started to fight the other resistance groups, preventing them from fighting the Assad regime unless they pledged allegiance to Baghdadi. Adnani voiced a number of predictions, which seemed melodramatic and wild at the time but which have come to pass, in part at least. In a video released on extremist websites, he said that all the al-Qa'ida affiliates would shift their allegiance and give their *bayat* to the future 'Caliph Ibrahim' (Baghdadi). And now he even included Zawahiri and Mullah Omar in this promise: 'This land of ISIS will grow until everyone gives *bayat* to al-Qurayshi al-Husseini al-Baghdadi, including you O Zawahiri and you O Mullah Omar.' Other groups have, indeed, shifted their allegiance and with unprecedented speed (affiliation with al-Qa'ida typically took one or two years).

The leader of al-Qa'ida in the Arabian Peninsula (AQAP), Nasir al-Wuhayshi, is very close to Zawahiri, their relationship dating back to shared times in Afghanistan where he was bin Laden's private secretary. Nevertheless, his group published a statement on its official al-Manbar website on 14 August 2014, announcing 'solidarity with our Muslim brothers in Iraq against the crusade. Their blood and injuries are ours and we will surely support them.'[14] Sources note that there has been ongoing co-operation between IS and AQAP, that IS trainers have travelled to Yemen and that AQAP fighters have joined IS ranks in Iraq and Syria. AQAP, arguably the second most powerful jihad group after Islamic State, has given IS advice on how to deal with the threat from drones; and the two groups have shared and employed similar military tactics.

Also in August 2014, AQAP's Sheikh Makmun Hatim suggested a complete union of the groups, and wrote this on Twitter: '... await the announcement of the Islamic State of Iraq, ash-Sham and the Arabian Peninsula'.[15] Although this has not yet come to pass, it is my contention that the *Charlie Hebdo* massacre and the simultaneous kosher supermarket murders (in Paris, January 2015) were a joint AQAP-Islamic State operation. AQAP commander Nasr Ibn Ali al-Ansi appeared in a video claiming to be behind the *Charlie Hebdo* attack; he said that the 'seeds' of the plot had been planted by the late Anwar al-Awlaki, an Islamic State icon. Behind al-Ansi was a large image of the Islamic State flag. He ended his address with the Islamic State salute. Amedy Coulibaly left a posthumous video claiming his attack on the kosher supermarket had been carried out under supervision by Islamic State.

In February 2015, Ansar al-Sharia in Libya uploaded a video showing the triumphalist entry into Benghazi of an IS cavalcade of gleaming new Toyota Landcruisers, focusing on the cheering crowds who welcomed them. Other jihadist groups in Eastern Libya had also given their *bayat* to Baghdadi, announcing the 'Islamic State Cyrenica Province' at the end of 2014. At the time of writing (March 2015) four major Libyan cities are under IS control – Benghazi, Derna, Sirte and Tibruk.

Meanwhile Ansar Bayt al-Maqdis (Supporters of the Holy House), based in the Sinai, also pledged allegiance in November 2014.[16]

Further afield, one of the world's most dangerous jihadist networks, the Pakistani Tehrik-i-Taliban (Taliban Movement of Pakistan), initially issued a somewhat ambiguous response to the in-fighting between al-Qa'ida and ISIS. In February 2014 it said: 'Our stance on ISIS and the groups fighting the group is abundantly clear. We support those mujahideen who fight for the sake of the survival of the caliphate.'[17] By October 2014, however, it had made up its mind and declared allegiance to Islamic State.[18] Boko Haram had already confirmed its support for IS on 25 August 2014 and since then has declared newly captured towns and villages as part of the caliphate's territories.[19] On 5 January 2015, Indonesian jihadists led by Alim Abu Bakr Bashir joined Islamic State and on 10 January, in a Twitter storm, mass defections were reported from 'repentant Ahrar al-Sham and al-Nusra'; in a very significant move, tweeted by one 'abu Dijani': '8000 mujahideen recently gave bayat in Afghanistan! Many ikhwa [brothers] fr Taliban AQ Afg and Tehreek Tal are here now. Big news soon...' At the end of January, IS announced it had established a new *wilayah* (province) covering Afghanistan and Pakistan with a regional *emir* (clearly a local challenge to the Taliban).

Not every al-Qa'ida affiliate or ally has transferred its loyalties, however. Opinion within al-Qa'ida in the Islamic Maghreb (AQIM) is divided. Leader Abdelmalek Droukdel rejected the announcement of the caliphate in July 2014 and renewed his *bayat* to Ayman al-Zawahiri, as did Mokhtar Belmokhtar, the *emir* of the Sahara 'branch', al-Murabitun (Independent Nasserites). However, other groups in the Maghreb, such as Ansar al-Sharia and Mujao (Movement for Oneness and Jihad in West Africa), have embraced the caliphate. Within AQIM, the leaders are divided over whether or not they will ultimately join Islamic State. French security sources told *Le Figaro* that the consultative Shura has been discussing defecting to Baghdadi, but that they will delay any announcement to avoid destabilising their own organisation through a split on such an important issue.[20] The same source also revealed that an important AQIM figure, former head of the Salafist Group for Preaching and Combat (GSPC) Abou Abdallah Othmane el-Acimi, has formally shifted his allegiance from Droukdel to Islamic State.

Unity or polarisation?

While several high profile al-Qa'ida leaders in Afghanistan have publicly backed IS, the Taliban has appealed for unity and the formation of a jihad Shura (consultation) council 'to be formed from the leaders of all the jihadist factions and the distinguished people among the experts and the scholars in Sham [Syria] in order to solve their [al-Nusra and ISIS] conflicts... Muslims also should avoid extremism in religion, and judging others without evidence, and distrusting one another,' it posted on its website.

Rather unexpectedly, the leader of ultra-extremist Somali group al-Shabaab (The Youth), Mukhtar Abu Zubayr, has also called for reconciliation. Al-Shabaab officially allied itself with al-Qa'ida under al-Zawahiri's leadership in 2012, which perhaps explains its adherence to his preferred solution to the crisis. Abu Zubayr began a video message on the subject of Islamic State with praises for Zawahiri and Mullah Omar, and asked jihadists in Syria to, 'Respect the leaders of Jihad and its scholars, have good opinion of them and appreciate their rights upon us, for we are all but merely a fruit from the fruits of their Jihad and steadfastness.'[21]

It is interesting to note that, whereas statements in support of IS and the new wave are definitive, those favouring the old guard stop short of outright condemnation of Baghdadi's group. This suggests that even the die-hard al-Qa'ida supporters are leaving their options open.

Without a process of conciliation and consensus, polarisation will increase, with the more radical members of all the groups migrating to IS; the supporters of Mullah Omar and al-Zawahiri will become, by comparison, the 'moderate' face of the jihadist movement, with opportunities for 'normalisation' and diplomacy, which Mullah Omar's Taliban has already started. This is a phenomenon that Saudi Arabia and the West might seek to exploit. But, sadly, if the old guard are no longer in control of the Islamic armies, such opportunities are unlikely to put a halt to the violent march of Islamic State.

FOUR

THE ORIGINS –
PART THREE: SYRIA

In Syria as in Iraq, Islamic State set out to exploit existing political chaos and sectarian violence in order to embed itself. Several additional factors make the situation in Syria even more combustible, not least the eruption of a full-blown civil war out of what were initially peaceful protests, demanding reform and an end to the autocratic regime of Bashar al-Assad.

As the regime brutally put down the rebellion, resulting in more than 200,000 civilian deaths,[1] in-fighting broke out among the opposition factions. The arrival of extreme Islamist entities into the fray – first al-Nusra and then the Islamic State of Iraq and Sham (ISIS) – was the final ingredient required for total chaos to ensue. In a very short space of time, secular and relatively modern Syria became the arena for the most extreme sectarian polarisation, tearing the country apart and causing regional and international superpowers to align themselves on either side of the proxy battleground.

The Syrian crisis has become a global crisis, with far-reaching international implications. The US has been forced to suspend its former objectives, which prioritised regime change, as Islamic State has become Public Enemy Number One for the West and the Assad regime alike.

The Assad dynasty

As in Iraq, the Syrian political landscape has been dominated by the secular Ba'ath party since 1963. The Assad family has ruled the country with an iron fist since 1970, with Bashar al-Assad having succeeded his father, Hafez, in 2000.

Hafez al-Assad wanted to become a doctor, but his parents were unable to pay the tuition fees. He joined the air force instead, seeing a military career as a route into politics. At the age of thirty-three, having attained the rank of commander, he participated in the March 1963 coup that brought the Ba'athists to power and saw Hafez appointed Commander of the Syrian Air Force. Seven years and two further coups later, Hafez seized power and appointed himself the absolute ruler of Syria.

Hafez al-Assad created a 'strong-man' autocracy that required unquestioning loyalty (on pain of death, imprisonment, torture or exile). It relied heavily on the type of personality cult more usual in the ex-Soviet Union and its republics, where giant posters and huge statues of the leader and his family dwarf and intimidate the populace – an approach also favoured by Hafez al-Assad's Arab contemporaries Saddam Hussein and Muammar al-Gaddafi.

The Assad family are Alawites – a vague relation of Shi'i Islam. As the demographics of Syria will become an important feature of this narrative in later chapters, I will add here that the 1.5 million Alawites constitute just 12 per cent of the population, whereas Sunni Arabs make up 65 per cent, with Sunni Kurds an additional 9 per cent. Other minorities include Christian Arabs at 10 per cent and Druze Arabs at 3 per cent – the latter also being an offshoot of Shi'i Islam.

The Alawite and Druze religions are curious hybrids and are regarded as heretical by extremist Sunni Muslims. The Druze embrace other Abrahamic creeds as well as neo-Platonic and Gnostic beliefs and practices. The Alawites maintain that they are Shi'i Muslims, despite not believing in traditional prayers or that the Qur'an is the holy book. The Alawites celebrate the Christian festivals of Christmas, Easter and Epiphany and believe in reincarnation (though not for women). Perhaps the most 'heretical' tenet of the Alawite faith is the claim that Muhammad's son-in-law Ali was God incarnate. 'Alawite' means 'follower of Ali'.

The Alawite *Shahada* (testimony) is 'There is no God but Ali' – guaranteed to enrage a Sunni-Salafist.

The Alawites have long been persecuted in Syria, but their fortunes changed for the better when Hafez al-Assad came to power. The Syrian constitution requires that the head of state must be a Muslim – a political and sectarian requirement, since it excludes Christians from power. There was some doubt about Assad's claim to be of the faith – as we have seen, the Alawite faith is far from 'traditional' Islam – until a Lebanese imam, Musa Sadr, endorsed his legitimacy. Riots, mostly involving Sunni Muslims, ensued in protest at what the protestors defined as the new 'atheist' regime.

Like Saddam Hussein, Hafez al-Assad understood the political power of Islam. Following the Islamic revolution in Iran he began to stress that Syria was a Muslim nation, fearing contagion as unrest grew in Aleppo, Homs and Hama. On that occasion the state's security apparatus efficiently extinguished burgeoning sectarian protests.

There are four main Alawite tribal confederations in Syria: Kalbiyah (the Assad family's tribe), Khaiyatin, Haddadin and Matawirah. As we will see, tribal allegiances in Iraq and Syria are an all-important factor in gaining and maintaining power. Hafez al-Assad was able to win tribal support from the majority Sunni tribes in exchange for power and money, and Islamic State has been able to exploit tribal networks in a similar manner.[2] The failure of the tribes to resist Islamic State was a cause of great dismay to the West, who may optimistically have anticipated an 'Awakening'-style stand-off in Syria.

While he did not exclude the Sunni majority from the administrative apparatus, Hafez al-Assad limited its members' participation to minor political institutions, keeping the leadership of military, security and intelligence services firmly inside the Alawite community and, indeed, his own family. In the succeeding decades, the Syrian security machine would become amongst the most brutal and feared in the Middle East, as well as the most complex, with forty-eight different branches centrally, in addition to scores of local branches.[3]

Bashar was born in 1965 to Hafez and his wife, Anisa Makhlouf, a strong-minded woman from a peasant family. He was not the natural choice to succeed his father, being shy and studious as a young man. Hafez's brother, Rifaat, was the preferred candidate until he attempted to overthrow a hospitalised Hafez in 1984. Bashar's dashing elder brother, Bassel, was the next in line, but he was killed in a sports car accident in 1994. Bashar's younger brother, Maher, born in 1967, was considered too wild, aggressive and unpredictable for the presidency and was instead installed as head of the Republican Guard, the core of Syria's security apparatus. He would later lead the fierce crackdown on demonstrators in the early days of the uprising and is believed to have authorised the chemical gas attacks on the suburbs of Damascus in January 2014, in revenge for an assassination attempt on the President.[4]

Bashar himself qualified as a doctor at Damascus University before heading for London where he trained as an eye surgeon. His progress in his chosen field was rudely interrupted by Bassel's untimely death; he was recalled to Syria in 1994 and enrolled in the military academy, in a manner echoing his father's career path. Bashar was obliged to toughen up; he gained first-hand battlefield experience when he led the 1998 Syrian occupation of Lebanon.

When Hafez died in June 2000, Syrians had some hope that Bashar would bring a more liberal and relaxed rule to Syria, following his sojourn in London and marriage to a British national, Asma (née Akhras), a fashionable and 'modern' young woman who had been a computer scientist and investment banker before her marriage. In March 2011, the very month the uprising began, American *Vogue* magazine ran a gushing portrait of Asma (known to her English friends as Emma) titled 'The Rose of the Desert', describing 'a thin, long-limbed beauty with a trained analytic mind'.[5]

Initially, Bashar did indeed encourage a more open political environment. Many political prisoners, including members of the Muslim Brotherhood, were released during what was fondly termed the 'Damascus Spring'. When the Muslim Brotherhood issued a statement (from the safety of London) in May 2001, calling for reforms in its native land, Bashar responded by instantly revoking all the freedoms he had formerly granted. From then on he followed the same path as his father, and it came as no surprise that he instantly threw all the military and security resources at his disposal at the embryonic revolution in March 2011.

Nor does the younger generation offer much hope of a more relaxed attitude. Bashar's eldest son, Hafez, named after his grandfather, was just eleven years old when the *New York Times* ran some quotes from his Facebook page in 2013: 'America doesn't have soldiers, what it has is some cowards with new technology who claim themselves as liberators,' he wrote, adding, 'I just want them to attack sooo much, because I want them to make this huge mistake of beginning something that they don't know the end of it...' Children of prominent officials 'liked' the post, with one commenting, 'Like father like son! Well said future President!'[6]

Radical Islam in Syria – recent history

Bashar clearly shares his father's antipathy for Islamists. Hafez al-Assad considered the Muslim Brotherhood and other fundamentalist groups to be the most likely threat to his power base and, despite being outlawed in 1964, the Muslim Brotherhood remained the most viable political opposition to the Ba'ath party. Hafez al-Assad's apprehensions were confirmed in 1976 when a sporadic insurgency erupted that would last nearly six years.

In 1972 a split had emerged within the Muslim Brotherhood between a more moderate wing, centred on Damascus, led by Issam al-Attar, and in Aleppo-Hama a more radical group, led by Abdul Fatah Abu Ghuddah, which was bent on violent confrontation with the regime. From the latter arose al-Talia al-Muqatila (The Fighting Vanguard), whose leader, Marwan Hadid, had been trained in a PLO camp in Jordan. The group has cells in Damascus, Aleppo and Hama, though its operational base remained in Jordan and became, in effect, the Syrian Muslim Brotherhood's military wing.

By 1979 Alawites and Ba'ath party officials found themselves regular targets of assassination and attack; by 1981 more than 300 had been killed, including a dozen imams who had criticised the violence. As the country prepared to celebrate the seventeenth anniversary of the first Ba'athist coup, strikes and protests paralysed most Syrian towns and cities and demonstrators battled with the security forces.

On 26 June 1980 Fighting Vanguard gunmen tried to assassinate Hafez al-Assad. Retaliation was extreme and brutal. The next day, Defence Brigades troops – whose insignia is a skull crossed by two swords – led by Hafez's brother, Rifaat, massacred 1,152 Islamist prisoners in Tadmor jail, shooting them down from the rooftops as they gathered in the yard.[7]

In July 1980, Hafez al-Assad decreed that membership of the Muslim Brotherhood was now a crime, punishable by death. The low-level insurgency continued with the Fighting Vanguard attacking government buildings, police stations and Ba'ath party buildings. Between August and November 1981 there were four major car bomb attacks on, in order, the Ba'ath Party headquarters, the Intelligence Agencies HQ, the Air Force HQ and the Prime Minister's office.

The Fighting Vanguard led a major insurrection in the city of Hama on 2 February 1982, taking control of the city and its 250,000 inhabitants. Hafez and Rifaat responded with full force, shelling the city repeatedly for the next three weeks until the Brotherhood surrendered – a sequence of events that would be repeated in February and March 2012. At least 20,000 people, most of them civilians, lost their lives as a result of the ferocious bombardment.[8] Hafez al-Assad blamed the Muslim Brotherhood for the massacre. His wily move ensured that the population lost whatever enthusiasm they might have had for the Islamist agenda. Bashar al-Assad must have expected a similar response from the public when the first jihadist bombs went off in Damascus in 2012 and he blamed al-Qa'ida.

After the Hama massacre, the Syrian government admitted to having incarcerated 30,000 leaders and members of the Muslim Brotherhood.[9] Thus ended the official presence of any Islamist group inside Syria for nearly two decades.

The Muslim Brotherhood leadership went into exile, but in Syria it remained – as in much of the Arab world – the most credible, organised political opposition. The Syrian branch in London in particular matured into a moderate group advocating democracy and an end to all political violence. Five years before the first 'Arab Spring' protests, the exiled leader of Brotherhood's Syrian branch, Ali Sadreddine Bayanouni, clarified in an interview with the *Guardian* newspaper that the Muslim Brotherhood did not see themselves as the 'alternative to 40 years of corrupt dictatorship... but as partners with others in the coming stage'. Speaking from his North London home, he added that his party sought a peaceful change of government in Damascus and the establishment of a 'civil, democratic state, not an Islamist republic.'[10]

Nevertheless, extremism was far from extinguished in Syrian hearts. Among the members of the Fighting Vanguard in 1980 was twenty-one-year-old Mustafa bin Abdul Qadir Set Marriam, aka Abu Musab al-Suri, who would become one of al-Qaʿida's leading strategists and thinkers; his prolific writings about tactics and the ideology of war still influence the online generation of jihadists, including the leaders of Islamic State. He was forced to flee after the Hama massacre, finding refuge in Jordan. Later, al-Suri would resurface in London (where I met him) and in Tora Bora, Afghanistan, where I was astonished to meet him again, this time at Osama bin Laden's side. Al-Suri became closer to the Taliban after 9/11 and he later told me that he had become Taliban commander Mullah Omar's administrative right-hand man. He was arrested in Pakistan by the CIA in 2005 and sent back to Syria just before the uprising in 2011. Reports of what became of him next vary; some say he was tortured and may have died in jail, whereas others, including the *Daily Telegraph* in London, say he was released as a 'warning to the US and UK' by the Assad regime in February

2012.[11] None of my sources has reported sighting him or hearing of him in Syria recently. If he is still alive, he is likely to be with the Taliban or the al-Qaʻida 'old guard' in Af-Pak hinterland.

Another significant figure of Syrian origin is Abu Khalid al-Suri, who would be killed by a suicide bomber in February 2014. Khalid, who had been a member of the al-Qaʻida elite since its inception, was acting as al-Qaʻida leader Ayman al-Zawahiri's representative in Syria. It is logical to assume that he was assassinated by ISIS, at that time embroiled in a bitter feud with al-Nusra (al-Qaʻida's 'official' branch in Syria) and al-Zawahiri himself.

Syrian jihadists have long been associated al-Qaʻida-linked groups in Afghanistan, Bosnia and throughout the 1990s in Chechnya.[12] They are known to have fought alongside Abu Musab al-Zarqawi when he was in Herat, Afghanistan in 2000. Among them was a figure of great significance to our present study: Abu Mohammad al-Jolani (often also transcribed Joulani and Julani), the *emir* of al-Nusra in Syria. Jolani's real name is not known, but his *kunya* indicates that he hails from the Golan Heights.

When Zarqawi arrived in northern Iraq in 2002 he was accompanied by several Syrian jihadists, including Jolani. They helped to establish a network of sleeper cells in Syria and Lebanon as well as securing trafficking lanes and safe houses along the border with Syria. These would be invaluable for moving men, arms and supplies into Iraq initially, and in the reverse direction too when the Syrian revolution erupted. As the insurgency against the 2003 US-led occupation in Iraq escalated, more and more Syrians joined its ranks, and it was through Syria that many foreign fighters entered Iraq to join al-Qaʻida. In 2007, the Syrian regime cracked down on the safe houses and al-Qaʻida cells that Zarqawi had established inside the country; a spike in Syrian jihadists entering Iraq was reported. They would not return home until the uprising offered them a new window of opportunity in 2011.

When Zarqawi was killed in 2006, Jolani moved for a short period to Lebanon. He spent time with al-Qaʻida affiliate Jund al-Sham (Soldiers of the Levant) before returning to Iraq (also in 2006) where he was arrested and sent to Camp Bucca – where Abu Bakr al-Baghdadi and thousands of fellow Islamists were also imprisoned. Like Baghdadi, Jolani established leadership credentials in prison by teaching Arabic and Qur'anic studies. It is likely he established a bond with Baghdadi behind the razor wire of Camp Bucca.

On his release in 2006 Baghdadi established a new extremist group called Jaish Ahl al-Sunnah wal Jamaa. When Jolani was released in 2008, Baghdadi's group was already under the Majlis Shura Council (MSC) umbrella and Jolani became close to the man who would become the ISI leader in 2010; he was appointed head of operations in Mosul province (also called Nineveh province). As the Syrian protests turned into an armed uprising, Baghdadi dispatched Jolani to his homeland to establish an ISI 'branch' there and to profit from the chaos. This group announced its presence with an online video in January 2012, and was called al-Nusra Front (Victory Front).

Syria's foreign relations

Syria's international allegiance with regional superpower Iran, and with global superpowers Russia and China, has made the search for a military or political solution to the ongoing crisis uniquely difficult. The resulting chaos and erosion of central government control have enabled Islamic State to advance and take over at least a third of the country. Syria's turbulent history of foreign relations is informing the present.

When Islamic State announced the caliphate, on a video taken at the Grand Mosque in Mosul in July 2014, Abu Bakr al-Baghdadi declared that this was the end of 'Sykes-Picot'. Jihadist commentators are not alone in blaming the secretive 1916 Anglo-French agreement for the tragedy and unrest that has characterised Middle Eastern politics for nearly 100 years. Concocted by diplomats Sir Mark Sykes and Georges Picot, the agreement was designed to fracture the Ottoman Empire – bringing to an end the succession of Islamic caliphates that had lasted 1,300 years – and ensure that its geo-political integrity could never be reassembled by a succeeding Islamic power. Greater Syria, Bilad al-Sham, was to be divided into what now constitutes Palestine, Israel, Jordan, Lebanon and Syria. In the grip of nationalism, the Arabs did not willingly submit to this plan; it was implemented in 1920 by armed force (French troops capturing Damascus), and the territories placed under mandate. Britain took Jordan and presided over the developments in Palestine, playing midwife to the birth of Israel and all the turmoil that would attend it. France took Syria – then divided into three states along sectarian lines with separate political entities for the Druze and Alawites – and Lebanon.

After the Second World War large numbers of Syrians took to the streets, demanding independence. The last French troops finally left Syria in 1946 and the Republic of Syria was declared, uniting the three states.

The following years were characterised by one military coup after another (three in 1949 alone). The rising tide of pan-Arabism – as a reaction against the colonialist past, and with a distinctly anti-Western flavour – saw a brief political union between Egypt and Syria, under the banner of the United Arab Republic (UAR) in 1958. Following a coup in Baghdad, Iraq also joined the UAR, but it was dissolved following another military coup in Damascus by a group of officers who were unhappy with the way Egypt was dominating the union. The idea of the UAR continued to inform Arab politics nonetheless. Libya announced its membership in 1971. Unity remained a shared dream in the Arab psyche, yet the ideal was constantly undermined by internecine squabbles and violence.

As with Saddam Hussein's Iraq, the West had plenty of reasons to wish for regime change in Syria. Damascus had been a robust supporter of the 'Palestinian cause' since 1947 and the Nakba (meaning 'catastrophe' – the expulsion of Palestinians from their lands during the formation of Israel); it had led the way in every major conflict with Israel. Syria's support for, and accommodation of, training camps for Palestinian guerrilla groups and Lebanese Hezbollah was another source of concern in Tel Aviv and Washington. Until 2005, when it withdrew all its troops after the assassination of the former Lebanese Prime Minister Rafik Hariri, Syria had been the major power broker in Lebanon, having maintained a numerous military presence since the end of the Lebanese civil war.

In the wake of 9/11, UK Prime Minister Tony Blair visited Damascus but was unable to persuade Bashar al-Assad to join the 'war on terror', leading George W. Bush, then US President, to declare that Syria was part of an 'axis of evil'. Linking Syria with Iraq, the US accused it of developing and acquiring 'weapons of mass destruction' and threatened Damascus with sanctions if it did not rein in Hezbollah. Washington's hostility and fear also derive from Cold War days when Syria sided with the USSR.

The Syrian civil war has brought new worries to Tel Aviv. If Assad was essentially hostile, at least he was in control of the country and had supressed the Islamists. When ISIS and al-Nusra began to dominate the rebel forces, this brought the extremists uncomfortably close to Israel's borders. In addition, Lebanese Hezbollah has been actively engaged militarily, fighting alongside the regime. The threat of the Syrian regime being equipped with Russian-made S-300 anti-aircraft missiles presents an additional military threat to Israel. Israel is in a dilemma because its security is weakened by either outcome of the Syrian conflict: a strengthened Syria-Iran-Hezbollah-Iraq entity, or the Islamists emerging as the strongest force.

From revolution to civil war

Tunisian and Egyptian revolutions achieved their primary aim in a matter of weeks; Libya and Yemen toppled their tyrants in under a year. Syria was always going to be different and it was highly unlikely that Bashar al-Assad would be unseated by peaceful dissent alone. The 'civil uprising' stage of the revolution began in earnest on 15 March 2011 after fifteen students were arrested and tortured in Deraa for writing political graffiti. Dozens protesting against the arrests were killed by security forces and demonstrations quickly spread to Banyas, Homs and some Damascus suburbs. An 18 March 'Day of Dignity' saw large protests in several cities across Syria. The security forces used water cannons and tear gas initially, but soon opened fire with live ammunition, and at least fifteen people were killed. The protestors became more daring. In Daraa on 20 March the Ba'ath party headquarters and several other public buildings were burned down. Friday 25 March saw the biggest protests ever, and now they were nationwide. Seventy were killed and hundreds were injured by heavily armed security forces and armoured riot police who openly beat demonstrators.

The Assad regime began to arrest anybody suspected of political activism. Tens of thousands were incarcerated. In April, attempts to erect tents and set up camps as protestors had done with great effect in Egypt were prevented by huge numbers of security personnel. Blockades were established to prevent protestors travelling between cities. Nevertheless, demonstrations continued across the country throughout the month.

At the same time as he ordered the violent crackdown on protests, President Bashar al-Assad attempted to dampen the revolutionary flame with several concessions in response to the protestors' demands, releasing scores of political prisoners and lifting the State of Emergency that had been in force for forty-eight years. State employees were offered an immediate salary increase, and new political parties were licensed. Also in April, Assad issued a decree allowing 'the right to peaceful protest as one of the basic human rights guaranteed by the Syrian constitution' – although anyone availing themselves of that 'right' continued to take their life in their hands.

Protests escalated as Assad's promises failed to convince the people that real change was likely. On 25 April, events took a turn for the worse when 6,000 soldiers were deployed to lay siege to Deraa, which had become the focal point of the uprising. The troops went from house to house arresting protestors; snipers took up positions on rooftops and tanks rolled into town. Water, food supplies, electricity and phone lines were all cut off. At the end of June, protests erupted in Aleppo, Syria's largest and wealthiest city and hitherto a middle-class, conservative enclave.

Unlike the other 'Arab Spring' revolutions, the Syrian uprising quickly descended into an unequal armed conflict. The hastily established opposition Free Syrian Army (FSA), which was announced in late July 2011, initially consisted of inexperienced volunteers bolstered by a handful of officers from the Syrian Army who had defected. By December 2011 it numbered 20,000, rising to around 50,000 over the next two years.

Assad's army remained relatively loyal – with fewer defections than in other 'Arab Spring' countries – and is a highly professional force, well equipped with air power and sophisticated weapons. By way of contrast, Muammar al-Gaddafi had deliberately run down the Libyan Army for fear of a coup, and the only troops he had to fight the rebels were security brigades run by close relatives and hired-in mercenaries. Hosni Mubarak was undone when the Egyptian army announced its sympathy with the protestors and refused to fire on them.

By August 2011, Syria was sliding into civil war and the regime ramped up its violence, with reports that it was deploying chemical weapons and dropping barrel bombs on random targets. At the time of writing, at least 300,000 Syrians have died and 9.5 million have fled their homes,[13] 3.5 million seeking refuge abroad. Given that the 2011 population was only 21 million, this is an astonishing number.

The chances of finding a solution became more remote as the crisis went on. They were even further compromised and complicated by the entry on to the scene of, first, the jihadist fighters and, latterly, Islamic State.

International response

Taken by surprise by the earlier revolutions, the international community benefitted from having had more time to take stock of the situation and its possible consequences by the time the Syrian civil war began. The Syrian rebels believed that the West would lead an early military intervention against Assad as it had done, unchallenged, in Iraq in 2003, and in Libya in 2011. They were to be disappointed.

Unlike the leaders who had already fallen to the Arab Spring, Assad had heavyweight allies in Russia, China, Iran and Hezbollah. Russia did not counter the US-led invasion of Iraq in 2003, still wounded after the break-up of the USSR in 1991, and was caught on the back foot over Libya, failing to veto United Nations Security Council Resolution 1973 which authorised international intervention in 2011. Now, however, it is once again a significant power and a firm Assad ally and its only Mediterranean naval base is in the Syrian port of Tartus. Regional heavyweight Iran, and Lebanese Hezbollah, also stand immovable behind Bashar al-Assad, for sectarian as well as political reasons

Russia and China sit on the UN Security Council and to date have vetoed every resolution designed to pressure Assad. Nevertheless, the US and EU imposed sanctions early on in the crisis, freezing the Assad family's, and top officials', assets and implementing an arms embargo in May 2011. Like every other feature of this civil conflict, however, sanctions policies have been confused and chaotic. The EU had to lift its arms embargo when it decided to arm the rebels in April 2012. An embargo on importing Syrian oil was also lifted in April 2012 because the EU wanted to buy oil directly from the rebels who had seized oil fields. This had the unintended consequence of deepening the schisms between different factions within the opposition as they began to fight for control of this lucrative resource (now dominated by the extremists). Their chances of deposing Assad were thus weakened.[14]

The 'Friends of Syria' – a group designed to offer political and material support to the rebels – was established under the aegis of the then US Secretary of State, Hillary Clinton. It immediately afforded the Syrian opposition umbrella, the Syrian National Council (later Coalition – in both cases SNC) the cloak of legitimacy and international acknowledgement by inviting it to attend meetings. The initial response was enthusiastic; more than seventy nations were represented at the inaugural meeting of the Friends of Syria in Tunis on 24 February 2012, and at the follow-up meeting on 1 April in Istanbul. By the time of the next two meetings, in Paris on 6 July 2012 and Marrakech on 12 December 2012, 114 nations were in attendance.

Just two months later, however, the group had dwindled to eleven (Turkey, the United States, the United Kingdom, Saudi Arabia, Jordan, Egypt, United Arab Emirates, Qatar, Italy, Germany and France), and the remaining members were re-packaged as the 'London Eleven' at their last meeting, chaired by then UK Foreign Secretary, William Hague. The decline of the Friends of Syria was due to splits in its ranks over the extent of help it should offer the opposition (ranging from an all-out invasion, through sophisticated arms, to non-lethal arms). These splits were in evidence at the very first meeting in Tunis when super-hawk Saudi Foreign Minister Prince Saud al-Faisal walked out saying not enough was being done to prevent Assad from killing his own people. No consensus on any major issue has been achieved – the Marrakech meeting spent a depressing amount of time discussing whether or not to change the group's name to 'the Friends of the Syrian People'. Most nations have simply walked away in frustration.

The Syrian crisis has proved deeply divisive and has seriously undermined regional, if not global, political stability, with powers aligning themselves along sectarian fault lines: Iran, Russia, China and Hezbollah champion the regime, whereas the US, UK, Europe, Turkey and the 'Sunni bloc' Arab countries (the Gulf States, Egypt, Jordan) support the 'moderate' opposition. The sectarianism that now characterises the Syrian civil war, and which has contributed to the 'success' of Islamic State, has been fomented and fed by many external actors.

In the absence of all-out international conflagration, the question of arms clearly affects potential outcomes. The regime has been armed by Russia and Iran throughout the conflict. Moscow claims it is not breaking the UN's sanctions because it is fulfilling previous contracts. Iran became a major supplier of rockets, anti-tank missiles, rocket-propelled grenades and mortars, mostly smuggled in via commercial planes and lorries.[15]

Despite promises to arm the rebels, the US, Britain and France have actually supplied only limited shipments of small arms; they were caught on the horns of a dilemma in summer 2013 as they ramped up threats to provide lethal weaponry to the opposition just as the extent of the jihadist presence became known. Fears that any arms they supplied would fall into the 'wrong' hands brought plans to a standstill. The CIA had already established an 'operations room' on the Turkish border for the purpose of ensuring that arms from Gulf countries went to 'West-friendly' FSA-linked fighters; but the West erred on the side of caution and limited its 'non-lethal' aid to food packages and clothing.[16]

Both Qatar and Saudi Arabia funded and armed the rebels, however. The *New York Times* reported that Qatar flew arms to Turkey for distribution to the Syrian rebels from January 2012. Regular Royal Saudi Air Force flights carried shipments of rockets and grenade launchers, as well as rifles and machine guns, to Jordan and Turkey whence they were smuggled into Syria. Unconfirmed estimates suggest that Saudi Arabia has spent $5 billion arming and supporting the Syrian opposition, just as it supported and armed the mujahideen in Afghanistan from which the most extremist Islamist groups, including al-Qa'ida, subsequently emerged. The Saudis urged the several Islamist groups in Syria that were not affiliated with al-Qa'ida to merge under the umbrella Islamic Army as a way of distinguishing them from the extremely radical jihadist groups which they fear – with good reason, since ISIS took to declaring that the House of Saud was next on its hit list.

A rift developed between Qatar and Saudi Arabia, initially

over the coup in Egypt in June 2013, which saw the legitimately elected Muslim Brotherhood figure, President Mohamed Morsi, overthrown by a military junta led by the current President al-Sisi. Qatar continued to support the Muslim Brotherhood, whereas the Saudis tried to pressure the US into designating them a 'terrorist entity'. Next, the Saudi authorities decided to reverse Prince Bandar bin Sultan's policy of establishing and supporting militant Islamic groups to speed up the overthrow of the Syrian regime, since it had produced exactly the opposite results. The Saudi-Qatari rift also found expression in the emergence within the SNC of two distinct blocs. The Saudis would like to see their man, head of the Syrian National Coalition Ahmad al-Jarba, replace President Assad.

Saudi Arabia found itself increasingly at odds with the international community over Syria during 2013. US President Obama had drawn a 'red line' on chemical weapons, heavily implying that if it were proved that Assad had used them, the US would lead a military intervention to effect regime change. When it seemed certain that Assad's troops had indeed launched a chemical attack on the unfortunate people of Ghouta in August 2013, President Obama stepped back from the brink of what might potentially have spiralled into an international conflagration (considering the alignments of the great powers outlined above) amid accusations of indecision and weakness. Instead, Obama succumbed to Russian diplomatic overtures on the sidelines of the G20 summit in St Petersburg and endorsed a Moscow-sponsored deal that saw Syria sign up to the Chemical Weapons Convention, agreeing to destroy all its stockpiles by mid-2014 and scrap its capacity for manufacturing chemical weapons by November 2014. Having dropped its primary insistence on regime change in Damascus, Washington suddenly appeared to be nearer Moscow over Syria than to its former (anti-Assad) partners in Paris, Ankara, Riyadh and Doha.

The usually taciturn Saudis did not conceal their fury at this development. Worse was to come when Washington began open rapprochement with Iran, Riyadh's nemesis. The Saudi royal family only learned about this unpalatable new development through television news reports, since they had been neither informed nor consulted before Obama and Iran's newly elected President, Hassan Rouhani, started chatting on the telephone. At the time, the Obama regime supported a diplomatic, negotiated settlement to the Syrian crisis; Secretary of State John Kerry even invited the Russians to host a conference in Moscow.[17] The Geneva II conference eventually took place in January 2014 after months of horse-trading.

Enraged that the US was not doing Saudi Arabia's bidding. in September 2013 Prince Saud al-Faisal refused to deliver a scheduled speech at the UN General Assembly and, in October, the Saudi Foreign Ministry announced that the country would not be taking up its place as a non-permanent member of the UN Security Council. It was the first time that Saudi Arabia had been elected to the two-year rotating membership which most countries use to highlight issues of particular concern to them and to influence world leaders.

The Arab League (founded in 1945 to 'safeguard the independence and sovereignty of member states') might have played a conciliatory role between the warring parties in Syria; instead, it contributed to the escalation of the crisis by slamming shut all diplomatic doors. Its first move was to expel Syria from membership in November 2011 and impose an economic and political blockade. Tunisia, Egypt and the Gulf States all closed their Damascus embassies and expelled Syria's ambassadors from their capitals. These actions immediately conferred legitimacy on the opposition as representative of the people of Syria, and in March 2013 the League invited SNC leader Moaz al-Khatib to take the Syrian seat behind the Syrian flag at its summit in Doha.

The Arab League decided to back regime change by force of arms early on, and approved the provision of modern weapons to the opposition to accelerate the process. This directly contributed to the militarisation of the struggle, and paved the way for the entry of jihadist groups to the battlefields.

In April 2014, UN-Arab League peace envoy Lakhdar Brahimi decided to drop his dual role and to operate, instead, under the UN banner alone, claiming that the Arab League's determination to back the opposition at all costs undermined his position as a neutral negotiator. In January 2014 Brahimi also snubbed the Arab League when he invited Tehran to participate in the UN-backed Geneva II conference on Syria – an invitation that was not extended to any League members. In the event, Iran did not attend because of fierce opposition by Riyadh; and Brahimi resigned in May 2014, just as his predecessor, Kofi Annan, had done, overwhelmed by the complicated diplomacy of the task.

The ongoing, major problem has been the lack of a strong, united and cohesive opposition body. The Syrian National Coalition was convened as an umbrella grouping of all the various factions in the opposition from the Muslim Brotherhood to the Kurds, yet emails leaked in early 2014 reveal the extent and depth of the splits and factional infighting. In one, Muhammad Faruk Tayfour (the leader of the Muslim Brotherhood bloc) demanded that Burhan Ghalioun (leader of the SNC) should sack spokeswoman Bassma Kodmani because she had appeared on French TV beside Israelis and had maintained that Israel was 'necessary to the Middle East'.[18]

Diplomacy was virtually impossible without a credible opposition and a putative alternative government. Two international peace conferences, Geneva I and Geneva II, failed to produce results. It became increasingly obvious that no negotiated peace could be brokered without the participation of the regime and its two main allies, Russia and Iran. Geneva II almost achieved a full house in this respect, but the Saudis objected so vigorously to Iran's participation that it was not, ultimately, invited to attend. Representatives of the regime and the SNC did manage to sit down together in the same room, but sadly no results ensued.

With all diplomatic opportunities used up and military intervention to achieve regime change no longer on the cards, the international community now faced a new and unexpected crisis in

Syria that would tear up all previous road maps: the establishment of Islamic State in July 2014. Now the West and its allies faced entirely new dilemmas. An intervention inside Syria would see the West in the same trench as Bashar al-Assad, whom it had been seeking to depose for the previous three years. An implicit political alliance would then exist between the US and its allies, plus Iran – Saudi Arabia's main regional rival – and Russia. Russia was particularly unattractive because of its annexation of the Crimea in March 2014 and subsequent interference in Eastern Ukraine, where it was accused of supporting the separatist rebels. The sectarian dimension of an – even unspoken – alliance with Syria in order to attack Islamic State was equally nonsensical. The West and the Sunni bloc (Saudi Arabia, Qatar, Turkey, Jordan) would be aligning themselves with their own main Shi'i enemies, Iran and Syria.

Then there is Israeli security, an obligatory element in any American foreign policy equation. Like Iraq under Saddam Hussein, and Libya under Colonel Gaddafi, pre-revolutionary Syria was a powerful country with a strong army and deeply antagonistic to Israel. Syria is capable of posing a real threat to Israel with whom it shares a border. The West and Israel were worried when Islamists, traditionally hostile to Israel, prevailed in post-revolutionary Egypt. They therefore welcomed the ousting of the Muslim Brotherhood's President Morsi by al-Sisi's military junta. President al-Sisi, as dictatorial and as repressive as the man the Arab Spring brought down – Hosni Mubarak – is more acceptable because he has agreed to abide by the peace treaty with Israel.

The jihadists prepare for Syrian opportunities

As I discovered from my own research, the jihadists were aware from the outset that a revolution in Syria would afford them unprecedented opportunities. Preparations in the digital world were already underway before the first large-scale demonstrations in Deraa. In February 2011, al-Nur Media Foundation presented a new essay from jihadist ideologue Abu Abdullah al-Qasimi: 'Message to the Proud People of Syria'. Al-Qasimi refers to a Syrian 'Islamic revolution jihadist', Abu Musab al-Suri (imprisoned by the Assad regime at the time), whose 'sacrifice and courage demonstrate the ability to fight tyranny'. Fomenting sectarian anger, he declares: 'for more than 50 years this Nusayri [derogatory name for Shi'i] junta has ruled over you... become your own masters and rid yourselves of this humiliation'.

After the revolution began in earnest in March 2011, more ideologues added their voices to the clamour for jihadist engagement. On 25 March Hamid Bin Abdallah al-Ali celebrated the 'Launch of the Syrian Revolution'. On 26 March, Libyan group Fatah al-Islam (Conquest of Islam) sent a message urging 'Victory for Our Brothers in *Islamic* Syria'. By 1 April, Sheikh Abu Basir al-Tartusi was describing the heresies perpetrated by the 'Nusayri' regime in an essay titled 'What People Do Not Know about the Sectarian Syrian Regime'. He urged the demonstrators to rise up, claiming that the Alawite elite maintained power through a deliberate policy: 'they teach their young that the rich and powerful humiliate and reduce to servitude the poor and weak, treating them like beasts of the field... there is no pity or compassion in their breasts, nor even charity...' Throughout April, May and June, ideologues and a variety of jihadist groups posted statements, calls for funding for the revolutionaries, and even poems celebrating their struggle – one offering was titled 'Deraa, You Are the Crown of Dignity'.

It was not until July that al-Qa'ida's new leader, Ayman al-Zawahiri, issued a statement on Syria. As with the Egyptian uprising, Zawahiri was slow to react to events on the ground. Now he praised the protestors and posited the revolution as an Islamic battle against US and Israeli interests. This more-globalised perspective, which would be shared by IS, contrasts with most other jihadist posting on the subject at this stage. They saw the Syrian revolution as essentially a sectarian conflict. Placing al-Qa'ida firmly in the same trench as the protestors, Zawahiri tells them, 'You are an example, explaining lessons to your Arab and Muslim nation in sacrifice, steadfastness and the struggle against oppression... How could you not? You are the sons of the Levant, the front for jihad and martyrdom.'

In September 2011 one 'Abu Jihad al-Shami' produced a fifty-two-page guide for the embryonic mujahideen in Syria. 'A Strategy for the Land of Gathering (Syria): An Attempt to Pinpoint the Pivotal Aspects' is, in many respects, a road map of the strategy the mujahideen actually adopted. It offers a revealing glimpse into the way jihadist groups establish a logistical infrastructure and bases from which to operate before issuing a call for volunteers or commencing their war plan.

Al-Shami advises jihadists already in Syria, and those arriving there, to 'establish secret logistics cells in the cities and mobile battalions in different regions... avoid centralisation, at least to begin with... but accept direction and guidance from the overall leadership.' The next stage of the insurgency is to 'attack the widest possible number of targets over as large an expanse of territory as you can... this will force the enemy to dilute their forces.' This is, indeed, the way that small battalions of jihadists were able to defeat regular army units in both Syria and Iraq. Al-Shami also foresees the symbiotic relationship between jihadists in Syria and Iraq: 'When the front develops,' he advises, 'trainers, experts, leaders, arms and explosives can all be brought across the border.' He points out that the mujahideen on both sides of the border can offer each other safe haven if they need to flee a losing battle, bombardment or surveillance.

With an eye already on expansionism, al-Shami notes that Jordan is an inhospitable country full of spies, but that 'brothers' already active inside the country should start low-key operations against the government to destabilise the security situation, which in turn will help the Syrian jihadists. The Syrian side of the border could be suitable for 'manoeuvres' since it is not, at present, well policed, although he comments that this is only until 'the Jordanian regime realises the danger on its doorstep.' In summer 2014, Islamic State indicated that Jordan is at the top of its wish list of territories.

Lebanon is a prime target from al-Shami's perspective: 'It already has two effective, internal enemies in Hezbollah and the Christian militia. These weaken it and require a lot of attention from the security forces... Open secret training camps in Lebanon,' he advises, 'and make it a rear operations base for planning and preparing attacks inside Syria.' By August 2014, local papers in Lebanon claimed there were at least forty secret ISIS cells in the country. Battles broke out between the Lebanese Army and ISIS after the latter seized Arsal.

Al-Shami warns the mujahideen to expect large numbers of 'martyrs' at the hands of the singularly vicious Assad regime and to ready the next generation of leaders to replace those who will be lost. Local leaders are urged to post YouTube videos calling for volunteers, celebrating martyrs and narrating operations carried out by the mujahideen inside Syria. The internet was, and remains, Islamic State's number one PR and recruitment vehicle.

Three years before 'Caliph Ibrahim' (Baghdadi) mounted the pulpit in Mosul's Grand Mosque, al-Shami writes, 'We must re-awaken the *ummah* [Muslim nation or community] by reminding them that the seat of the Abbasid Caliphate was Baghdad, and the Umawi Caliphate was based in Damascus.' The notion of re-establishing the Caliphate was inextricably linked to the Syrian jihad from the outset. Al-Shami also proposes that the jihadists become financially self-sufficient, recommending that they seize 'enemy' oil, but adding that the 'best source of liquid cash is kidnapping'. Sadly, like many jihadist groups, Islamic State has adopted this practice, with its harrowing consequences. Whether or not al-Shami's writings were a primary influence, there can be no doubt that events in Syria were well planned and systematically brought to fruition.

In the latter part of 2011 armed Islamist factions started to appear and the whole range of jihadist websites, bulletin boards, chat rooms and all manner of accounts on social media platforms was harnessed to muster a mujahideen army to help the people of Syria depose Assad. Al-Qaʻida announced its arrival on the scene with two suicide bombings in December 2011, blowing up intelligence compounds in Damascus, killing forty-four and wounding 160. In early January 2012, another suicide bomber struck an intelligence target and on 10 February 2012 two suicide bombers targeted security installations in the Syrian commercial capital, Aleppo.

Confirmation of al-Qaʻida's engagement inside Syria came in the form of a video from Ayman al-Zawahiri, disseminated across the internet and social media, titled 'Onward Lions of Syria'. Al-Zawahiri urged jihadists from neighbouring countries such as Iraq, Turkey, Lebanon and Jordan to migrate to Syria to join the fight; he exhorted the Syrian people to 'continue your revolt and anger, do not accept anything but independent, respectful government.'

With al-Qaʻida resurgent in Iraq, a large number of battle-hardened and experienced jihadists were only hours away from Syria, with which Iraq shares a 500-kilometre border. Since the Iran-backed regime in Iraq had expressed its support for Assad, there now existed a sectarian motive for jihad in both countries. In Iraq, around 35 per cent of the population are Sunni; by contrast, the sectarian map in Syria works in al-Qaʻida's favour; Sunni Muslims (including Kurds) are in the majority at 75 per cent of the population.

North-eastern Syria had been something of an al-Qaʻida stronghold after 2003, when fighters passed through on their way to join the insurgency against the occupation of Iraq; with the success of the US 'surge' in 2006, Iraqi intelligence reported a steady exodus of al-Qaʻida fighters from the Islamic State of Iraq (ISI) across the border into Syria from late 2011; the infrastructure that had been established to facilitate the flow of jihadists into Iraq via Syria was now in service the other way. There were reports, too, of arms being smuggled from Mosul through the Rabia crossing and into Syria.

In the early days of the mujahideen presence, Saudi Arabia was enthusiastically arming and funding the fighters; Jordanian officials intercepted several cargos of arms originating from Riyadh.[19]

Neighbouring countries became embroiled either wittingly (as in the case of Turkey, which facilitated the transit of fighters and arms) or not. The Jordanian city of Irbid, near the Syrian border, is a long-standing transit point for migrating fighters. A group of militant jihadists in Jordan, led by Abu-Muhammad al-Tahawi, renounced their commitment to non-violence and travelled to help the mujahideen in Syria.

Al-Qa'ida-linked fighters from Lebanon's refugee camps also found their way to Syria. In late April 2012, a high-profile leader of the Lebanese group Fatah al-Islam, Abdel-Ghani Jawhar, was killed in Qusayr, near the city of Homs, which correspondents described as 'crawling with mujahideen'.

As in Libya, the international jihadist community was poised to play a major role in the revolution. This time, however, the Salafi-jihadist presence would evolve into one of the biggest, best-armed, richest, most violent and most effective Islamic army the world has witnessed in modern times.

Map of the armed Syrian opposition

The armed opposition in Syria emerged over the first twelve to eighteen months of the uprising. It was uniquely uncoordinated and complicated, consisting of at least 1,000 different groups and 100,000 fighters. Some of the groups were small, local outfits, and many found their way into wider alliances and coalitions.

Here is a brief overview of the main groupings.

The Free Syrian Army (FSA)

Formed in July 2011 by Syrian Army deserters and volunteers, the FSA was initially based in Turkey, where it trained and gathered funding and weapons before joining the fray. Its manifesto was essentially secular and had one aim: to depose Assad. Dozens of groups sprung up across Syria fighting under the FSA banner, but there was no centralised operational, strategic or political control. This meant that the group did not make as much progress against the regime as it might have done.

In response to critique from the West and its Gulf Arab backers, the FSA formed a 'Supreme Military Council' (SMC) in December 2012. A government in exile, headed by Ahmad Tohme, was in political control of the SMC, while General Salim Idris was Chief of Staff and military commander on the ground. The SMC was intended to provide the united, 'moderate' opposition that the West and its allies desperately wanted to see in Syria, both as an alternative to the regime and to counter the burgeoning jihadist groups.

The SMC broke the command down into five 'fronts': Northern (Aleppo and Idlib), Eastern (Raqqa, Deir al-Zour and Hassaka), Western (Hama, Latakia and Tartus), Central (Homs and Rastan) and Southern (Damascus, Deraa and Suwaida). Six members for each front joined a central council, and each front had a commander and an advisory council composed of civilians and soldiers. Despite this apparently workable structure, General Idris did not assert operational control and the SMC remained fragmented and riven with in-fighting. The various brigades under the SMC umbrella did not have a shared agenda or even identity; some have aligned themselves increasingly closer with the Islamist and extremist groups as the civil war has gone on.

Groups affiliated with the SMC were: Martyrs of Syria Brigades, consisting of around 7,000 fighters and based in Idlib; Northern Storm Brigade, an Islamist group that was in control of the Syria-Turkey border crossing at Azaz until overrun by IS; and Ahrar Suriya (Free Men of Syria) Brigade, established by a former air force officer, Colonel Qasim Saad al-Din.

In November 2013, the *Daily Telegraph* investigated 'How the FSA became a largely criminal enterprise.' Interviewees on the ground described how FSA commanders had become 'princes of war' by profiteering. A rebel fighter from the Jisr al-Shugour market district in Idlib told the *Telegraph* how the 'band of brothers' that had liberated his town were overrun in April 2013. 'People arrived who were... only interested in selling guns,' he said. 'They called themselves FSA, but they had no interest in fighting Assad. They seized areas that were already free of the regime and set up checkpoints on roads there and started charging people for access... some of the men in my brigade started working with them.'[20]

Correspondents for Rai al-Youm, the news website I run, confirmed that many commanders who had formerly been sincere in their fight against the regime had been corrupted by the large amounts of money and weapons they received from backers in the Gulf. Men who were formerly peasants have become warlords, with brigades of armed men at their disposal; now they drive expensive cars and have constructed enormous family homes for themselves. It may be that, for these men, an end to the civil war and the chaos that has afforded these 'opportunities' is not to be desired.

Corrupt commanders have their own digital media crews embedded with them to record their military operations; videos are then posted on YouTube for the sole purpose of convincing sponsors, and potential donors, that they are active in the fight against Assad. 'Sponsors will give us money for a specific operation, so when we do it, we film it as proof that we have used their money well,' a media officer with the Farouk Brigade, one of the best-known rebel outfits in Syria in 2013, told the *Daily Telegraph*.[21] He seems to have volunteered no information as to who these 'sponsors' might be.

In the absence of centralised rule of law, every town and village in the north of Syria found itself under the control of various, feuding, warlords. According to activists reported in the same *Telegraph* article, when the oil fields round Raqqa were seized, 'It changed from revolution to a battle for oil.'

The West always viewed the FSA as its best potential ally, with Western diplomats emphasising the need for central command and control under the SMC. But it failed to gain traction, disintegrating rapidly under bombardment not by regime explosives but by greed, corruption and self-interest. Given this background, the arrival of ISIS, with its promise of law and order and religious conservatism, may have appeared to many as a welcome break.

The SMC attempted to soldier on and the West still lent it its unerring support, believing it could become the ally it so desperately needed. General Idris was fired by the FSA in February 2014 over his 'failure to create an institution' and he was replaced by Brigadier General Abdelilah al-Bashir. On 25 June 2014, the US decided to fund the SMC to the tune of $500 million but, the very next day, Ahmad Tohme announced that the SMC was to be disbanded, al-Bashir was to be sacked, and its leadership investigated for corruption.[22]

The FSA has limped on, but has lost support and credibility, both at home and abroad. It has little to show for its four-year battle against the Assad regime which is, if anything, regaining ground. The US has lost interest in the FSA as an effective anti-regime vehicle and has, anyway, shifted its focus onto destroying Islamic State, for which task it began training new Syrian units in 2015. The FSA declared war on Islamic State in late 2014 and sent units to fight it in the northern Syrian city Kobani, finding itself in the extraordinary situation of fighting with the regime and the US against a common enemy.

The Islamic Front

The Islamic Front was formed in November 2013 in response to Saudi Arabian concerns over ISIS and al-Nusra. Seven groups came together to form a rival Islamic Army of 45,000 men. The groups were: Harakat Ahrar al-Sham al-Islamiyya (Islamic Movement of the Free Men of the Levant); Jaysh al-Islam (Army of Islam); Suqour al-Sham (Falcons of the Levant); Liwa al-Tawhid (Unity Brigade); Liwa al-Haqq (Right Brigade); Ansar al-Sham (Supporters of the Levant); and the Kurdish Islamic Front. Although the Front employs the language and rhetoric of jihadist groups, it was intended to provide a 'moderate' Islamist presence which aimed to topple Assad and establish an Islamic State. In December 2013 it withdrew from the SMC umbrella and began fighting SMC brigades for control of several warehouses and the Bab al-Hawa crossing with Turkey. The US and UK suspended their 'non-lethal' aid to rebel groups in the north in response.

There was another, similar, alliance of about twenty Islamist rebel groups called the Syrian Islamic Liberation Front, formed in September 2012. Its membership ranged from moderates to ultra-conservative Salafists, but it recognised the SMC and fought alongside it. Just one year later, it announced it was ceasing all operations, its fighters dispersing among various opposition groups, al-Nusra and ISIS.

Harakat Ahrar al-Sham al-Islamiyya

Led by Hassan Abboud, who had been a commander in the ISI, and with an estimated 20,000 fighters, Harakat Ahrar al-Sham al-Islamiyya (Islamic Movement of the Free Men of the Levant) quickly gained a reputation for discipline and bravery, making an immediate impact on the battlefield when it was formed in late 2011 in Idlib. It became the most powerful armed opposition group and, despite having a Salafist-Jiihadi identity and agenda, was able to co-operate with FSA forces in military action. Latterly it has distanced itself from the FSA and is firmly in the jihadist camp, being bombed by American planes along with al-Nusra and Islamic State. Many of its members migrated to Islamic State after it was declared.

Jaysh al-Sham

The 'Army of Islam', Jaysh al-Sham was formed in September 2013 by an alliance of more than fifty Islamist factions from the Damascus area. It numbers more than 9,000 fighters. The main group is Liwa al-Islam (Battalion of Islam) which is led by Zahran Alloush, a Salafist who had been in prison and whose father is a religious scholar in Saudi Arabia. Alloush also heads Jaysh al-Islam. Again, this coalition was formed at the behest of Saudi Arabia to counter the al-Qaʻida-linked groups operating round the capital. Lliwa al-Islam was the main group operating in Ghoutta, where Assad's forces unleashed the first, verified, chemical weapons attack in 2013. It claimed the July 2012 bombing of the National Security Bureau HQ in Damascus that killed Assad's brother-in-law and several other officials.

When the US and its Gulf allies switched the focus of their campaign on to eradicating ISIS, Alloush's group lost its international support network and its funding. The group disbanded in July 2014, with many members migrating to Islamic State, while Alloush surprised his erstwhile comrades and commentators alike by proposing negotiations with the Assad regime.

Suqour al-Sham

With around 10,000 fighters the 'Falcons of Syria' hail from the Jabal al-Zawiya region of Idlib. They are led by Abu Issa (aka Ahmed al-Sheikh), who has called for an Islamic state but does not believe this should be imposed by force, as Islamic State does. Formed in September 2011, it expanded its reach into the provinces of Aleppo and Damascus. In late 2013 it joined the Islamic Front.

The Kurdish Islamic Front

This Kurdish Salafist group is notable because it fought alongside ISIS.

Other groups

There are several other independent groups and, again, most of these are Islamist in character. They include: Ahfad al-Rasoul (Grandsons of the Prophet) Brigades; Asala wa al-Tanmiya (Authenticity and Growth) Front; Durou al-Thawra (Revolution Shields) Commission (set up with the help of the Muslim Brotherhood); Tajammu Ansar al-Islam (Gathering of the Supporters of Islam);

and the Yarmouk Martyrs' Brigade. The latter is of interest because it operates along the Syrian-Jordanian border and the Golan Heights. In March and May 2013, its fighters briefly detained UN peacekeepers.[23]

The only secular brigades are the original FSA and the National Unity Brigades. The latter is so small as to be insignificant, with just 2,000 fighters. The Islamist nature of the armed rebellion as it has evolved is striking. When President Obama reiterated his call in September 2014 to arm the 'moderate' opposition, veteran Middle East specialist Patrick Cockburn told an interviewer that 'there is no such thing'.[24]

FIVE

ABU BAKR AL-BAGHDADI: A PORTRAIT OF 'CALIPH IBRAHIM'

Abu Bakr al-Baghdadi has been extremely successful in maintaining a high degree of anonymity and secrecy. He achieved this first in his role as leader of the Islamic State of Iraq (ISI) from 2010 and now as the *emir* and caliph of Islamic State as he declared it on 1 July 2014. He rarely appears in public. Until recently he made few public statements, whether in writing, audio recordings or videos. This is largely a consequence of advice from his security staff, who are well aware that any kind of public profile might present foreign intelligence with leads as to his whereabouts. It was a careless, boastful video, shot in the desert, that led American assassins to Abu Musab al-Zarqawi in 2006.

However, I have been able to piece together an idea of the man through interviews – including speaking to a valuable source who is very close to the IS leadership and was in prison with Baghdadi for two years – and various Arabic online sources. What follows is therefore a mosaic, and many fragments are, for the moment, missing. However, when assembled, this information paints a striking portrait of the world's most dangerous man.

Personal life

Abu Bakr al-Baghdadi, also known as Abu Du'a, Docteur Ibrahim, Awwad Ibrahim, Abu Duaa, Al-Shabah (the phantom) and 'the invisible sheikh' (because of his habit of wearing a mask when addressing his commanders), was born in 1971 in Samarra, fifty miles north of Baghdad. His real name is Ibrahim bin Awwad bin Ibrahim al-Badri al-Qurayshi. He is from the Bobadri tribe, largely located in Samarra and Diyala, which includes the Radhawiyyah, Husseiniyah and Adnaniyah tribes, as well as, crucially, the Prophet Muhammad's Quraysh tribe. One of the key 'qualifications', historically, for becoming caliph is to be a descendant of the Prophet. Commentators have pointed out that Baghdadi used a *miswak* (cleaning twig) to clean his teeth before delivering his famous sermon at the Great Mosque of al-Nuri in Mosul on 4 July 2014, declaring the caliphate. In this he was emulating the Prophet Muhammad's reported practice. Thus he was linking himself through word, gesture and blood lineage to the Prophet, as well as referencing the Salafists' desire to return to the lifestyle of the first Muslims.

. According to a biography posted online by al-Hayat and widely circulated among jihadist websites, Baghdadi is from a religious family that includes several imams and Qur'anic teachers. His mother is from a distinguished family within the Bobadri tribe. He attended the Islamic University of Baghdad, receiving a BA, MA and PhD. His doctorate focused on Islamic jurisprudence and Islamic culture and history. His religious credentials are taken to confer legitimacy on his claim to be not only a military and political leader but also a religious guide. This is something even Osama bin Laden could not lay claim to. Both bin Laden and al-Qa'ida's current leader, Ayman al-Zawahiri, had more secular professional backgrounds. Bin Laden was involved in the construction industry, while Zawahiri was a surgeon.

People who have met Baghdadi describe him as quietly spoken and serious. A contact close to the IS leadership, whom I cannot identify for security reasons, was imprisoned with Baghdadi in the US detention centre Camp Bucca, Iraq, for around two years from 2004. He said Baghdadi always had a serene smile on his face and was 'calm and self-possessed'. This person, who had also been in Osama bin Laden's coterie, said that Baghdadi reminded him of the late al-Qa'ida leader. The same source told me that Baghdadi is extremely charismatic and that, sitting in a room with him and listening to him talking, 'It is very difficult not to be influenced by him, his ideas and his beliefs.'

Baghadi can also be ruthless and menacing. My contact told me that when Baghdadi was released from prison, he told the American guard at the gates that he would be seeing him again: 'We will find you on the streets somewhere, someday,' he threatened, 'either here or in New York.' Enemies are not forgiven or forgotten by this quiet leader: after Abu Omar al-Baghdadi was assassinated in 2010, two of the eleven members of the Shura council convened to choose a new *emir* did not approve the choice of Abu Bakr. One of them, Jamal al-Hamdani, was murdered shortly afterwards.

As a military leader Abu Bakr al-Baghdadi is shrewd and calculating. Though he has never fought abroad – unusual in a global jihadist leader – he has extensive battleground experience. He is an intelligent opponent too, having carefully evaluated and analysed the experiences of 'successful', long-standing jihadist organisations like the Taliban and al-Qa'ida. He recognises the effectiveness of *hijra* (flight); he will immediately order full withdrawal from a battle that cannot easily be won, concluding that *hijra* is key to the survival of al-Qa'ida affiliates from Somalia to China.

Baghdadi understands the value of a well-run organisation. Like the Taliban and al-Qa'ida in its late 1990s' heyday in Afghanistan, under Baghdadi ISI and then IS have adopted a complex, hierarchical, administrative and decision-making structure, with departments and committees for everything from kidnapping to salaries and propaganda.

Comparisons with Osama bin Laden are inevitable and frequent. Baghdadi is held in as much esteem as bin Laden was among Sunni fighters for his prowess as a military and religious leader; this is something Zawahiri has not been able to achieve. Baghdadi did not embark on his journey to the leadership with the benefit of wealth, like Osama bin Laden. His progress has been due to his reputation alone, which appears to have won him praise and loyalty among the extremists. He has claimed that he, rather than al-Qaʻidaʼs present leader, is the true successor to bin Ladenʼs legacy and the person most likely to fulfil his agenda. A Syrian fighter with IS once said that 'Sheikh Baghdadi and Sheikh Osama are similar. They always look ahead, they both seek an Islamic state.' Speaking to the same reporter, a non-Syrian fighter added that, 'The group al-Qaʻida does not exist any more. It was formed as a base for the Islamic state and now we have it, Zawahiri should pledge allegiance to Sheikh Baghdadi.'[1]

The indications are that Baghdadi has, or has had, two or three wives. He first married when he finished his PhD, and his first son was born in 2003;[2] according to the Iraqi Interior Ministry, his first wife is called Israa Rajab Mahal al-Qaisi. He married Saja Hamid al-Dulaimi in 2010 or 2011. Sajaʼs former husband was jihadist commander Fallah Ismail Jassem, of the Iraqi insurgency Jaish al-Rashideen (Army of the Guides). He was gunned down by the Iraqi Army in the province of Anbar in 2010, according to media reports. Saja is from an extremist family whose members all adhere to Salafist-Jihadist ideology. Her father was a commander in ISIS, killed in battle with the Syrian Army in September 2013. It has also been reported that her sister, Duaa, carried out a suicide attack on a Kurdish gathering in Erbil and her brother is reportedly facing execution for a series of bombings in southern Iraq.

The Dulaimi tribe, from which Saja hails, is one of the largest tribes in the Arab world, with over 7 million members. This is of immense significance in a country where tribal networks are a dominant socio-political factor; the US-orchestrated 'Awakening' campaign, which began in 2006, saw a significant (if temporary) reversal of fortune for al-Qaʻida in the Land of Two Rivers (Iraq), when tribal leaders were persuaded to turn against the jihadists. Jihadist leaders have a tradition of making political marriages to ensure tribal support. Osama bin Ladenʼs fifth wife, for example, was a young Yemeni woman from Taez: Amal al-Sadah. Taez is Yemenʼs second largest city and, by marrying Amal, bin Laden secured the protection of her tribe for al-Qaʻida members migrating to Yemen. According to the Iraqi Interior Ministry, Baghdadi married another

Dulaimi, Asma Fawzi Muhammad, some time in the 2010s. It is not known if this marriage has endured. The Dulaimi connection, along with Baghdadi's own extensive tribal network, may ensure greater loyalty and protection.

Saja's identity was revealed when she was photographed during an exchange of prisoners. At some time in 2014 the al-Qa'ida group al-Nusra kidnapped a group of Syrian nuns in the town of Maaloulah. They were subsequently swapped in a deal with the Damascus regime. Among the female prisoners released by Bashar al-Assad's government was Saja. Abu Maan al-Suri, an al-Nusra member, told reporters that Baghdadi's wife had been imprisoned along with her two sons and a younger brother. In November 2014, Saja was arrested crossing into Lebanon with two sons and a daughter, the latter Abu Bakr's child.[3] According to a source interviewed by the *New York Times,* Lebanese, Iraqi, Syrian and American intelligence co-ordinated in Saja's capture, in the belief that she will have a lot of valuable information;[4] the Lebanese government also sees members of Abu Bakr's family as useful bargaining tools should any of their nationals be seized by Islamic State.

A large amount of rumour and disinformation designed to paint Saja as a less high-value prisoner has followed her detention, including the suggestion that her marriage to Baghdadi lasted only three months and that she is now married to a Palestinian by whom she is pregnant. Saja and her ten-year-old daughter have remained remarkably tight-lipped about their relationship with Baghdadi; at one point Saja told interrogators that her husband was dead. The real status of Saja's marriage to Baghdadi is unlikely to be revealed by her and in any case her position is now compromised – the *New York Times* article cited above related that, when American intelligence captured one of Abu Musab Al-Zarqawi's wives in Iraq, 'We got little out of her... and when we sent her back, Zarqawi killed her.' Saja's high status among the 'jihadi brides' suggests that she is far from ostracised by her husband or his close associates. This situation would be unlikely if the couple were divorced – and the idea that she would have absconded for another man is simply ridiculous.[5]

Becoming radicalised

In the 1990s, Baghdadi lived at the mosque in Tobchi, an impoverished suburb in east Baghdad. Locals recall him arriving; they say the young man was quiet and polite. He gained his first experience as a preacher at the small mosque, taking prayers and the occasional sermon when the imam was away.

Like Osama bin Laden, Baghdadi enjoys sport. In bin Laden's case, this was basketball; Baghdadi loves football, according to *Daily Telegraph* interviews with his contemporaries.[6] By some accounts he was an impressive striker. It was not all fun and games though. Tobchi locals remember him espousing fundamentalist values, losing his temper when he saw men and women dancing together at a wedding and, finally, falling out with the mosque when its owner became associated with the political 'Islamic Party' – his extremist ideology held that political parties are sacrilegious. The mosque owner's tribal allegiances worked to squeeze Baghdadi out, and he began preaching at the Imam Ahmad ibn Hanbal Mosque in Samarra, which was frequented by several hardliners. It was around this time that he began to be known as 'Sheikh Ibrahim', the most common name for him in jihadist circles before he became 'Caliph Ibrahim'.

Baghdadi moved to a small town called Qaim, in Anbar province, following the 2003 US-led invasion of Iraq. Angered by the invasion of his country by foreign soldiers, he adopted the pseudonym Abu Duaa and became part of an insurgent, extremist group, probably under the umbrella of Jaish Ansar al-Sunna (Army of the Followers of the Teachings). It seems highly likely that it was here he became associated with Abu Musab al-Zarqawi and his group al-Tawhid wal Jihad (Monotheism and Jihad), which was also based in Anbar province. However, it is known that he did not at this point offer any form of allegiance to Zarqawi.

In late 2004 he was arrested for 'militant activities' and imprisoned without trial by the Americans in their Camp Bucca prison, deep in the desert. It was here that my source first met him,

having been interrogated in Abu Ghraib prison jail first and then
sent on to Bucca – a process my contact says was normal American
practice at the time. If he was not entirely radicalised before prison,
al-Baghdadi certainly became so during his incarceration, where
he met many al-Qa'ida men. As a Qur'anic teacher, Baghdadi gave
classes and lectures to many prominent Iraqi and foreign extremists
in Camp Bucca.

He was released in 2006, according to my source – conflicting
accounts, including official US intelligence reports, have him in
jail until 2009, but this is not possible given the chronology below.
He co-founded a new extremist group called Jaish Ahl al-Sunnah
wal Jamaa (Assembly of the Helpers of Sunnah), which was active
in the areas around and including Diyala, Baghdad and Samarra,
where he was a regular preacher in the mosque. Baghdadi was the
head of the Shariah committee of Jaish Ahl al-Sunnah wal Jamaa.

He was close to some leaders of al-Qa'ida in Iraq, but did not
give his *bayat* (allegiance) to al-Zarqawi, or his successor Abu
Hamza al-Muhajir. Baghdadi liked and greatly respected the latter;
he described him to my source as 'a wise leader' because he sought
to avoid conflict between the various jihadist groups then fighting
in Iraq. It was Abu Hamza who persuaded the Jordanian Zarqawi
to give his *bayat* to Osama bin Laden and who took his oath of
allegiance on behalf of the al-Qa'ida leader. Abu Hamza then gave a
special kind of *bayat* to Zarqawi, whereby he pledged loyalty to him
as a military, rather than a spiritual or religious, leader.

When al-Zarqawi was killed in 2006, Baghdadi brought his
group under the Majlis Shura Council (MSC) umbrella, at Abu
Hamza's invitation. The MSC incorporated al-Qa'ida and would
soon be repackaged the 'Islamic State of Iraq' (ISI). Baghdadi was
on the Sharia committee and the central advisory (Shura) council of
the MSC. When ISI was inaugurated it was considered necessary to
have a native Iraqi leader, because local people, as well as indigenous
insurgents, were becoming indignant about the large numbers of
foreign jihadists mustering in their country. The first indigenous
leader went by the *kunya* (honorific) Abu Omar al-Baghdadi; he

was from the same Qurayshi tribe as Abu Bakr al-Baghdadi, and Abu Bakr gave him his *bayat*. Abu Hamza al-Muhajir – a non-Iraqi – was made the chief representative of the foreign jihadists on the consultative Shura council. Al-Muhajir and Abu Bakr had a close relationship based on mutual respect. Al-Muhajir recommended that Abu Bakr, who was by then already the general supervisor of the ISI's Shariah committee, be 'promoted' to deputy leader of ISI.

When Abu Omar al-Baghdadi was killed in a US air strike in 2010, Abu Bakr al-Baghdadi was chosen as the group's *emir* by the Shura council, meeting in Ninevah in northern Iraq. Even though there were older, more experienced jihadists also under consideration, nine of the eleven men on the council decided in Baghdadi's favour.[7] In little more than a decade he had gone from quiet, pious obscurity to becoming the leader of one of the most feared terror groups in history. Yet those who know him affirm that he has always disliked the limelight and would never have pushed himself forward as a leader.

Bold leadership

Like all successful leaders, Baghdadi knows how to 'seize the moment'. He decided to exploit the chaos in neighbouring Syria to establish a 'branch' there, creating the Islamic State of Iraq and al-Sham (ISIS) almost overnight in 2013, seizing territories before the regime, or the opposition, knew what was going on. ISIS thus established a stronghold in Raqqa, a city that was soon under its full control.

From the outset, Baghdadi's military style was robust and confrontational, favouring 'hit and run' strikes and full-on raids. With breathtaking daring, the newly configured ISIS set about robbing banks and commandeering oil fields in the Syrian province of Deir al-Zour. Baghdadi knew that al-Qa'ida under Osama bin Laden had, in its heyday, been very wealthy and extremely well equipped. Such circumstances greatly increase a group's recruitment potential (it can pay its fighters) and its reach (via a much more sophisticated arsenal and intelligence). In bin Laden's case, much of the money at al-Qa'ida's disposal came from his own, personal, fortune and connections in the Gulf. Baghdadi decided not to rely on Arab sponsors (although Islamic State certainly has them) but simply to seize millions from whatever source came within his range.

Next, Baghdadi squared up to the new al-Qa'ida leadership. He ignored orders from al-Zawahiri to limit his operations to Iraq, effectively mounting a leadership challenge for the growing global jihadist army mustering on both sides of the border. It seemed clear that Baghdadi intended to wrest control of the Global Jihad Movement (a pan-Islamic rather than predominantly Sunni movement), which Zawahiri had co-founded back in 1998, from the ageing fugitives in the Hindu Kush.

In contrast to his placid demeanour, Baghdadi fully understood and exploited the power of extreme violence. Using the internet and social media platforms, IS's slick propaganda wing launched a grisly campaign disseminating images of massacres, beheadings, public executions – some by young boys – and amputations. Baghdadi's background as a scholar of the Qur'an and jurisprudence lent some authority to his organisation's harsh justice. With the populations of both Iraq and Syria exhausted by lawlessness and fear, Baghdadi is aware that any kind of judicial system might be viewed by them as a relief, at least initially. The Taliban was welcomed after the Afghan civil war for much the same reasons.

The boldest move of all came when Baghdadi proclaimed the establishment of the caliphate at the beginning of Ramadan 2014 and then declared himself the caliph, leader of all the world's Muslims, in the Grand Mosque in Mosul, which IS had overrun days before. Statements since attest to an unlimited vision of world domination with Rome, as well as Mecca and Medina, in the new caliph's sights. Is he a visionary or a megalomaniac crackpot? Most of the Western and international media know where they stand on that one; the jury is still out in much of the Arab world.

Popularity

Most successful popular movements have a charismatic leader who acquires legendary status – in their own very different fields we might think of Che Guevara, Malcolm X or Gandhi. At the height of its success, al-Qa'ida became almost synonymous with Osama bin Laden. Even though jihadist groups are careful to train two or three deputies for every man in a leadership role, al-Qa'ida has undeniably suffered from the loss of its poster-boy and his replacement by the dour Dr Ayman al-Zawahiri.

Baghdadi's boldness, defiance, steadfastness and reputation as a clever battlefield strategist (borne out by his many military successes) have won him thousands of admirers across the Muslim world. For example, polls show that 92 per cent of Saudis approve of him. As with bin Laden, Baghdadi's face, and the black-and-white *Shahada* ('I testify') flag that IS has made infamous, can be found on a whole range of merchandise, from T-shirts to mugs and badges, all of which were freely available on Facebook at the time of writing.[8]

Baghdadi also benefits from the support of an extensive tribal network. Baghdadi's influence in his own tribal group – the same group as that of his predecessor, Abu Omar al-Baghdadi al-Qurashi – is such that its elders immediately gave their *bayat* to the self-proclaimed 'caliph' and the 'Islamic State' as soon as it was born. Tribes from Samarra and Dilya had earlier supported ISI under Abu Omar, out of loyalty to Abu Bakr.

After Baghdadi took over the leadership of IS, his first public utterance was a written eulogy for Osama bin Laden on 9 May 2011; four audio messages are all that followed for the next two and a half years. Abu Bakr's video debut – the Grand Mosque sermon in which he declared the Islamic State and himself as caliph – was streamed the next day on the internet, went viral on Twitter, was archived in the 'cloud' and afterwards digitally disseminated to the world's media. That apart, his absence from the world's television and computer screens creates a mystique.

That, then is what we know of Abu Bakr al-Baghdadi: a man of calm and pious manner and appearance, but calculating in his use of extreme violence; a shrewd and intelligent military tactician; a scholar of both law and scripture; a persuasive talker and preacher whose deliberate eschewing of publicity only enhances his charisma; and a careful manipulator of tribal loyalties unafraid to topple others and take control himself.

Like Osama bin Laden, he has been the subject of tributes by the poets of the jihadist world. September 2013 saw him praised in this *Nasheed* (a song sung in close harmony with no musical accompaniment, music being considered *haram*, sinful, by the extremists). It was first posted on the IS YouTube channel (since deleted) and then widely circulated on the internet. It seems to sum up the status and popularity the man enjoys, as well as the way he is perceived by the thousands of extremists who support Islamic State:

They have closed ranks and pledged *bayat* to Baghdadi,
For he is our *emir* in our Iraq and ash-Sham [Syria].

For the Caliphate of God: I am its symbol
Its glory has been decreed by our blood.
They have promised each other to protect the Caliphate

From corner to corner
They have not held back from giving their lives
for its survival.

They have closed ranks and pledged *bayat* to Baghdadi,
For he is our *emir* in our Iraq and ash-Sham.

They have pledged *bayat* to our *emir*,
They are your heroic knights and our own weapon.
For he is the one to whom *bayat* is pledged in our land of Iraq
And our land of ash-Sham

And the land of all the Muslims.
He is our *emir*.

They have closed ranks and pledged *bayat* to Baghdadi,
For he is our *emir* in our Iraq and ash-Sham.

Preserve the soldiers of Allah, oh our custodian.
The cross has returned to our land and our homes.
We offer our lives on our skulls,
We will vanquish oppression
while our enemies lie low.

They have closed ranks and pledged *bayat* to Baghdadi,
For he is our *emir* in our Iraq and ash-Sham.

SIX

CONSOLIDATION AND EXPANSION

The ideological and organisational evolution of today's 'Islamic State' has now been examined in detail, and can be summarised as follows: from 2000 to 2004, Abu Musab al-Zarqawi led al-Tawhid wal Jihad, which migrated from Afghanistan to Iraq (via Iran) in 2002. Following official acceptance by Osama bin laden, Zarqawi's group was renamed al-Qa'ida in the Land of Two Rivers in 2004. In 2006, following accusations that foreign fighters were taking over the Iraqi insurgency, an umbrella group of all Iraqi Salafi-jihadist groups was announced, called Majlis Shura al-Mujahideen, briefly led by Zarqawi until bin Laden demoted him; Zarqawi's assassination by the US followed in June 2006. The umbrella group was now rebranded the Islamic State of Iraq (ISI) – underscoring the geo-political ambition of the group – under the command of a native Iraqi, Abu Omar al-Baghdadi, until his death in 2010. Then another Iraqi, Abu Bakr al-Baghdadi (the present 'Caliph Ibrahim'), was elected to succeed him.

Baghdadi was quick to exploit the opportunities afforded by the uprising in Syria. In summer 2011, he dispatched a senior member of his group – Abu Mohammad al-Jolani – to establish a jihadist fighting group in Syria. The result, Jahbat al-Nusra, announced itself online in late January 2012.

Baghdadi's strategic decision had been taken in consultation with al-Qa'ida's leader, Ayman al-Zawahiri (before the rift between the two men developed). Initially the association between al-Nusra and ISI was deliberately obscured. It was felt that the historic connection with al-Qa'ida would alienate other rebel groups fighting the regime, as well as some potential recruits. By the end of 2012, al-Nusra, largely composed of Syrian fighters, was not only one of the best rebel fighting groups but was also functioning as a municipal and judicial authority in towns and villages under its control, arbitrating in local disputes and challenging corrupt practices.

Encouraged by the success and influence that the Salafi-jihadist groups had obtained, foreign fighters began to arrive in significant numbers. In 2013, *Jane's Defence and Security Weekly* estimated that more than 50 per cent of the opposition forces were jihadists, many of them foreign. In April 2013 – with al-Nusra well established and respected locally, despite a rabid Syrian government media campaign against it – Abu Bakr al-Baghdadi unilaterally announced that ISI and al-Nusra were going to unite under the banner of the Islamic State of Iraq and al-Sham (ISIS). Again, the geopolitical intentions were clear in the new name, but few took them seriously. Al-Nusra's leader, al-Jolani, rejected the merger and Ayman al-Zawahiri ordered Baghdadi to focus his efforts in Iraq. Zawahiri understood the younger man's desire to hasten the re-establishment of the caliphate, but disagreed that the time had come for this dramatic advancement of the 'global jihadist' project. Baghdadi has never given his *bayat* to an al-Qa'ida leader and he rejected Zawahiri's command.

Baghdadi had already dispatched thousands of his fighters into Syria under the banner of ISIS. He was emerging as a potential rival to Zawahiri, with his eye on the prize of a caliphate stretching across the Iraq-Syria borders. When the al-Qa'ida leader requested that ISIS withdraw its men from Iraq and leave the fighting in Syria to al-Nusra, Baghdadi humiliated him by stating that he did not recognise artificial borders created by the 'infidel' Sykes-Picot agreement of 1916.

An ideological divide now appeared between ISIS and al-Nusra, and between Baghdadi and Zawahiri. ISIS vigorously pursued the plan of seizing territory and establishing a caliphate from the outset. Al-Nusra, however, had more local aims, primarily to free Syria from the *tawagheet* (ungodly, i.e. un-Islamic) regime of Bashar al-Assad. Al-Nusra is comparatively restrained beside the grisly excesses of ISIS. When the former kidnapped a group of thirteen nuns and swapped them for 150 female prisoners in Syrian jails, the nuns reported that the jihadists had treated them well and given them everything they had asked for. Al-Nusra's religious strategies are also less radical, working on the principle that Sharia can be implemented gradually and responsively over time.

Jolani responded by pledging his allegiance to Ayman al-Zawahiri, and it was announced online that al-Nusra was now part of al-Qa'ida. Over time, however, most of al-Nusra's foreign jihadists would defect to Islamic State.

Islamic State's outrageous land grab

Initially, ISIS fought alongside the Syrian rebel brigades, but soon it was openly confronting, and fighting, the secular element in the rebel ranks. In early July 2013 ISIS fighters stopped Free Syria Army commander Kamal Hamami (Abu Bashir al-Jeblawi) at one of their roadblocks and shot him in the head;[1] this was the first of many assassinations of rival leaders, which would include Abu Obeida, of fellow jihadist group Ahrar al-Sham, in September of the same year.

Key to the relentless progress ISIS was to make over the coming months was its ability to carry out high-profile actions on both sides of the Iraq-Syria border. At the same time as it was asserting its dominance over the rebel faction in Syria, in Iraq it carried out a spectacular jail break at the notorious, politically significant Abu Ghraib prison, which had been the scene of well-publicised US and UK torture and mistreatment of prisoners. Around 500 key jihadists, including top al-Qa'ida men, were released to join the ranks of ISIS, full of bitterness and rage.[2] Sources close to the ISIS leadership told me that this daring prison break had been a year in the planning and that it was designed to attract admiration, support and new recruits.

ISIS commanders pursued a carefully planned strategy not only to take key targets but to win hearts and minds. In August 2013, with the Syrian regime indiscriminately dropping barrel bombs filled with high explosives, shrapnel and nails on its citizens in Aleppo, ISIS captured Menagh Air Base northwest of the city. This temporarily put a halt to the bombardment. In September 2013 it wrested control of the town of Azaz, on the Turkish border, from the FSA. Azaz is a key strategic asset and was a well-established transit point for foreign fighters – as well as for funds and weapons from Gulf countries, which the jihadists simply seized for themselves.

The land grab continued in Syria and Iraq. From December 2013, ISIS began to overrun towns in Anbar province in Iraq, and in the New Year took Fallujah. Yet in the chaos its spectacular gains were somehow overlooked, and Western intelligence agencies confidently asserted that it had no more than 3,000 fighters.[3] In a January 2014 interview for the *New Yorker*, US President Obama would notoriously dismiss the group as 'junior varsity players'.[4]

On the ground, however, the danger was more obvious. The Saudi-sponsored Islamic Front, together with the Free Syrian Army, began to battle ISIS positions in Aleppo and Idlib. The Free Syrian Army assassinated Abu Bakr al-Baghdadi's right-hand man, Haji Bakr, a former officer in Saddam Hussein's Republican Guard. Meanwhile, the rift between ISIS, al-Qa'ida and al-Nusra translated into fighting, with al-Nusra joining FSA forces in a bid to expel Baghdadi's troops from Deir al-Zour province in Syria.

In May 2014 ISIS began its online campaign to increase its profile and notoriety. A steady stream of images and videos of suicide bombings, raids, beheadings and other grizzly punishments and executions was posted on a wide variety of social media and online platforms. The aim was to grab world headlines and inform as wide a pool of potential recruits as possible of the 'opportunities' ISIS was offering in Iraq and Syria.

This digital psychological warfare was also designed to terrify citizens and any forces that might confront ISIS, allowing the group's onward march to seize many territories unopposed. When a brigade of around 500 ISIS fighters entered Iraq's second city,

Mosul (population more than one million), in early June 2014, 30,000 regular Iraqi Army soldiers surrendered instantly, throwing down their weapons and stripping off their uniforms before running away.[5] This pattern was repeated in three other, smaller nearby towns. My correspondents in Mosul told us that even the ISIS men themselves appeared surprised by the ease with which they were able to take over the city, a strategic point on the route from Baghdad to Syria. They seized government offices, the airport, police stations and the Central Bank, where they reportedly looted nearly half a billion dollars.[6] ISIS seized the city's Turkish Embassy and took hostage the head of mission and forty-eight staff – a bargaining chip that would later contribute to Turkey's refusal to join the US-led Alliance against Islamic State. Half a million residents fled Mosul, including the Christian minority of around 400 families.

Next ISIS secured the oilfield and the huge dam just outside Mosul, before overrunning much of the province of Nineveh, the cities of Fallujah and Tikrit, and several towns around Kirkuk – where they intended to capture both oil fields and another important dam – as well as ten towns in Saladin province.

ISIS captured Iraq's largest oil refinery in Baiji on 21 June 2014, after 400 Iraqi soldiers agreed to desert the army, and then the oil fields at Ajeel. Also in June, ISIS took the Iraqi town of Mansouriyat al-Jabal and seized its extensive gas fields from the foreign companies that operated them. A month later, ISIS began selling crude oil on the black market.

On 19 June 2014 ISIS captured Saddam Hussein's former chemical weapons facility at al-Muthanna, sixty miles north of Baghdad[7] (in October 2014 there were reports that IS had used chlorine gas in an attack on Iraqi security forces in Balad, north of Baghdad).[8] Fearing that Baghdad was now in ISIS's sights, the UN evacuated sixty staff; instead, ISIS brigades concentrated on opening a corridor to the Syrian border, taking nearly every town *en route*, including the strategic city of Tal Afar with its airport. Not that action ceased in Iraq: ISIS brigades also seized strategically important Turaibil on the border with Jordan.

Hundreds of fighters from other Iraqi Islamist groups defected to ISIS, lured by its rapid conquest of around a third of the country and in awe of its raw, if brutal, power. Meanwhile ISIS continued its campaign of psychological terror, publicly beheading Iraqi soldiers it had captured near Kirkuk and then staging a mass execution of 670 Shi'i inmates of Badush prison in Mosul. Thousands of Iraqi troops fleeing Camp Speicher military base were captured by ISIS and it executed 1,500 of them over the course of three days. In Mosul thirteen imams – including the imam of the Grand Mosque – were executed when they refused to give their allegiance to Baghdadi.

The West begins to understand

Belatedly, the West and regional governments realised ISIS was much bigger and more powerful than they had believed possible. But the CIA's June 2014 reassessment was still woefully inaccurate, suggesting ISIS fighters might be 'as many as 7–10,000'.[9]

On 1 July 2014 ISIS released an audio recording on the internet that quickly went viral online as well as seizing the world's media headlines. The group's spokesman Abu Muhammad al-Adnani announced that ISIS held territories from Diyala in Iraq to Aleppo in Syria and would from now on be known as Islamic State. He also declared a caliphate, with Baghdadi, 'Caliph Ibrahim', in command. 'Listen to your Caliph and obey him,' Adnani urged. 'Support your state, which grows every day.'[10] On 4 July Caliph Ibrahim addressed the congregation in Mosul's Grand Mosque, as well as thousands of supporters, reporters, and onlookers all over the globe via the internet.

During the following month the armies of Islamic State continued their run of spectacular military achievements, including the seizure of Syria's largest oil fields at al-Omar from al-Nusra (who put up no resistance), and the Shaer gas field near Homs. The campaign of extreme violence, ruthless extermination of enemies and 'making of examples' continued apace. Informers were abducted from a village near Tikrit; sixty Iraqi Army officers were abducted from near Mosul; 700 Turkmen villagers were murdered in Beshir; and forty-two captive Iraqi soldiers were executed. Islamic State brigades captured an entire Syrian Army division near Raqqa and beheaded a large number of soldiers, displaying their severed heads on the top of fences and stakes. Eighteen Iraqi policemen suffered a similar fate near Tikrit, and Sunni imam Abdel Rahman al-Jobouri of Baquba was killed for denouncing Islamic State. To mark the end of Ramadan, *eid al-Fitr*, on 28 July Islamic State's media arm, al-Hayat media centre, released a gruesome video of mass executions for online dissemination. The UN released figures suggesting that in Iraq, in July 2014 alone, and excluding Anbar province, 1,737 had been killed in the violence, of which 1,186 were civilians.[11]

Ideological cleansing

Now Islamic State soldiers commenced a vigorous campaign of ideological cleansing, demolishing sites of religious significance to other sects and creeds: for example the Mosque and Tomb of the Prophet Jonah in Mosul, a Shi'i site that is holy in Jewish tradition as well, and the shrine of the Prophet Seth. They were careful to loot any valuable antiquities within before flattening the buildings.

Deadly in-fighting among the extremist groups presents a viable mechanism for the demise of Islamic State; in August 2014, however, Western and local intelligence services noted with anxiety that al-Nusra appeared to be working in tandem with Islamic State in some military operations. My correspondents in northern Syria reported that envoys from al-Qa'ida attended a late-night meeting with ISIS and al-Nusra representatives in Atareb on 2 November 2014. They agreed to co-operate primarily to defeat Kurdish and rival rebel forces: since September 2014, Islamic State brigades had been laying siege to the strategically placed Kurdish capital, Kobani, near the border with Turkey. Apart from al-Nusra, a group of elite al-Qaʻida veterans called the Khorasan Group (the name relates to a leadership council within al-Qaʻida) was also represented, along with Ahrar al-Sham, whose former leader had been assassinated by ISIS in September 2013. Al-Nusra denied widespread reports that it had entered a truce with Islamic State, but affirmed that it shared the same goals.[12] Islamic State's usually vociferous social media network has remained silent on the matter.

In the light of past, catastrophic, interventions in Iraq, Afghanistan and Libya, and given the chaotic political situation in Syria, the West had done little more than hover on the sidelines as the terrifying Islamic State marched on. When its soldiers rampaged through the villages of the Iraqi Yazidi-dominated province of Sinjar, however, in August 2014, the Western press began to adopt a more warlike tone. Islamic State fighters brutally massacred hundreds of Yazidi men – survivors told reporters that Islamic State soldiers had informed them that if they didn't convert to Islam they would be killed – and abducted up to 500 women and girls, allegedly to be sold as slaves. In one particularly repellent attack, Islamic State soldiers buried a number of Yazidi women and children alive;[13] and reports of savage rapes proliferated.[14] Up to 40,000 Yazidis fled for their lives and took refuge in the Sinjar mountains, where many died of hyperthermia, starvation and dehydration.

Christian minorities were also given the ultimatum to leave or die when Islamic State soldiers took control of Mosul and several towns in Nineveh province, including Qaraqosh, Bartella, Tel Keppe, Karemlash and Makhmour. Syrian Christians were similarly terrorised. Syria used to be 'the easiest place in the Arab world to be Christian', according to charity group the Barnabus Fund. Now 600,000 Christians have either fled the country or lost their lives.[15]

Western intervention

The Western media and public were outraged. If their governments wanted to act militarily to crush IS, they now had a public mandate to do so. With Islamic State conquests positioning the extremists within striking distance of Kurdish capital Erbil, and the second largest oil fields in Iraq, the first US-led strikes began. While Kurdish fighters from the Pershmerga (military forces of Iraqi Kurdistan) and the PKK (Kurdistan Workers' Party) fought the actual battle on the ground, American President Obama authorised limited air strikes on Islamic State targets. The UK and France also flew over Iraq, but only to drop humanitarian aid to refugees fleeing the violence.

On 9 September 2014 a *Washington Post* poll found that 71 per cent of Americans asked supported more robust intervention in Iraq, and 65 per cent in Syria. Yet President Obama hesitated. Forty per cent of Americans now considered him 'too cautious'. In the UK a 20 August vote in the House of Commons decided against a military intervention. It was not until the end of September 2014 that a US-led coalition of more than forty nations, now including Britain following a further vote on 24 September, agreed that something must be done, but reached consensus on little else.

Meanwhile Islamic State had found another way to guarantee a 'Twitter Storm' and the front pages: it began to barter for the US and UK nationals it had taken captive. On 12 August, the parents of American journalist James Foley received an email from his captors making clear the link between Western interference in Muslim countries and the current violence, which it painted as retaliatory. The email was written in English, and Foley's parents decided to make it public; here is the text:[16]

A message to the American government and their sheep-like citizens:

We have left you alone since your disgraceful defeat in Iraq. We did not interfere in your country or attack your citizens while they were safe in their homes despite our capability to do so!

As for the scum of your society who are held prisoner by us, THEY DARED TO ENTER THE LION'S DEN AND

WERE EATEN!

You were given many chances to negotiate the release of your people via cash transactions as other governments have accepted, we have also offered prisoner exchanges to free the Muslims currently in your detention like our sister Dr Afia Sadiqqi, however you proved very quickly to us that this is NOT what you are interested in.

You have no motivation to deal with the Muslims except with the language of force, a language you were given in 'Arabic translation' when you attempted to occupy the land of Iraq!

Now you return to bomb the Muslims of Iraq once again, this time resorting to Arial attacks and 'proxy armies', all the while cowardly shying away from a face-to-face confrontation!

Today our swords are unsheathed towards you, GOVERNMENT AND CITIZENS ALIKE! AND WE WILL NOT STOP UNTILL WE QUENCH OUR THIRST FOR YOUR BLOOD.

You do not spare our weak, elderly, women or children so we will NOT spare yours!

You and your citizens will pay the price of your bombings!

The first of which being the blood of the American citizen, James Foley!

He will be executed as a DIRECT result of your transgressions towards us!

Sadly, James Foley was indeed executed circa 19 August, on camera, dressed in the orange jumpsuit of a Guantanamo Bay prisoner to underscore the political message. A second American, Steven Sotloff (who held an Israeli passport) was executed in the same way in early September 2014. Maximum media impact was assured by the additional detail of the executioner having a British accent, and he became known in the tabloid media as 'Jihadi John' – his identity was unknown to the general public until, at the end of February 2015, UK and US media named him as Mohammed

Emwazi, a Kuwaiti-born Londoner in his mid-twenties, previously known to British security services. According to Bünyamin Aygun, a Turkish photojournalist who was held in the same facility before being freed by a rival militia working with Turkish intelligence,[17] there is a British cell, of which 'Jihadi John' is a member, which fellow extremists have dubbed 'The Beatles', naming individual members after the pop group's personnel. Two more Westerners, David Haines and Alan Henning, both British aid workers, were executed in September and October respectively.

The birth of the digital caliphate

When Islamic State and the new 'caliphate' were declared on 1 July 2014, much of the world's media made fun of the idea, claiming it is a 'medieval' concept, with no place in the modern world. In fact there has been an almost unbroken succession of Islamic caliphates, in one form or another, for 1,300 years, with the only significant gap occurring between the demise of the Ottoman Empire in 1922 and 2014.

A very brief history of the Islamic Caliphate is in order here. The caliph is, literally, a 'successor' of the Prophet Muhammad and is the undisputed head of state. After Muhammad's death the First, Rashidun, Caliphate was established by his followers and family to continue the religious, judicial and social systems he had established. The first caliph was Abu Bakr al-Siddiq. He nominated his successor (Umar ibn Khattab) on his deathbed. A council (*majlis*) elected Khattab's succesor, Uthman ibn Affan, but he was killed by a rebel group and Ali ibn Abi Talib proclaimed himself caliph. A civil war between the Muslims, known as *fitna*, ensued over succession to the caliphate. This is where the Sunni-Shi'i schism occurs, with the followers of Ali – *Shiat Ali* – known thereafter as the Shi'i.

The next caliph, Muawiyah ibn Abi Sufyan, was governor of Syria and a relative of Uthman. He established the principle of a hereditary caliphate, which the Umayyad dynasty ruled from AD 661 to 750, a period of rapid expansion through three continents (Africa, Asia and Europe). The Umayyad Caliphate became one of the biggest unitary states in world history. Islamic State aspires to reclaim all these territories.

The Abbasid Caliphate which overthrew the Umayyads in AD 750 is considered the 'golden age' of Islam, rich with intellectual, cultural and scientific achievements and innovations; Baghdadi frequently refers to this idealised period. The Abbasid family were from Mecca and their dynasty produced an unbroken line of caliphs for almost 300 years. Then the regional rulers of various parts of the huge Islamic state began to agitate for greater autonomy, fragmenting the whole – which remained a nominal caliphate nonetheless – into sultanates and monarchies.

Abu Bakr al-Husseini al-Qureishi al-Baghdadi – to give the current self-proclaimed Caliph of Islamic State his full, chosen, names – references (and lays claim to) previous caliphates with this moniker. Abu Bakr was the first caliph and Imam Husseini was the Prophet's grandson. The Qureysh are the tribe from which Muhammad emerged and the 'true caliphs' are meant to be from this tribe too, descendants of the Prophet. Like any leader of a new state, Baghdadi is particularly keen for new immigrants with useful skills: 'We make a special call to the scholars, fuqaha [experts in Islamic jurisprudence], and especially the judges, as well as people with military, administrative and service expertise, and medical doctors and engineers of all different specialisations and fields.'[18]

Two days after proclaiming himself caliph, on the first Friday in Ramadan, 'Caliph Ibrahim' (Baghdadi) emerged from the shadows and addressed the congregation for prayers at the Grand Mosque in Mosul (whose Imam had been beheaded) dressed in the black *thob* (robe) and turban traditionally worn by the caliphs. In a dramatic and war-like speech, punctuated with Qur'anic references, Baghdadi emphasised that the caliphate had only been re-established thanks to 'the conquests and victories of the mujahideen which came after many years of hardship and patience'. Note that 're-established' and the reference to the mujahideen as the vital link to the past. It must be stressed that the network is adhering to plans and strategies put in place many years ago by previous generations of extremists.

Finally, Baghdadi spoke about his personal feelings on being appointed caliph, describing it as 'a heavy burden'. 'I have been tested by Allah in my election as caliph,' he declared. 'I am no better than you. Advise me when I err, follow me if I succeed and assist me against the *tawagheet* [atheist leaders and followers of idols].'

Reaching out and linking up

Ideological expansion beyond neighbouring countries is furthered by *dawaa* (outreach) and I have had reports of Islamic State literature being handed out on the streets of more than one continent. But there is already an ideological infrastructure in places in every territory where there is an established al-Qa'ida affiliate. Although al-Qa'ida boss Ayman al-Zawahiri has tried to keep control of his organisation, many constituents have already defected to IS; and as long as the newcomer continues to notch up successes, more are likely to follow. This offers Baghdadi an array of possibilities from China to Libya.

Al-Qa'ida in the Arabian Peninsula was formed in January 2009 by a merger between the Saudi and Yemeni offshoots of the organisation. Although it has been weakened by a sustained US drone campaign, it is considered the most significant terrorist threat to the Gulf region, to local Western interests and to the West itself. In April 2011, shortly before his death, Osama bin Laden noted with satisfaction that Yemen had become 'the rear base for all jihadist work in the world'.[19] Its late ideologue Anwar al-Awlaki pioneered English-language online magazines and other recruitment materials, believing that using the *lingua franca* of much of the world would open up enormous recruitment opportunities. It seems he was correct in that. In August 2014 AQAP announced its support for, and solidarity with, Islamic State.[20]

In January 2015 AQAP claimed responsibility (in an online video) for the killing of twelve people in Paris – including most of the editorial staff of the controversial weekly satirical newspaper *Charlie Hebdo* – by two brothers, Cherif and Said Kouachi. In the video, one of AQAP's commanders, Nasr Ibn Ali al-Ansi, said that the 'seeds' of the attack had been planted by Awlaki, who was killed by a drone in September 2011. Al-Ansi spoke with an image of the Islamic State flag behind him and ended with the group's salute, which is the index finger of the right hand pointing heavenward. Amedy Coulibaly, a friend of the brothers, carried out a simultaneous, linked attack, on a Parisian kosher supermarket, killing four hostages; Coulibaly left a video which posthumously announced that he had been under supervision by Islamic State. It is possible that AQAP and Islamic State operated together in these terrible atrocities in the French capital.

Somalia's al-Shabaab (The Youth) emerged from the Islamic Courts Union that took control of the country, briefly, in 2006. It has long been a magnet for foreign jihadists. In February 2012 a video featuring al-Shabaab *emir* Ahmed Abdi Godane (aka Mukhtar Abu al-Zubeyr) and Ayman al-Zawahiri announced the 'glad tidings' that 'al-Harakat al-Shabaab al-Mujahideen has officially joined al-Qa'ida'.[21] When IS first emerged, Godane maintained loyalty to Zawahiri. However, he was killed by US drones on 1 September 2014 and many analysts believe that the group will now shift allegiance to Islamic State, which is popular with its younger members. Al-Shabaab's fortunes have waned since the US began a hefty and prolonged drone campaign against the group, and many believe that IS backing would bring it new credibility.

Further afield, Islamic State has allies in Indonesia's Jamaa Islamiyyah (JI, meaning 'Islamic Congregation'), the jihadist group behind the horrific Bali bombing of 2002 in which more than 200 young people were killed, at least half of them Australian. Eighty-five per cent of Indonesia's 235 million people are Sunni Muslim – the world's biggest Muslim population in any one country – and the jihadists' agenda is to establish an Islamic caliphate throughout the region. In August 2014 JI's leader, Abu Bakr Bashir, pledged allegiance to Islamic State from the maximum security prison where he is now held.[22] The Indonesian state has made it a criminal offence to support Islamic State or ISIS, but there are many extremists in the country who are unlikely to comply.

Among the Pakistani Taliban (TTP), the hot debate over whether or not to join Islamic State has caused huge rifts. While the TTP is unlikely to control a whole country, as the Afghan Taliban look set to do, it is still a formidable ally and ruthless fighting force. American radio network NPR carried a story on 27 October 2014 that started, 'Few scenarios worry the US and its allies more than the prospect of the rise of the Islamic State on the war-battered landscape of northwest Pakistan.'[23] Islamic State is already popular in Pakistan where radicalism flourishes and the 'caliphate' has been working hard both on the streets and online to recruit from Pakistan's 180 million people. Traditionally allied to the Afghan Taliban, the more moderate leadership shied away from joining Islamic State – but in October six high-ranking TTP commanders pledged allegiance to Abu Bakr al-Baghdadi. Also in October, Mullah Fazlullah, the TTP's *emir*, tried to play both sides of the game by saying he 'supported all Islamist groups fighting in Syria and Iraq'.[24]

In addition to these territories available to IS either through proximity or allegiance, Baghdadi's ambitions extend beyond the Mediterranean to reclaiming for the caliphate the territories of al-Andalus (Spain and Portugal) and even, as he announced in his July 2014 audio, Rome.

SEVEN

WITHIN ISLAMIC STATE

Administration

The administrative and decision-making structure adopted by Baghdadi for his caliphate is based on Qur'anic and historical precedent. It is a framework that becomes familiar if one studies the Taliban, al-Qa'ida, and similar groups such as Somalia's al-Shabaab or Nigeria's Boko Haram.

The Caliph, as representative of the Prophet, is the ultimate authority of Islamic State. Baghdadi has a sophisticated security detail, headed by Abu Yahya al Iraqi; despite his sermon exhorting 'advise me when I err', any threat, opposition or even contradiction is instantly eradicated. It is a highly centralised and disciplined organisation. Because it covers a large geographical area, and because all important personnel must have able deputies in case they are killed, delegation is essential. Baghdadi has two deputies; both were former members of the Iraqi Ba'ath party, and both were fellow prisoners in the US prison Camp Bucca. Abu Muslim al-Turkmani (aka Fadil Ahmad Abdallah al Hayyali), Baghdadi's second-in-command, was a senior special forces officer and a member of military intelligence under Saddam Hussein; he is from Tal Afar in northwest Iraq, has roots in Turkmenistan, and was close to both Saddam Hussein and the Iraqi military commander Izzat Ibrahim al-Douri. He is the 'governor general' of Islamic State's Iraqi territories, overseeing local governors and councils and acting as a political envoy.

Baghdadi's second deputy is Abu Ali al-Anbari (aka Ali

Qurdash al Turkmani and Abu Jasim al Iraqi), who comes from a village near Mosul though, as his alias suggests, his roots also lie in Turkmenistan. Before the 2003 invasion he was a major-general in the Iraqi Army. He joined the insurgency and was a member of Abu Musab al-Zarqawi's Ansar al-Islam (prior to Zarqawi joining al-Qa'ida), as a result coming under the ISI umbrella with his leader. He is a member of the Shura Council and head of the Intelligence and Security Council, working closely with Abu Yahya al-Iraqi. He is the 'governor' of Islamic State's Syrian territories and has also gained a reputation for successful behind-the-lines intelligence operations in Syria, enabling Islamic State brigades to operate swiftly and with deadly efficiency; a speciality is ambushing unsuspecting enemies.

Baghdadi and his two deputies set the overall aims and objectives of the group, which are then communicated to the lower rungs of the hierarchy. The manner in which objectives are autonomously fulfilled is left largely to the discretion of local commanders or administrators. This system allows Islamic State to operate effectively in many places simultaneously and is particularly empowering in military terms; an officer will know what he has to achieve, but has the authority to decide on the best manner and time to implement it given the circumstances and opportunities on the ground.

Under Baghdadi are advisory councils and several departments, run by committees, which oversee various aspects of the state. The leader of each department forms part of Baghdadi's 'cabinet'.

The most powerful advisory body is the Shura (consultative) Council, which endorses the Sharia council's choice of caliph, whom it then advises. It oversees affairs of state and communicates decisions and orders down the chain of command and ensures they are implemented. It comprises up to a dozen members, selected by Baghdadi and headed, at the time of writing, by Abu Arkan al-Ameri.

The Sharia Council deals with all religious and judicial affairs; it is charged with selecting the caliph. It ensures that the whole administration of the State complies with Sharia law and is responsible for maintaining discipline within the body politic, determining punishments for infringements. The council supervises the Sharia Police and court system, appointing judges and clarifying Qur'anic punishment tarifs. It also oversees religious outreach – *dawaa* – inside the State's territories and beyond. Unsurprisingly the Western media has focused on the draconian implementation of *Hudd* penalties (amputations, capital punishment and so on), but Sharia judges in Islamic State can also apply a *Tazeer* punishment, which is aimed at shaming a criminal with a view to reform and rehabilitation.

According to verbal accounts from my contacts in locations controlled by Islamic State, the first thing Islamic State does on taking control of a newly secured community is to establish a Sharia police force to supervise Islamic conduct. This is separate from the regular police force and works for the 'purity' of religion within Islamic State. This it pursues through control of the mosques, for example, and poster campaigns in the streets giving the exact times for five-times-a-day prayer and quoting Qur'anic verses urging women (and men) to wear 'modest dress'. The 'moral' police are under its command, ensuring 'correct' dress and behaviour on the streets of the State. Anecdotal evidence suggests that in Raqqa, at least, this task is carried out by women in the al-Khansaa Brigade,[1] who are also on the lookout for enemy combatants concealed under a burqa. The regular police force is also brought under Islamic State administration and kitted out in new, black uniforms with Islamic State badges or writing, in white, on the arm. Police cars are resprayed with the Islamic State insignia, as are boats in towns and cities with river police.

The Sharia courts deal with all complaints, whether religious or civil, and cases can be brought by the police or by individual citizens. In conurbations where there has been no policing and no judiciary owing to the collapse of central government, these courts are largely popular; citizens can bring cases directly to the courts, which are able to process cases quickly and, in most cases, reasonably. In socio-psychological terms, once a citizenry submits to the law of a government, it is accepting its authority and asking it to guarantee security. In this way Islamic State compounds its control of overrun areas.

The Sharia Council is an important instrument in the face of any challenges regarding the legitimacy of Islamic State and Baghdadi himself – and there have been plenty. The council seeks endorsement from scholars and clerics, and has recruited a former Saudi Army officer, Bandar bin Shaalan, to enlist statements of support from respected preachers.

The Security and Intelligence Council is informed by the professional expertise and experience of its four main leaders, who were all high-ranking officers in Saddam Hussein's notoriously cruel security services. It has a network of branches throughout the Islamic State and is quick to eliminate dissidents, challengers and spies. It plays an important role in maintaining the integrity of the caliphate establishment, mounting and manning roadblocks and regional border controls.

The Military Council oversees the territorial expansion of the State and defends what it already controls. It is overseen by Abu Ayman al-Iraqi, who was a lieutenant colonel in Saddam Hussein's air defence intelligence and a close ally of Izzat al-Douri. He is part of the core ISIS group who met in Camp Bucca and is known for his extremely violent behaviour. He was formerly Islamic State's governor in Anbar province and, in early 2014, was the military commander of its operations in western Syria. The Chief of Staff is a well-known face among the jihadists' online community: the red-bearded Chechen Tarkhan Tayumurazovich Batirashvili (aka Omar al-Shishani) was an officer in the Georgian Army before joining the Caucasian Emirate (CE – an al-Qa'ida affiliate). He arrived in Syria in March 2012 with a group of battle-hardened, well-trained Chechen fighters. He swore allegiance to Baghdadi in mid 2013. Pictures of him accepting *bayat* on behalf of Baghdadi have appeared on Twitter, which suggests he is a very influential figure within the State.

The Military Council also covers supplies, provision for the families of martyrs, the manufacturing and distribution of explosives and their deployment, and the movement of fighters. In January 2015, in a bid to win round anxious residents, the Military Council banned fighters from entering central Mosul in uniform and carrying arms.[2] This has not prevented the Sharia police from carrying out public executions, including crucifixion for theft and being pushed from a high building for homosexuality.[3]

The Economic Council deals with the State's impressive income, which stems from a variety of sources described in more detail below. They include oil wealth, cash from sixty-two government and non-government banks in the various towns and cities IS has overrun,[4] 'fees' at roadblocks, ransoms, Islamic 'taxes' (*Jizya* is a *per capita* tax for non-Muslims while *Zakat* taxes wealth and income of Muslim citizens) and spoils of war. In January 2015 it produced its first annual budget, set at $2 billion across its territories; a surplus $250 million is to be added to its war chest.[5] It also produces annual reports in March each year; its 'annual report', *al-Naba*, details attacks and military operations set off against revenue, indicating 'money well spent' for its leaders, followers and financial backers. Analysts concur that this level of bureaucratic process and accountability is indicative of a large, well-organised, state-like entity.

The Education Council oversees the provision of education and the curriculum – based, of course, on the strict Salafist interpretation of the Qur'an. Several subjects have been banned, including evolutionary biology and philosophy.[6] According to my communications with residents in Islamic State territories it has not – as widely reported in the Western media – banned education for girls, and it makes a feature of its all-female schools and universities in its online magazines.

The Islamic Services Council oversees 'services for citizens', which include maintaining and running an infrastructure, road repairs and power and sanitation. In towns and cities under its control, Islamic State runs a ration system and discourages traders from selling to people who do not carry the correct card with the group's logo on it. As part of the ongoing strategy to win the hearts and minds of its residents, since December 2014 daily meals have been provided to residents in need, and there are weekly free grain and vegetable distributions. Poor and disabled people, widows, orphans and families who have lost a bread-winner receive a monthly 'salary'.[7] Tweets from Islamic State accounts suggest that the entity has also established its own postal system, though this could only function inside the territories under its control. In the September 2014 edition of the *Islamic State Report* (one of several online magazines) there was an article about the Consumer Protection Services the Council had been trialling in Raqqa, headed by one Abu Salih al-Ansari. The Council also oversees the provision of basic health and social services including an 'office for orphans', food kitchens for the impoverished, and a vaccination programme. 'Suggestions and Complaints' boxes are provided – an innovation that has come from the Taliban, who started this system a few years ago in an attempt to be more 'consumer friendly'.

The Islamic State Institution for Public Information is responsible for the State's media and propaganda output. It is led by the most significant figure in Islamic State after Caliph Ibrahim and his deputies; formerly the leader of ISIS in Syria, thirty-seven-year-old Abu Muhammad al-Adnani al-Shami, who hails from Idlib, is the caliphate's main spokesman. Al-Adnani has been responsible for some of most inflammatory Islamic State propaganda, including the speech, released online on 22 September 2014, that urged lone-wolf jihadists in the West to kill 'citizens of countries which have entered into a coalition against Islamic State' by 'any means you chose'.[8] Adnani suggested deliberately running over people with a car. Demonstrating the extent of the group's online influence on a global scale, several attacks involving hit-and-run drivers followed. In October an extremist ran over two soldiers in Canada; in November two Israelis were killed; a dozen pedestrians were hit by a driver in Dijon, France, in December 2014; and in January 2015 a policewoman was mown down in Paris.

The Provincial Council oversees the administration of the (to date) eighteen provinces (*wilayat*) the State comprises: in Iraq, Anbar, Baghdad, Diyala, Fallujah, al-Janoub (the South), Kirkuk, Nineveh, Salahuddin; in Syria, Aleppo, Homs, al-Baraka, Damascus, Hama, Idlib, al-Khair, Raqqa, Latakia. An additional *wilayat*, al-Furat, spans the border, which Islamic State claims to have erased.

The day-to-day administration of Islamic State is facilitated by a 'cabinet'; the responsibilities of its members are to provide a vivid picture of the group's wider activities. There is a general management official, an officer for prisoners and hostages, general security and finance representatives, people from the departments responsible for new arrivals of foreign and Arab jihadists, and for the 'transport of suicide bombers'. Members of the cabinet from the 'War Office' include a 'Co-ordinator of Martyrs and Women' and somebody responsible for rigging improvised explosive devices and bombs.[9]

Daily life in Islamic State

In bid to emulate the days of the Prophet and his Companions, even time itself is calculated differently in the territories of the digital caliphate. On 27 October 2014, IS's media wing al-Hayat announced (on Twitter) that the lunar calendar would be in use henceforth. The Islamic calendar starts in the year of *hijra* when Muhammad and the Sahabah ('companions' – the Prophet's family, disciples and scribes) migrated to Medina, and for this reason it is known as the *hijri* calendar. Each month begins when the new moon can be seen with the naked eye; this may vary depending on geographical location, so different countries might have slightly different dates for the New Year. It is common for new, totalitarian regimes to impose a new calendar; North Korea and Pol Pot's Cambodia have both reset to 'year zero' in recent times.

There have been various reports of life in the Islamic State. Al-

Hayat produced a film called *A Visit to Mosul* in August 2014 in which the presenter freely wandered round the 'beautiful city', indicating the places where the 'infidels' lay down their arms and surrendered to – according to him – 200 'brothers'. He entered all the municipal buildings that have been taken over, including the town hall and courts. Residents interviewed said (predictably) that life in Mosul was better under Islamic State than under Maliki, when road closures, beatings, car searches and arrests were commonplace. The few reporters who have made it into the territories speak of terrible punishments, but concede that there is improved law and order and public amenities. I have been able to contact several people living in Islamic State via various social media platforms and have put together the following facts and impressions, although it should be borne in mind that these are people who are happy to be living there, rather than those who have been trapped.

An Iraqi jihadist living in Mosul answered questions about life for women in the Dawlatul-Islamiyyah (Islamic State). He is man of about thirty who appears to have been delegated the task of fielding enquiries from, and allaying the doubts of, potential recruits, in particular young women. He said that single women arriving from abroad live in a 'sisters' *maqar*' (house designated for single women only) and that there are people 'in charge of marriage affairs' who arrange meetings for those interested in marriage. The two parties are allowed to speak for five minutes and, if they are still interested, 'can see each other if they wish' (i.e. unveiled) and then 'accept or refuse' marriage. He assured us that women are allowed to drive and that married couples are given a house (abandoned by the million residents who fled) or, if none is available, are helped to rent in the private sector with a grant from the state. Families of fighters are given monthly food and money. There are no training camps for women, he said, but women who wish to 'can receive training from their husbands'.

A non-extremist Sunni Muslim living in Manbij, a small Syrian city near Aleppo which has been under IS control since January 2014, said that crime was now non-existent owing to the uncompromising methods of the extremists and their 'consistency'. He said the group has been collecting *Zakat* taxes (on income and wealth) and redistributing the proceeds to the poor and displaced families from other parts of Syria which, he said, now made up half the city's population. By his account the emphasis on education was approved of by the populace, despite a focus on Islam, and he reported that the teaching was strong on sciences. Teachers were receiving salaries again after months of non-payment. The city's residents were aware that rival 'rebel groups' might attempt to seize the city from Islamic State. They were not generally enthusiastic about such a turn of events, which might mean having to flee, yet again. This outcome might fragment the fragile civic administration, law and order and security the extremists had put in place. He also said that the regime did not attack cities under Islamic State control so they had avoided the suffering experienced by their countrymen in Aleppo; as a result people from other towns and cities insulted them and called them '*Shabihat daesh*' – daesh thugs, 'DAESH' being an acronym of an Arabic version of ISIS's name, most commonly used by those opposed to it.

Despite generally positive impressions, our Manbiji said most people doubt that Islamic State can survive for two reasons. The first is that people will eventually rebel against its harsh strictures. The second, he says, is because IS is in a symbiotic relationship with the regime: Sunnis, out of antipathy for Assad, have flocked to IS, yet Assad is refraining from fighting the jihadists because they have all but demolished the 'moderate' opposition, which is a greater political threat to him in the long run.

On social media platforms frequented by foreign jihadists, a rosy picture is painted of life in Islamic State. But reports have also emerged of young people who realise they have made a terrible mistake, yet find themselves unable to leave both because their countries of origin would arrest them on return, and because their commanders threaten to kill them if they try to run away. One twenty-five-year-old British mother travelled to Raqqa with her toddler son in November 2014, became disillusioned, and managed to escape over the border to Turkey, where she is in custody. She spoke of her terror at 'bombs going off all over the place... and women were treated like cattle'.[10]

An Iraqi journalist living in Mosul complained of power cuts, galloping inflation, school closures and the cessation of rations – including sugar, rice, oil and flour – that the government had previously provided. That writer interviewed former government officials and employees, so it is difficult to ascertain the impartiality of this story, which appeared under the pseudonym Mohammad Moslawi.[11]

The richest terror group in history

Islamic State has apparently decided to follow one of the basic rules for business success: diversification. It has numerous legal and illegal revenue streams that involve both local and global partners. Unlike al-Qa'ida, IS makes its own money. It receives donations from individuals and groups, thanks to the anonymity of the internet and virtual currency such as bitcoin; however, they account for only a small proportion of its war chest. Its wealth in turn makes it independent and extremely powerful. In October 2014, the US Treasury Department remarked that IS 'has amassed wealth at an unprecedented pace'.[12] It has done this mainly through the oil fields and refineries it has seized, as well as looting, gun-running, bank robberies, slave trading, and ransoms for kidnap victims.

At the time of writing, Islamic State had control over eleven oil fields in Syria and Iraq. In Syria, it controls all the major oil fields, including the country's largest, the al-Omar, which can produce 75,000 barrels a day. In Iraq, the group controls at least six oil fields in the central province of Salahuddin and the eastern Diyala province, including the Qayyarah and the Ajil and Hamrin fields. It has also seized control of refineries in both countries including the Baiji refinery, one of Iraq's most important installations, and the smaller Gayara refinery near Mosul. In order to combat efforts by coalition planes, fighters ignited a huge oil storage tank at Baiji containing 100,000 barrels, causing a fire to rage for days.[13] In Syria, confirmed details of what IS does or does not control are hard to come by, owing to intelligence black-outs; but given that coalition planes target only assets held by the extremists it would appear that Islamic State holds at least twelve refineries in Syria.[14]

Islamic State extracts an estimated 50,000 bpd (barrels per day) in Syria and 30,000 in Iraq and sells its oil at knockdown rates – $25 to $60 for a barrel of oil that normally fetches more than $100. Nevertheless it is taking $3 million to $5 million a day.[15] Remarkably, the Assad regime in Syria buys oil from Islamic State in Iraq because, since the US and European Union banned Syrian oil exports in 2011, official production virtually came to a halt.[16] In Iraq, it sells crude oil to traders or middle men who sell it on, via long-established smuggling networks, into Turkey, Jordan and Iran; apparently, there is nothing the Kurdish regional government in northern Iraq (where the fields are) can do about it.[17]

Another significant source of Islamic State's income is looting and trading antiquities, sometimes to order. Iraq and Syria are full of ancient sites, dating back 6,000 years, which had been carefully preserved by governments intent on maintaining the nations' cultural integrity and heritage, and in attracting tourists. Looting antiquities fits well with the group's belief that it has to 'cleanse' 'pagan' relics such as shrines and tombs. But it destroys them only after having removed everything of value from them; these are then considered spoils of war and a legitimate asset. Archaeologists believe the worst hit sites are Apamea, Dura-Europos and Raqqa. In Iraq, looting of antiquities also occurred during the insurgency, but not on the industrial scale observed from satellite imagery in Iraq, where bulldozers demolish entire sites in order to ransack their treasures.[18]

Looted items end up offered for sale on the Turkish-Syrian border and include figurines, gold and silver coins, mosaics, jewellery, cylinder seals and tablets.[19] Experts told the *New Yorker* magazine that 'high-end' antiquities can exchange hands for astronomical figures. A three-inch-tall, 5,000-year-old Mesopotamian lion made of limestone was auctioned in New York for $57 million in 2007. The arrest of a messenger in June 2014 led to the discovery of financial records showing that antiquities sales in just one province of Syria had added $36 million to Islamic State coffers.[20]

The Western press has been full of lurid tales of female captives being sold as 'sex-slaves'. It would be easy to dismiss the more sensationalistic claims as propaganda, were it not for the fact that the Islamic State itself considers human trafficking and slavery to be legitimate practice. In issue four of its online magazine *Dabiq*,[21] an article titled 'The Revival of Slavery before the Hour' describes how a group of 'scholars' considered whether the Yazidis they had captured were a fallen sect of Islam, 'people of the book' (Jews or Christians), or pagans. Having decided on the latter, Islamic State announced that their 'women could be enslaved unlike female apostates who the majority of the *fuqahā'* [legal experts] say cannot be enslaved and can only be given an ultimatum to repent or face the sword'. The *Dabiq* article describes how, after capture, 'the Yazidi women and children were divided according to the Sharī'ah amongst the fighters of the Islamic State who participated in the Sinjar operations, after one fifth of the slaves were transferred to the Islamic State's authority to be divided as khum [war booty]... The enslaved Yazidi families are now sold by the Islamic State soldiers as the *mushrikīn* [pagans] were sold by the Companions (*radiyallāhu 'anhum* [may Allah be pleased with them]) before them. Many well-known rulings are observed, including the prohibition of separating a mother from her young children.' (Square brackets in these quotations are my own additions, explanations in round brackets are in the original.) The writer also links this phenomenon to the coming of the end times as it is mentioned as one of the 'signs of the Hour'. Finally he addresses the sexual aspect of the proposed slavery: 'A number of contemporary scholars have mentioned that the desertion of slavery had led to an increase in *fāhishah* (adultery, fornication, etc.), because the shar'ia alternative to marriage is not available, so a man who cannot afford marriage to a free woman finds himself surrounded by temptation towards sin. In addition, many Muslim families who have hired maids to work at their homes, face the *fitnah* [trial] of prohibited *khalwah* [seclusion] and resultant *zinā* [unlawful sex] occurring between the man and the maid, whereas if she were his concubine, this relationship would be legal. This again is from the consequences of abandoning jihād and chasing after the *duny* [earthly rewards].'[22]

Accounts by Yazidi women who escaped their captors suggest that something akin to a slave market was held over a period of ten days in Mosul in September. In one account, a Yazidi woman called Alyas told a reporter about her experiences. 'Men perused the captive women and placed their offers,' wrote the reporter, 'buying women for as little as $15. Among the buyers were both foreign and local men – she recognized several people from Sinjar. The men who didn't want to take children separated them from their mothers, leaving them in Mosul, where they would be educated at an ISIS-run school, the women overheard. As the days dragged on, several women attempted suicide, creating nooses from their headscarves. At least four women were successful.'[23] While slave-trading is unlikely to be a major revenue stream for Islamic State it is certainly one of the most inhumane and bizarre.

Ransoms from kidnappings brought in an estimated $20 million in 2014 alone. Several countries, including France, have agreed to pay the demands, but Washington refuses, saying it will only encourage further hostage-taking.[24] Associated Press reported that Islamic State had demanded $132.5 million for the release of the American journalist James Foley.[25]

Military tactics and objectives

According to Kurdish commanders reported in the media, the armed force of Islamic State currently numbers more than 200,000 fighters, nearly one third of whom are experienced in battle.[26] In September 2014 official estimates put the number of foreign fighters at around 15,000, from ninety different countries;[27] in January 2015, however, well-placed sources suggest there are around 30,000 foreigners, at least 7,000 of whom have European nationality. In addition, local Sunnis in both Iraq and Syria work for Islamic State in intelligence and logistics capacities. Estimates suggest these men (and women) number 10,000 to 15,000 in each country. New recruits have flocked to the jihadists since US-led bombardments began in Syria. Sunni fighters who were previously with 'moderate' opposition groups have switched to Islamic State out of anger and frustration at the West's failure to defeat the regime and eagerness to crush the jihadists instead. In both Iraq and Syria, where unemployment rates are rocketing, the prospect of earning a decent, regular salary is a significant incentive. Islamic State pays its fighters a very generous $500–$650 per month (the average salary in Iraq is $590, while in Syria it is just $243).[28]

The officers from Saddam Hussein's military and security cadres in its ranks are experts in key fields such as manufacturing the complicated, deadly improvised explosive devices (IEDs – which quickly became the hallmark of al-Qa'ida in Iraq), security issues and intelligence, both within its own ranks and territories and behind enemy lines. An American military expert commented that they 'know the military terrain and demographic dynamics in Iraq as their own and how to exploit it... For me, the military campaign design exhibited by ISIS over the last two years bears the signature of multiple commanders because successive campaigns have consistently demonstrated scope, distribution, deception, and timing as overarching strategic characteristics.'[29] These professional soldiers have also advised on the development of a military hierarchy and command that enables Islamic State to function as a highly disciplined army, rather than as a terror group. This is unprecedented on such a large scale, the only comparable entities being the Irish Republican Army (IRA), Shining Path in Peru, and Hezbollah.

Like ISI in its heyday, Islamic State also enjoys the support and military collaboration of local Sunni tribes, and some of the other Salafi-Jihadist entities. In recent months, the enmity between Islamic State and al-Qa'ida's branch in Syria, al-Nusra, has diminished, and the groups have agreed to co-operate.[30]

Within its army Islamic State has dozens of heavily armed battalions (a battalion is about 500 fighters). They have sophisticated military hardware, largely stolen from captured Iraqi Army bases and stores but also including equipment and arms from the stockpiles of former Libyan ruler Muammar al-Gaddafi. These were abandoned during the Libyan revolution and spirited away into the desert, whence they have found their way to most major jihadist combat zones. Islamic State and al-Nusra fighters have also cherry-picked arms sent over the Turkish border for the 'moderate' rebels.[31]

Islamic State's ultimate military capabilities are weakened by the absence of an air force or navy. However, it is not beyond the realms of possibility that they will eventually commandeer planes and ships, together with their crews.

Islamic State battalions and units are extremely adaptable to changing situations and new developments on the ground, and field commanders are given total autonomy in implementing the operations they are charged with. This flexibility, and confident delegation, makes IS's war effort extremely effective and frees up the Military Council to concentrate on the overall strategy, rather than the detail of individual battles. Its opportunistic 'liquid' structure makes it difficult for global intelligence networks to get solid information and tangible details in order to counter and pre-empt Islamic State operations. Thus Islamic State always has the advantage of surprise and is able to seize opportunities as and when they arise. Rather than 'fight to the death', its brigades will slip away from a battle they are clearly not going to win, regrouping in a more advantageous location – a tactic successfully employed for many years by the al-Qa'ida network. In January 2015, for example, with the US-led alliance bombarding Islamic State targets in Iraq, the Military Council decided to redeploy its efforts to Syria. Fighters inside Iraq were ordered to lie low (mostly in cities where it is harder for war planes to strike without significant 'collateral damage') while battalions and sleeper cells in Syria were reactivated. As a result, the group doubled the territory under its control in Syria between August 2014 and January 2015.[32]

The West's reluctance to commit ground troops has also hampered Western-led attempts to halt Islamic State's expansion. The group's ferocious reputation and catalogue of atrocities act as a substantial deterrent. In addition, Islamic State fighters are adept not only in conventional battles but also in urban and mountain guerrilla combat – as are most jihadists. Guerrilla warfare requires larger battalions to rapidly disconnect into small, fast-moving, adaptable fighting groups. This gives them the upper hand against conventional troops who founder in such circumstances – hence, for example, the inability of US troops to prevail in the battle of Fallujah during the Second Gulf War. As an American military commentator concluded, 'Islamic State combines and hybridizes terrorism, guerrilla warfare, and conventional warfare... and it makes IS a new breed.'[33]

In terms of tactics and strategy, the most common feature of Islamic State assaults on towns and cities is to surround the conurbation and then lay siege to it. When the target is a large city, or even the capital – Baghdad seems a likely target – the strategy would be to seize control of the outer provinces and 'belt regions', or key areas, surrounding the main target. Through road blocks and bases along the 'belts', the group controls access to the conurbation and can facilitate the passage of money, arms and fighters.

Islamic State has also focused on securing strategic targets essential to food and water security in both Iraq and Syria such as key dams on the Tigris and Euphrates. Dams in particular can also be used as bargaining chips. In the July 2014 edition of its online magazine *Dabiq*, titled 'The Flood', the group threatened to destroy the Mosul dam which it had captured, unleashing a torrent that could destroy Baghdad.

EIGHT

THE MANAGEMENT OF SAVAGERY

Crucifixions, beheadings, the hearts of rape victims cut out and placed upon their chests,[1] mass executions, homosexuals being pushed from high buildings, severed heads impaled on railings or brandished by grinning 'jihadist' children – who have latterly taken to shooting prisoners in the head themselves[2] – these gruesome images of brutal violence are carefully packaged and distributed via Islamic State's media department. As each new atrocity outdoes the last, front-page headlines across the world's media are guaranteed.

It may seem like an undisciplined orgy of sadism, but it is far from being that. This is systematically applied policy. The extreme violence perpetrated by Islamic State is discussed and advocated in jihadist literature, most notably the 2004 internet document 'The Management of Savagery' written by al-Qa'ida ideologue Abu Bakr Naji. Naji's work is often referenced by Islamic State's online speakers and writers.

Most countries and empires have been established in oceans of blood and the most gruesome acts of terrifying violence. A conquering army's arsenal always includes psychological terror. And as far as the leaders and ideologues of Islamic State are concerned, they are building a new state or, rather, restoring an empire on Muslim lands: the Caliphate.

The history of extreme violence in war

In his book *The Psychology of Genocide, Massacres and Extreme Violence*, Donald G. Dutton shows that 'sophisticated' and 'civilised' societies will blithely accept atrocity when it is under the banner of a shared cause: most Americans opposed the punishment of Lt William Calley, who ordered the rape and murder of women and children by his troops at the Vietnamese village of My Lai.[3] More recently, Americans scarcely blinked when stories of the most barbaric CIA torture practices in Guantanamo Bay were revealed.[4] Extreme violence is also used by governments seeking to stamp out dissent and discourage disobedience. In the course of the twentieth century governments killed 170 million of their own citizens with 62 million killed in the USSR alone between 1917 and 1987.[5]

The pattern of extreme violence and savagery has not changed since the first well-documented atrocities in the name of religion occurred in the course of the crusades. The concept of 'positive violence' found expression in eleventh-century Rome when Pope Urban II painted 'Holy War' as an adventure that God not only tolerated but actively supported. Psychological warfare was common during the Crusades and included so-called 'threat display'. Christians catapulted the severed heads of Muslim fighters' heads over the walls of besieged towns for example. The Muslims, meanwhile, hung dead Crusaders on top of the walls so that 'their friends could watch them rot'.[6]

War *is* violence, so we can hardly be surprised that the victor is usually capable of more cold-blooded psychopathy than the defeated armies. The numbers killed reached unprecedented extremes in the twentieth century, as did the variety of methods used to exterminate a target group. Stalin systematically starved millions in Ukraine (in an attempted genocide known as Holodomor) and massacred an additional 30 million 'dissenters'; one million Armenians were slaughtered by the Ottomans in 1914 and 20 million Eastern Europeans died in the Second World War at the hands of the Nazis, as did millions of Jews, disabled people, Gypsies and homosexuals; in 1995, Serb armies slaughtered 8,000 Bosniak Muslim men and boys in former Yugoslavia and forcefully expelled 30,000 more from their homes... the list goes on, is lengthy and depressing.

Japanese soldiers who fought in the Second World War were deliberately desensitised and shown how to decapitate living prisoners; they were at first repulsed but became inured to atrocities committed both by themselves and by their comrades. One soldier, who would become a doctor in later life, wrote of his conduct during the war: 'It is terrible that I could turn into an animal and do these things. There are really no words to explain what I was doing. I was truly a devil.'[7]

Dehumanising the victim relaxes intrinsically felt moral restraints; enemies are often depicted as repulsive animals like rats or cockroaches. US soldier Steven Green, along with four colleagues, gang-raped then murdered fourteen-year-old Abeer Qassim al-Janabi in front of her parents and family who were then also killed; he said, 'I didn't think of Iraqis as human.'[8] In the context of war, the overarching imperative is to terrify the enemy and assert superior levels of ruthlessness. This is what we are currently witnessing in the excesses of Islamic State. The Americans have a term for it: 'Shock and Awe'.

Atrocities can equally be used for recruitment purposes: by demonising and agitating against the enemy, acts of war become justified. As one British general pointed out after the First World War, 'To make armies go on killing one another it is necessary to invent lies about the enemy.'[9] In the case of the 'global jihad' movement (which includes al-Qa'ida and Islamic State), revenge for national and Western armies' atrocities against citizens and comrades, and their uninvited military interventions, as well as the perceived theft of Muslim resources by greedy multinational companies and a failure to broker a just solution for the Palestinians, all feed into the appetite for war.

For Islamic State atrocities are a deliberate, premeditated 'Message in Blood', to use the title given by the group's media department, al-Hayat, to a grizzly October 2014 video depicting the beheading of Kurdish fighters. It is 'propaganda by the deed' and the more heinous the deed the more impact (and global coverage) it has. Islamic State often creates a political subtext to its high-visibility acts of violence. The live-streaming of hostages in orange jumpsuits as they wait to be slaughtered instantly makes a connection between this act and the ill-treatment of Muslims detained without trial for years in Guantanamo. It implies that the US government is responsible for the executions of its citizens because the killings are revenge for past actions; and that culpability is extended to the whole American populace.

The 'Management of Savagery'

Abu Bakr Naji's internet treatise 'The Management of Savagery' appeared in 2004. It draws heavily on the work of the fourteenth-century Islamic scholar Taqi al-Din ibn Taymiyyah, who is considered the first Salafi-jihadist and is revered by today's hardliners. Naji is believed to be the pseudonym of Muhammad Khalil al-Hakaymah (aka Abu Jihad al-Masri), an Egyptian who merged his group, Jamaa Islamiyyah, with al-Qa'ida and was close to Ayman al-Zawahiri. Naji was killed by a US drone strike in Waziristan, Pakistan, in 2008.

His essay discusses the role of extreme violence in the three-stage route to re-establishing the Caliphate: a 'stage of vexation and exhaustion' is followed by 'the administration of savagery' and, finally, 'the establishment of the Islamic State'. The document would certainly have influenced Abu Musab al-Zarqawi. He was causing controversy among his fellow jihadists at the time it was written by advocating – and indeed, practising – extreme violence, not against 'the infidel' but also against fellow Muslims, in Iraq and Jordan.

Naji begins his treatise by suggesting that 'the administrations of savagery' are a developmental stage in state and nation building and 'human nature'. His aim, and the aim of his fellow-travellers, is to remove the *ummah* (nation) from 'the quagmire of darkness and decadence' which the world became following the 'fall of the Caliphate'. This pagan state is called the *Jahiliyyah*.

Every caliphate was established and maintained by the sword.

Salafi-jihadists maintain that the Prophet Muhammad himself had to establish Islam by violence and it is true that he became a great military leader and introduced the obligation of defensive jihad for all Muslims. The argument here is that jihad became a necessity: Muhammad was initially instructed (by God) to seek the path of peaceful reconciliation. For the first thirteen years of his mission (610–623), when he was based in Mecca, he advocated non-violence and told his followers that their patience would be rewarded in heaven. The Surahs (Qur'anic verses) revealed in this period include: 'overlook with gracious forgiveness' (Qur'an 15:85) and 'bear then with patience all that they say.' Even when Mecca's polytheist Qurayshi oligarchy began to display murderous intentions towards Muhammad, he was told to 'invite all to the way of thy Lord with wisdom and beautiful preaching' (Qur'an 16:125) rather than violence.

Forced to flee for their lives in the first *hijra* (emigration) Muhammad and his companions relocated to Medina. This *hijra* marks the most significant development in the history of Islam, and is the start date for the Islamic calendar. In Medina, Muhammad became the political, judicial and military leader of a mixed community where Arab tribes had converted to Islam and most Jewish tribes accepted it as a political system. The Surah revealed in Medina deal with the law and what is permitted, whereas those that had gone before were to do with the nature of belief.

With the 1,000-strong Meccan army determined to exterminate the Muslims, whose fighters at that point numbered just 300, verses in Surah 8 contained the following prophecy: 'if there are twenty among you, patient and persevering, they will vanquish 200; if a hundred they will vanquish a thousand of the Unbelievers, for these are a people without understanding' (Qur'an 8:65). Now the Muslims were permitted to 'fight them until there is no more tumult and oppression, and there prevail justice and faith in Allah altogether and everywhere' (Qur'an 8:37). In the subsequent stand-off, the Battle of Badr (624), Muhammad's 300 did indeed prevail over the Meccans' 1,000.

The Battle of the Trench came three years later, shortly after the eighth Surah had been revealed concerning jihad in the military sense, assuring the Muslims that Allah would both be on their side and guide them to victory. Again, the Muslims prevailed and the burden on enemies was now greater: 'when you meet the unbelievers, smite at their necks; at length when you have subdued them, bind them firmly; thereafter either generosity or ransom' (Qur'an 47:4). The same Surah contains the promises of reward for the martyr 'slain in the Way of Allah' in the 'Garden which he has announced for them' (Qur'an 47:6).

We are now firmly in the ideological territory inhabited by Islamic State and its predecessor, al-Qa'ida. In his 1996 *fatwa* declaring war on America, Osama bin Laden warns that the mujahideen 'have no intention but to enter paradise by killing you... these youths are different from your soldiers. Your problem will be how to convince your troops to fight, ours will be how to restrain our youths to wait for their turn in fighting and in operations... our youths know that if one is not killed, one will die, and the most honourable death is to be killed in the way of Allah.'[10] This *fatwa* was first faxed to and published in *al-Quds al-Arabi*.

In all, Muhammad fought for the last ten years of his life, initially at the head of a small band of 'insurgent' or 'guerrilla' fighters that grew into the Arab world's first conventional army, numbering up to 10,000. It had cavalry and infantry units, and a highly effective intelligence service. Muhammad returned to Mecca in triumph and most of the city's inhabitants now converted to Islam. Military historians describe the Prophet as a great general and military strategist.[11]

Having established his authority, Muhammad did not balk at violence and understood the power of fear. He assured loyalty among his followers by public punishment of traitors; the penalty for apostasy was execution and many of his political opponents were assassinated. To strike terror into the hearts of non-believers, Muhammad declared the 'war of the knife' on them.

Subsequent caliphates were also established and maintained

through military prowess, with the Abbasid Caliphate ushered in on the wave of blood issuing from one of the most famous battles in world history – the 751 Battle of Talas, which saw the Arab armies engage with, and vanquish, the Tang Dynasty of China.

In his treatise, Abu Bakr Naji describes the first stage towards re-establishing the caliphate (which he refers to as the 'Islamic State') as 'vexation and exhaustion': the superpowers will be worn down militarily by constant threat, terror and aggression from the jihadists. The US and its allies will implode politically owing to their 'moral collapse, social iniquities, opulence, selfishness and giving priority to worldly pleasures'. Economic collapse will follow due to the intolerable financial burden of incessant war: 'the most likely way to defeat the strongest enemy militarily is to drain it militarily and economically', Naji asserts (as have many other al-Qa'ida ideologues, including Osama bin Laden and Ayman al-Zawahri; both were admirers of Yale historian Paul Kennedy's book *The Rise and Fall of Great Powers*, which observes that great empires fall in large part because they overstretch themselves militarily abroad and in maintaining security at home). The social unrest that will result from economic meltdown will further damage 'the enemy'. The reader may recall that this process almost exactly describes the downfall of the Soviet Union, which was simultaneously drained by its decade-long war in Afghanistan and keeping its increasingly restive member states in line.

The second stage Naji describes is the 'administration of savagery', which sees the jihadist army dismiss anything that stands in its way. The Americans, he says, 'have reached a stage of effeminacy which makes them unable to sustain battles for a long period of time and they compensate for this with a deceptive media curtain'. The aim here is to provoke the US to 'abandon its war against Islam by proxy... and the media psychological war... and force it to fight directly'. This is the same strategy outlined to me in 1996 by Osama bin Laden, who sought to defeat 'the ponderous

American elephant' by bringing it to fight on Muslim land. Islamic State has yet to provoke its enemies into putting military 'boots on the ground', which is surely its ultimate aim, but Naji suggests 'direct American interference in the Islamic world' together with its 'support for the Zionist entity' would ensure its defeat at the hands of 'the renewal movement'.

The 'region of savagery' in which the Salafi-jihadists will operate, according to Naji, will be 'a region submitting to the law of the jungle in its primitive form' and commences with the breakdown, or weakening, of regular armies, enabling the mujahideen to prevail in areas left undefended. Saddam's Iraq, Assad's Syria and Gaddafi's Libya were possessed of the strongest armies in the Arab world before the invasion of Iraq and the Arab Spring revolutions saw them dismantled; these countries had no 'Islamist problem' before this stage.

The benighted people who are unfortunate enough to live in this 'savage chaos' will 'yearn for someone to manage this savagery', and, Naji posits, this will be Islamic State. As we have seen, the ability of Islamic State to impose and maintain law and order is one of the reasons it has been welcomed in many of the towns and cities it has overrun, much as the Taliban were initially welcomed in Afghanistan following the civil war.

Naji emphasises the necessity for the jihadists to be 'savage' themselves. Referring to the establishment of the Abbasid Caliphate, he says 'one of the reasons for the success of the Abbasids and the failure of the others is the Abbasids' violence and the others' softness and protection of the blood.' Acknowledging the natural revulsion most recruits experience at the thought of extreme violence, he cites the Prophet's companions who 'burned people with fire even though it is odious because they knew the effect of rough violence in times of need... they did not undertake it because they love killing; they were certainly not coarse people. By God! How tender were their hearts... The reality of this role must be understood by explaining it to the youth who want to fight.'

Naji details how the Prophet's companion, Abu Bakr, gained a reputation for 'ruthlessness in war' that almost rivalled that of 'the Messenger of God'. He ordered troops to 'sever the neck without clemency or slowness'. For Naji (and the soldiers of Islamic State) 'we are now in circumstances resembling the circumstances after the death of the Messenger (peace and blessings be upon him) and the outbreak of apostasy the like of which the believers faced in the beginning of the jihad. Thus, we need to massacre...'

In Naji's project, the increase of their own 'savagery' sees the 'reputation and stature of the mujahids rise' with 'waves of operations which fill hearts with fear and this fear will have no end'. The aim is to get as much media coverage of outrages as possible so as to 'make them think one thousand times before attacking us'. He urges excesses, for example, 'using a quantity of explosives which not only destroys the building or even levels it to the earth; it makes the earth completely swallow it up. By doing so, the amount of the enemy's fear is multiplied and good media goals are achieved.' If ransoms are not paid for kidnapped hostages, they should be 'liquidated in the most terrifying manner which will send fear into the hearts of the enemy and his supporters'.

By making the enemy 'pay the price', Naji asserts that he will be 'more inclined towards reconciliation'. Not that he advocates peace-making: 'a temporary stop to fighting without any kind of treaties or concessions... will only be to allow the fighters to catch their breath and progress.'

Noting that US-led coalitions are based only on 'self-interest' (as opposed to the mujahideen who, according to him, are united through shared faith) Naji does not anticipate long-lived resistance to the Islamic State: 'As for their persistence in continuing war, that is only when they think that their opponent is weak and it is possible to crush his will. When there is violent resistance which leads to invasions that cost a great deal and are of little use, the factions of the coalition began to withdraw one after another, preferring security or delaying the conflict until more suitable circumstances.'

Once the mujahideen are in the position of 'managing' the stage of savagery, the aim is to implement several 'primary goals' which, theoretically, culminate in the establishment of the Islamic State (Caliphate). I leave the reader to determine which of the goals identified by Naji have already been reached by today's putative Islamic State:

1. Spreading internal security and preserving it in every region that is managed

2. Providing food and medical treatment

3. Securing the region of savagery from the invasions of enemies by setting up defensive fortifications and developing fighting capacities

4. Establishing Sharia justice among the people who live in the regions of savagery

5. Raising the level of faith and combat efficiency during the training of the youth of the region of savagery and establishing a fighting society at all levels and among all individuals by means of making them aware of its importance. But it must be made clear that it is an obligatory duty [*wujbihi al-muta'ayyan*], which does not mean that every individual member of society must practise fighting; rather, only a part or portion of the fighting ranks [must practise it] in the form which the society knows best and needs

6. Working for the spread of legal, Sharia science and worldly science [Schools and universities in the Islamic State are prioritising these two subjects]

7. Disseminating spies and seeking to complete the construction of a minimal intelligence agency

8. Uniting the hearts of the people by means of money and uniting the world by Sharia governance and compliance with rules which are at least exemplified by individuals in the administration

9. Deterring the hypocrites with proof and other means and

forcing them to repress and conceal their hypocrisy, to hide their discouraged opinions, and to comply with those in authority until their evil is put in check.

10. Working until it is possible to expand and attack the enemies in order to repel them, plunder their money, and place them in a constant state of apprehension and desire for reconciliation

11. Establishing coalitions with those with whom coalitions are permitted, those who have not given complete allegiance to the administration

12. To these we add a future goal, which is the advancement of managerial groups towards the attainment of the 'power of establishment' and readiness for plucking the fruit [of their efforts] and establishing the state.

Mastering barbarity

The strategy and ideology for the ongoing attempt to establish a caliphate in the heart of the Middle East with expansionist ambitions have been in place for at least a decade and they envisage great barbarity.

The year after Abu Bakr Naji's treatise was published, a second, 2005, document appeared. It was titled 'Al-Qa'ida's Strategy to the Year 2020', and was written by a shadowy ideologue called Makawi (in all probability one of Saif al-Adel's pseudonyms). This sets out a five-step plan that also begins with 'provoking the ponderous American elephant' on to Muslim lands where its troops can be killed, and ends with the re-establishment of the caliphate following a definitive battle with the 'unbelievers'.[12]

As it has turned out, al-Qa'ida appears to have been usurped by Islamic State – perhaps temporarily – but the two groups' ideology and projects are close. One might expect a strategic reunion in the future if Ayman al-Zawahiri can swallow the bitter pill of giving his *bayat* to Abu Bakr al-Baghdadi.

The gruesome public exhibition of extreme violence is part of a plan to instil fear and trepidation in the heart of the enemy. In this, as I have shown, Islamic State is by no means unique today, but is devastatingly adept.

NINE

THE CALIPH'S FOREIGN FIGHTERS

'There are thousands of us, literally from every corner of the world... and we are all al-Qa'ida,' an ISIS Foreign fighter told BBC correspondent Richard Galpin in December 2013. He added that his entire 8,000-strong foreign jihadist brigade had recently pledged allegiance to ISIS. My research includes interviews with Islamic State fighters and anecdotal evidence provided by sources in Middle Eastern countries during field research for this book in late 2014; it suggests that, a year on from Galpin's interview, the foreign jihadists who were flocking to the region hailed from a wide variety of backgrounds. While many are al-Qa'ida, an equal number have never fought before.

Islamic State recruitment and propaganda material insists on the 'religious duty' of *hijra* (migration) to join the caliphate, and many young people are taking this call seriously. Anyone seeking to migrate to Iraq or Syria can get advice on how to do so from someone who is already living in *Dawla* (short for *Dawlatul Islamiyyah*, Islamic State), easily contactable via Twitter. The would-be recruit is then instructed to contact someone 'off-page' on Ask.fm or Kik – anonymous sites where anything goes and nothing is traceable – for more specific detail and offers of help.

The phenomenon of migrating foreign fighters, motivated by a shared religious ideology and membership of a non-geographical national identity (in this case, the *ummah*), was until recently so rare that no term exists for it in political science. In jihadist vocabulary, foreign fighters are *muhajireen*, the term the Prophet Muhammad used for fighters who migrated for the purpose of jihad. The concept of the *ummah* is key to jihadist ideology. The 'nation of Muslims' does not have borders, and the jihadists fiercely dismiss the artificial boundaries created by the former colonial powers. Islamic State, then, is not a nation state but a state for all Muslims. That is the theory.

A history of migration

The practice of Muslims travelling to help each other in their various local struggles is not new. Arab volunteers (as opposed to the regular armies) from other countries joined the Palestinians in their battles with Israel, but in small numbers, peaking at under a hundred in the Six-Day War in 1967.[1] Non-Arab Muslim volunteer fighters joined the mujahideen for the first time in significant numbers during the ten-year war against the Soviets in Afghanistan in the 1970s. An estimated 20,000 joined their Pashtun and Arab fellow travellers in jihad. Approximately 2,000 of these fighters stayed on to fight in the civil war that followed Soviet withdrawal. Most of them joined al-Qa'ida – which established itself in Afghanistan, under the patronage of the Taliban, from 1996 until 2001, when the US bombed Tora Bora in retaliation for 9/11 and the mujahideen dispersed.

The 1992–95 Bosnian jihad attracted around 6,000 foreign fighters (Bosnian intelligence reports suggest 25 per cent were Saudi). Algeria's 'Armed Islamic Group', the GIA, which emerged during the 1990s civil war, and its successor the GSPC (Salafist Group for Preaching and Combat), numbered thousands of foreign jihadists, including Westerners. When the US invaded Iraq in 2003, thousands more flocked to join the insurgency, reviving the fortunes of al-Qa'ida, which had been almost extinguished. Numbers are hard to ascertain, largely because of efforts by the West and the fledgling Iraqi government to downplay the phenomenon in a bid to scale down recruitment. But the US army suggested that 20 per cent of fighters they captured were foreign.[2]

Large numbers of foreign fighters joined AQAP (al-Qa'ida

in the Arabia Peninsula), mostly in response to the strenuous recruitment efforts of the charismatic Anwar al-Awlaki. He was a fluent English-speaker, having spent many years in the US. Somalia's al-Shabaab group also appealed to Western fighters,[3] including the well-known American Omar Hammami (Abu Mansour al-Amriki) and the 'white widow' (of London Transport bomber Germaine Lindsay) Samantha Lewthwaite. Many of those who have been intercepted leaving America to join Islamic State are Somalis from Minneapolis.[4]

The increasingly transnational nature of 'jihad' is due to a number of factors: the enthusiastic export of Wahhabism (a strict form of Islam examined in Chapter 11) throughout the Muslim world by the Saudi establishment, and the resultant expansion of extremist mosques, schools and universities that posit jihad as a religious obligation; a large number of Islamic charities that offer funding and help with the logistics of travel to people recruited in mosques; finally, the explosion in the online recruitment of foreign fighters, which first swelled the ranks of AQAP and Somalia's al-Shabaab, before the phenomenal response achieved by ISIS and Islamic State.

The number of foreign fighters who have travelled to Iraq and Syria in the past two or three years is unprecedented. By 2012 there were already more foreign fighters in Syria alone than had gone to join the jihad in Afghanistan and Iraq. At that time the think tank Carnegie Middle East Center expressed concern over the 'unprecedented speed with which large numbers of fighters had mobilized'[5] compared with previous calls to arms. There was a further surge when the caliphate was declared in July 2014 and another when the US began its aerial bombing campaign in August 2014. *The Times* in London reported in September 2014 that 6,000 new recruits had signed up in just two weeks, 1,300 of them foreign fighters.[6]

My correspondents in Iraq and Syria suggest that hundreds of new recruits turn up every day across the territories under Islamic State control. Fighters I have communicated with via Skype and instant messaging say that Islamic State's selection process is less rigorous than al-Nusra's; the latter requires three references from within its ranks to vouch for strangers, for security reasons. However, many report sensing 'suspicion' from their new comrades until they have proved themselves. Contacts say spies are often sent by security agencies, though they frequently give themselves away by not speaking the jihadist 'lingo', wearing obviously new clothes or acting too zealously. The most difficult to identify are 'double-agents' – real jihadists who have agreed to inform on their colleagues. Anyone suspected of being a spy in the Islamic State ranks is instantly executed, which certainly acts as a deterrent.

Although most media sources suggest Islamic State's fighting force numbers 100,000, jihadists and journalists in the region suggested to me when I visited in late 2014 that it is significantly larger. Of these, more than one third are foreign, originating from a total of eighty countries. A modest estimate, then, puts the number of foreign fighters at around 30,000. International security agencies say that just 20 per cent of al-Nusra fighters are foreign.[7] This is corroborated by reports that suggest al-Nusra is not well equipped to handle non-Arabic-speaking recruits, whereas Islamic State is home to speakers of all European languages.

The Washington Institute has produced a breakdown of the foreign cohort. Although I disagree with the figures, the percentages largely tally with anecdotal evidence. Among the Arabs, the most numerous are Libyan (21 per cent),[8] Tunisian (15.7 per cent), Saudi (15.7 per cent), Jordanian (11.4 per cent), Egyptian (9.6 per cent) and Lebanese (7.86 per cent). On the number of Turkish recruits, I disagree with official estimates of just 3 per cent: most sources I spoke to during a May 2014 field trip – including Turkish parliamentarians – said there were at least 2,000 Turks in ISIS. The proximity of Syria to Europe has seen unprecedented numbers of Europeans leaving their homes and families and heading for the uncertainties of 'jihad', sometimes under the banner of aid or humanitarian NGOs. Because they tend to be 'normal' young citizens, most are not on national security services' radar. Of these, the French are the most numerous (6 per cent) and there are as many as six 'French Brigades' within IS's 'army', composed of French and Belgian nationals of North African descent. *Paris Match* reported that these brigades are mostly in the Aleppo governorate.[9] The UK is the next most numerous (4.5 per cent). Australian authorities were shocked to discover that at least 200 of their nationals had left to join IS, making the country the biggest per capita exporter of foreign jihadists. Seventeen-year-old Australian 'Abdullah Emir' became a poster-boy for Islamic State when he ran away from home to join it in October 2014. The US has been consistently evasive when questioned by reporters about the numbers of American citizens who have joined. Former Defence Secretary Chuck Hagel admitted to only 'around a hundred... we don't know' in October 2014.[10] Canada is believed to have a similar number of nationals to the US in Islamic State.[11]

A network established over time

Much of the current success of Islamic State comes from seeds planted long ago. The transnational support it receives is no exception. Over the decades, foreign jihadist fighters who have migrated to various conflicts have created intricate, mutually supportive networks, contributing to the strength of the overall movement (despite its inherent factionalism and internal disputes) and the expanding pool of recruiters and recruits. Of great significance in this transnational network are the well-established foreign jihadist groups.

The Chechen Islamists are a good example. Although geographically situated at a considerable distance from the Middle East (the whole of Georgia separates the former Soviet republic from Northern Turkey), they share the ideology of global jihad espoused by al-Qa'ida and Islamic State. In 1994 Chechen separatists launched the first of two wars against Moscow; the uprising soon took on an Islamist aspect, most Chechens being

Sunni Muslims while the Marxist-Atheist Soviet Union wished to eliminate all religion. Jihadists from other countries migrated to Chechnya with the majority hailing from Saudi Arabia (59 per cent according to figures collated by researcher Murad Batal al-Shishani).[12] Among the most effective fighting groups was the 'Islamic Battalion' consisting of Arab and other foreign fighters. When the Bosnian war (which had also attracted large numbers of foreign jihadists) ended in 1995, many fighters went to Chechnya rather than returning home or seeking political asylum in Europe.[13] Many Arab fighters established families with local women in Bosnia and Chechnya. Incorporating a shared ideological purpose, these international marriages transcended tribal networks and created deep-rooted connections between various jihadist communities throughout the Middle East, Eurasia and beyond.

The Chechen link with the al-Qa'ida-Taliban nexus was present from the outset. The organisation's 'Benevolence International Fund' (a front) was used to channel money to Chechen fighters. Al-Qa'ida member Saif al-Islam al-Masry worked in its Grozny office until 1998. Chechens reciprocated by joining the mujahideen in other battles. At least three Guantanamo detainees captured in Afghanistan in 2001 were from the North Caucasus. *The Times*, reporting from Iraq in 2003, said that 'The Americans... have captured Chechens fighting with Fedayin units close to Baghdad.'[14] Chechens from the 'Chechen Emirate' (which was established in 2007) have been identified in thwarted attacks by al-Qa'ida-affiliated sleeper cells in Europe. In April 2011, for example, a cell was disrupted in the Czech Republic that included one Chechen, two Dagestanis, Moldovans and Bulgarians. Some of the men told investigators that they had attended training camps in Pakistan.

In an August 2011 interview the group's *emir*, Umarov (who would be poisoned in late 2013 and succeeded by Ali Abu Mukhammad), noted with some prescience that, 'A true jihad is developing in Iraq, the emirate was proclaimed there.'[15] When ISIS emerged, Umarov sent funding and fighters to help, siding with it against rival al-Nusra. Now, many of the leaders of foreign battalions within Islamic State are Chechen. They include twenty-eight-year-old Tarkhan Batirashvili aka Omar al-Shishani (al-Shishani meaning the Chechen), a veteran of the 2008 South Ossetia War, fighting with the Georgian Army against Russia. Omar is one of the best-known and respected rebel leaders in Syria, and there are hundreds of Chechen fighters in his Jaish al-Muhajireen wal Ansar (Army of Emigrants and Supporters), which he brought under ISIS command in October 2013. Islamic State is keen to emphasise the participation of these Chechen warriors, and its Facebook pages and Twitter feeds are full of news about these Caucasian fellow travellers. Baghdadi clearly respects their ferocity and cunning, having deployed Omar to lead several key battles such as that against the Kurdish YPG (People's Protection Units) in northern Syria in October 2013. Islamic State will also see the Caucasian jihadists as an important gateway into Eastern Europe and Europe itself.

Jihadists from Indonesia, too, have used the opportunity of the Syrian jihad to revitalise their long-standing connections with global jihadist groups. In February 2014 a veteran Indonesian jihadist, seventy-six-year-old Abu Bakar Bashir – who is in prison for funding an 'al-Qa'ida in the Veranda of Mecca' training camp in Aceh – released a statement urging Indonesian extremists to take the opportunity to go to 'the university of jihad education' in Syria.[16] Indonesian intelligence reported in January 2014 that at least 50 militants had travelled to Syria. That number is likely to have greatly increased since the establishment of the caliphate.

The number of Islamist guerrillas in Algeria during the civil war that erupted in 1995 reached 28,000 at its peak, with a small but significant group of foreign 'volunteers' sent by al-Qa'ida.[17] Shared battles here resulted, ultimately, in the formation of one of al-Qa'ida's strongest 'branches', with deep transnational roots. Al-Qa'ida in the Islamic Maghreb emerged when the GSPC joined Osama bin Laden's network in 2007. Algerians and Tunisians feature strongly in the Islamic State roll call. I have observed Tunisians in the ranks in previous jihads, but only in very small numbers – for example the Sinjar Records (captured from al-Qa'ida in 2007) number them at just 1 per cent of the foreign fighters in the Iraqi insurgency. This is certainly fall-out from the Arab Spring: former Tunisian dictator Ben Ali supressed all jihadist activity and imprisoned even moderate Islamists. The 2011 revolution and the subsequent electoral victory of Islamist parties inspired a revival of hard-line Islamism in that country. Now, groups like Ansar al-Sharia (Partisans of Law, based in Libya) are able to recruit openly and have funded and facilitated the passage of Tunisian jihadists to the frontline.

Also in the Maghreb, Libyans have long been sympathetic to the most radical ideology, supplying what a leaked diplomatic cable from 2008 described as 'a wellspring of foreign fighters for al-Qa'ida in Iraq'[18] as well as several of the organisation's key leaders. I was not surprised to see hundreds of Islamic State of Iraq (ISI) flags being waved in Benghazi during celebrations to mark former leader Muammar al-Gaddafi's brutal murder. The east of the country is now an extremist stronghold with local groups (including Ansar al-Sharia, who murdered US diplomat Christopher Stevens in 2012) swearing allegiance to Baghdadi in October 2014 and declaring their territory part of the Islamic State. An attack on a hotel in Tripoli in January 2015, in which ten people – mostly foreigners – were killed was claimed by Islamic State.[19] The jihadists and other Libyan militias are phenomenally well armed, having commandeered whatever they could from Gaddafi's vast and sophisticated arsenals – fighters in Syria and Iraq have told me that Libyan-marked weapons are common among jihadists there. Libyans also form one of the largest cohorts of foreign fighters in Islamic State. The deputy of Libyan politician and military leader Abdel Hakim Belhaj, Mahdi al-Harati (who is half Irish), led a vanguard of Libyan fighters called the Tripoli Brigades into Syria in June 2012. [20]

Radical Islamist groups are also prevalent across the Sahel, from Mali to Mauritania, with Nigeria's Boko Haram the biggest, most militant and most resembling Islamic State in its ruthlessness and extremism. The most dangerous prospect would see these groups in Africa and the Maghreb webbing up and joining Islamic State.

In August 2014, Boko Haram leader Abubakar Shekau announced that his group was now part of the Islamic caliphate.

The FATA (Federally Administered Tribal Areas) on both the Afghan and Pakistani side of the Hindu Kush remain a magnet for foreign jihadists, who train and fight with al-Qa'ida, the Afghan Taliban, and factions within the Pakistani Taliban. By 2008 reports suggested there were already 4,000 British-born fighters[21] in the region, and hundreds of Turks – an unprecedented occurrence.[22] In September 2009 the *Daily Telegraph* reported that there was a whole 'German village' among the Pakistani Taliban (TTP) fighters in Waziristan.[23] These fighters represent a further reserve for the Islamic State army, should these groups web up in the future. As we have seen, elements among the TTP have already pledged allegiance to 'Caliph Ibrahim', resulting in a rift within its ranks.

There is a distinct correlation between groups with significant numbers of foreign fighters and their propensity to strike abroad. Al-Shabaab, for example, carried out the terrifying Kenyan Westgate shopping mall massacre in September 2013, and two of its associates had already hacked British Army Private Lee Rigby to death with a machete on the streets of London in May the same year. The TTP was implicated in the Mumbai massacre, claimed responsibility for the failed Times Square bomb attack in 2009 and said it had trained Mohammed Merah, the French 'lone wolf' who shot seven people dead over a period of days in Toulouse, France, in 2012. AQAP masterminded several devious attempts to bring down planes, including the Christmas Day 2009 antics of so-called 'underwear bomber' Umar Farouk Abdulmutallab.

The new recruits

The usual route for individuals migrating from their homelands to Islamic State is via the insecure Turkish border. The would-be citizens of IS hail from a wide variety of backgrounds with no obvious single profile across the board. Recent research into the subject carried out by London University offers the finding that British jihadists tend to be better educated – to at least 'A' level standard – and most do not have former convictions or a criminal past. A separate survey of 600 British Muslims found that only 2.4 per cent sympathised with the jihadist cause but, interestingly, those who did fell mostly into three cohorts: the young; students; and those earning more than £75,000 a year. By contrast, German jihadists typically have a criminal background in violence or drugs; are poorly educated, with only 2 per cent possessing degrees; and are usually unemployed, with only 12 per cent having jobs when they leave Germany for Syria.

Evidence from a variety of sources suggests that most new recruits from abroad are aged between fifteen and twenty and have had no previous battle experience. They are therefore significantly younger than the cadres who made up the Afghan mujahideen, who were mostly aged twenty-five to thirty-five. In issue three of its online magazine *Dabiq*, Islamic State identified its target group for recruitment, describing a typical individual who 'lives in the West among the *kufr* for years, spends hours on the internet, reads news and posts on forums'.

Research suggests that females are just as likely to become radicalised as males.[24] Dr Katherine Brown, lecturer in Defence Studies at King's College, University of London, found that between 1981 and 2007 women constituted 26 per cent of all suicide attacks and there had been a marked increase since 2005.[25] Abu Musab al-Zarqawi was the first al-Qa'ida leader to actively encourage and train female *shaheedas* (martyrs) and, as we have seen, he is considered a leading light among the ranks of the Islamic State.

Online recruitment for Islamic State was stepped up when the caliphate was declared in July 2014; when US planes dropped their first bombs in Iraq in August there was a recruitment spike of 6,300, of whom 1,000 were foreign.[26] Foreign fighters recruit others by sharing their lives and battles in 'real time' via Twitter, Facebook and Instagram, generating a sense of familiarity and involvement with their followers as well as the 'normalisation' of jihad.

Although it recruits primarily in cyber-space, Islamic State has not limited its proselytising to online opportunities. Unlike other, comparable, groups like al-Qa'ida, IS activists have taken to the streets with brazen confidence. Shoppers in Oxford Street, London, in August 2014 were amazed to see black-clad, bearded and long-haired youths handing out 'passports' for the Islamic State and announcing the 'glad tidings' that the caliphate had been established. The passport leaflet – which someone posted to our news room at Rai al-Youm on 12 August 2014 – contained seven 'commands' for all Muslims in the UK to heed:

1. Pledge our *bayat* [allegiance] to the Caliph [Abu Bakr al-Baghdadi]
2. Obey the Caliph according to the Sharia
3. Advise the Caliph if he does anything wrong
4. Dua [prayer] – Make *dua* to Allah to help and guide the Caliph
5. Migrate – those that [sic] can migrate and resettle should migrate
6. Educate Muslims and non-Muslims about the Caliphate
7. Expose any lies and fabrications made against the Islamic State.

Correspondents for Rai al-Youm have reported seeing groups of Islamic State activists on the streets of Peshawar in Pakistan, handing out leaflets. And IS's distinctive black-and-white flag (originally that of the Islamic State of Iraq) has become a common sight across much of the Muslim world at rallies and demonstrations. On a July 2014 march in London against Israel's most recent strikes on Gaza, I personally saw a group of youths marching under the Islamic State banner. Fellow journalists in Paris reported that several IS flags were flown during similar protests in the French capital. The Islamic State flag and insignia have become a political and socio-cultural rallying point as much as (or more than) a religious statement.

The sense of belonging to a resilient *ummah* presents a sense of certainty in an increasingly chaotic and insecure Muslim world. Muslim youths have witnessed the failures of the Arab Spring: the democratic project has been discredited by the military coup which unseated the elected President of Egypt, Islamist Mohamed Morsi, and secular revolution has produced only continued injustice and corruption to date. Conspiracy theories and anti-Western sentiment flourish in a climate of disappointment and bitterness.

While most governments have tried to silence jihadist imams, well-known figures have nevertheless been able to urge Muslims to join the 'jihad' in Syria. The well-known and fiery Egyptian television cleric Yusuf al-Qaradawi has repeatedly exhorted the mujahideen to migrate to Syria since the revolution began, as has Saudi imam Muhammad al-Arifi. UK-based imam Anjem Choudray said in a televised debate that for British Muslims to travel to Syria or Iraq was like British members of the Jewish community travelling to fight in Israel.[27] Lebanese imam Sheikh Mazen al-Mohammad, Mauritanian Abu Mundhir al-Shinqiti, and even Mohamed Morsi, have all championed the 'Syrian jihad'. For some young Muslims, this exhortation by respected religious and authority figures acts as a powerful endorsement of their inclination to 'migrate'.

In the case of around 30,000 Western jihadists, we need to factor in the growth of the Far Right in Europe. In the UK, France and Greece, right-wing or neo-fascist parties took large numbers of seats in the 2014 European Parliament elections. Some of these parties foment racism towards Europe's 10 million Muslims and there has been a rise in Islamaphobic attacks on mosques, community centres, Islamic institutions and individuals. In the two weeks following the Paris attacks of January 2015 there were 128 anti-Muslim attacks in France – more than in the whole of 2014. Shots were fired at mosques and Islamic centres across the country, a grenade was thrown at a mosque in Le Mans and a pig's head was impaled on railings outside a prayer room in Corsica.[28] Extremism among Western Muslims has increased exponentially.

Other motives for travelling to the Islamic State emerged in the course of my online conversations with foreign fighters in Iraq and Syria. Reasons varied from mundane explanations, speaking of 'ordinary life' being 'boring', or of wanting to fight 'like in video games' – Islamic State's propaganda department regularly posts footage from 'Go-Pro' cameras, mounted on fighters' helmets or chests, which creates the sense of gaming rather than reality. Ironically, the so-called 'Pompey Lads' – a group of five Britons from Portsmouth who travelled for jihad in Syria – were part of a Muslim proselytising group who wore T-shirts reading 'Is Life Just a Game?'

Islamic State is not averse to using 'celebrities' to endorse its product. Perhaps the most bizarre western recruit to star in IS propaganda is a well-known German rapper who went by the name Deso Dogg until he arrived in Syria and took the *kunya* (fighting name) Abu Talha al-Almani. He was in several recruitment videos and had thousands of Twitter followers before his account – on which he posted live news feeds from the frontline – was taken down so repeatedly that he appears to have given up.

Appealing to youth

Rejection of the West, democracy, liberalism and secularism is hardwired into the extremist vocabulary and has produced a small but significant urban youth culture. Extremist youths I have spoken to in London refer to the dominance of gang loyalty and the prevalence of Islamophobia – the two combined have produced a mentality where jihadist credentials are akin to gang membership, providing a sense of brotherhood, shared aims, 'respect', kudos, and a group of friends who are 'handy in a fight'. In a significant proportion of cases, this translates into more drastic action as the young person prepares to travel to the Islamic State, either alone or in a group. Potential recruits are also targeted by Islamic State sympathisers attending mosques or Islamic centres in Western cities. Three youths from Cardiff – Nasser and Aseel Muthana and Reyad Khan – are believed to have been 'talent-spotted' and encouraged to travel to Syria where they were filmed for a propaganda video urging others to follow their example.[29]

In June 2014 IS's al-Hayat media centre released a recruitment video aimed at Western youths, titled 'There is No Life Without Jihad'. Several fighters from the West are interviewed, including two Britons, one of Yemeni descent (Abu Muthanna al-Yemeni), the other an Indian Muslim (Abu Barra al-Hindi). Al-Yemeni reports that, 'We have participated in battles in al-Sham and we'll go to Iraq in a few days and we'll fight there...We'll even go to Jordan and Lebanon, with no problems – wherever our sheikh wants to send us.' Al-Hindi advises listeners that there's no 'cure for depression' like 'the honour of coming to jihad'.

'There is No Life Without Jihad' also featured a Canadian convert, Andre Poulin, who was later killed in battle. In his last will and testament video he asked potential Western recruits, 'How can you answer to Allah the Almighty when paying taxes to them [Western governments], and they use these taxes for war on Islam?' Poulin recommends life in the Islamic State where 'There's a role for everybody. Every person can contribute something to the Islamic State. It's obligatory on us. If you cannot fight, then you give money, if you cannot give money then you can assist in technology, and if you can't assist in technology you can use some other skills... We can use you. You'll be very well taken care of here. Your families will live here in safety just like how it is back home. You know, we have wide expansive territory here in Syria and we can easily find accommodations for you and your families.'

The 'heroic fight'

The sense of a heroic fight to protect the weak (in this narrative the people of Syria) was often mentioned to me by migrant jihadists, as were the global jihadist constructs originated by al-Qa'ida of the 'near enemy' (apostate regimes) and the 'far enemy' (the West). Others felt they were part of a genuine, religious war, restoring the caliphate to its ancient capitals of Damascus and Baghdad and defending Islam against global attack. This produced a paradoxical conflation of the Abbasid Empire with the digitalised, globalised experience of modern life.

However, it seems that not all recruits are well versed in the religion. Two Britons, Yusuf Sarwar and Mohammed Ahmed, ordered *Islam for Dummies* from Amazon as part of their preparations before travelling to Syria.[30] A further paradox appears in the often-repeated belief that the jihadists are fighting in order to bring peace under Sharia law; this aspect is greatly romanticised by online imagery of long-haired, muscular fighters on horses or tanks, waving Kalashnikovs and praying five times a day. With their songs, dramatic appearance, their willingness to die for their cause, their bravery in battle and, crucially in the context of Islamic State, their actual *successes*, it is not difficult to understand their appeal to the inexperienced mind.

Some new arrivals reported finding comfort in the strict-order Sharia and organisational infrastructure of the Islamic State: one Yemeni contact marvelled at the fact that it 'runs its own police, courts, banks, road repairs and rubbish collection'. Like any good nationalist, an Egyptian jihadist reported 'a great sense of pride and emotion when I see the Islamic State flag'.

Emphasising the sense of a 'just cause' one Syrian national, who had defected to ISIS from the Free Syrian Army (largely comprising defectors from the state forces), said, 'Islamic State is the only one strong enough to bring down the butcher, Assad.' In addition, there is the sectarian framework that al-Qa'ida has been constructing for nearly a decade. This is particularly potent in Iraq, where the Shi'i are widely blamed for the misfortunes of the Sunnis in that country. The US realised, probably too late, that the exclusivist government and policies of former Iraqi president Nouri al-Maliki, a Shi'i, were stirring up the hornet's nest of Sunni militancy. They then backed his removal from power, insisting on a 'unity government' that would represent all the peoples of Iraq, in a bid to put out the flames of sectarian civil war. They had already been ignited, however, and Iraqi politics have yet to discard self-interest in favour of the greater good.

With so many disappointments and failures to complain about in the Arab world, the jihadists are seen as 'doing something', rather than just talking about the things that are perceived as 'wrong' such as corruption, decadence, immorality, materialism and, of course, the absence of the 'true' religion, that is, the Salafist interpretation of Islam.

Welcome to Islamic State

The general chaos in Syria and Iraq, and the resulting security vacuum, has meant that travelling into these war zones is relatively easy. A plane ticket or a coach trip to Turkey is the first step. The Turkish authorities admitted to *The Times* that 'controlling our border with Syria to stop the flow of foreign fighters... is impossible.'[31] There are hundreds of 'safe houses' on the border with Syria for fighters either crossing to Syria or intending to fly back to wherever they came from, having served their term fighting with the Islamic State. One of my researchers, posing as a willing recruit wishing to travel from Britain, was invited to a house in Reyhanli (in Turkey, on the border with Syria) by a person contacted first on Twitter and then via the social networking site Ask.fm. The supposed recruit complained of lack of funds for the trip and was told that help could be arranged. The group had 'people' in the UK who would get in touch and arrange to meet and hand over the necessary money. The new recruit would then be given instructions on where to go next by the person running the house (usually a jihadist). At this point I decided it was too dangerous for the researcher to continue the dialogue. Other foreigners told me they had entered Syria via Jordan and Lebanon.

Locals are not always as welcoming as recruits are led to believe. I have heard grumbles concerning Westerners being 'useless' fighters, requiring much more training than their Arab counterparts. Training courses start at two weeks, with additional courses for specialisms such as the recently introduced snipers' course, which lasts two months. There have been complaints, too, about some Westerners' failure to assimilate, with some being considered 'spoilt' with their expensive laptops and mobile phones. One Western jihadist tweeted about his sorrow on learning of Hollywood actor Robin Williams's death; others ask those about to migrate to bring Nutella (a big favourite) and Marmite.

Veteran fighters we contacted described the Western newcomers in unflattering terms, with one declaring they are 'useless at fighting' and thus more likely to be asked to carry out a 'martyrdom operation'. Twenty-two-year-old Moner Mohammad Abu Salah from Florida became the first American-born suicide bomber on 25 May 2014. His martyrdom video, widely available on the internet, showed him burning his passport and issuing threats to the American people and President Obama, saying, 'We are coming for you.' In the video he credited AQAP's Anwar al-Awlaki with radicalising him and describes the 'leap of faith' that saw him taking a plane to Turkey with no idea where he was going or what he would do. 'I was scared. I don't have money, I don't have a hotel... I don't know what to do. *Subhanallah* [glory to God], I see two men, three men speaking Arabic, and I said, "*Subhanallah*, I know what these people are here for." People speaking Arabic, they're either Syrian or you know, from tons of research, *muhajirun* [emigrants] from Tunis or I don't know where... So I didn't say nothing to them I just simply sat down and waited until they got off the train. When they got off I was going to speak to them. It was very dangerous what I was doing – I could've went to jail, you know, could've been a spy... So when I got off the train, I follow them I went to ask them, "I want to make *hijra*, I want to go to jihad."' Abu Salah finally met a Turkish man who told him he was from al-Qa'ida and would help him cross into Syria and find a training camp.

A forty-one-year-old father of three from Crawley became
the first UK suicide bomber when he blew himself up as part of
a February 2014 operation that liberated hundreds of Islamist
prisoners from Aleppo's jail. Abdul Waheed Majid had been radical
cleric Omar Bakri Muhammad's personal assistant; interviewed
by the London paper *Evening Standard*, Bakri praised his former
colleague's 'noble deed'.[32]

Most fighters I have spoken to really believe that they are part
of a state-building exercise. Islamic State is well funded and able
to pay its fighters and support workers a generous wage. New
arrivals are given a house and the state has ensured its own food
and water security by seizing grain silos and dams. All of these
factors make family life possible and Baghdadi has emphasised
the necessity for a new generation to consolidate the State. There
have been several reports of husbands and wives travelling together
to Syria, including American citizens Yusuf and Amira Ali. Many
fighters from abroad are reported to be bringing their children with
them, but not their wives, who do not share their enthusiasm for
the caliphate. A French national took his three-year-old daughter
to the Islamic State in August 2014 and another was detained in
October 2014 transiting from Morocco with two- and four-year-
old daughters to join Islamic State.[33] Girls and young women are
being recruited to act as 'babysitters' for all the children arriving
without their mothers. In addition, there is the phenomenon of the
so-called 'jihadi brides'.

Jihadi brides

At least 10 per cent of recruits from abroad are young women who
wish to marry jihadist fighters.[34] They want to live in, and produce
the next generation for, the Islamic State. Many of them have been
brought up in the West. Some female recruits are trained for battle
(my sources say this is usually by their husbands), with increasing
numbers being deployed as 'human bombs'.

In the summer of 2014, Abu Bakr al-Baghdadi launched an online recruitment drive to encourage more women to 'join the caliphate'. In order to soften the image of life in Islamic State, its social media platforms showcased photographs of jihadists relaxing at home alongside the usual collection of stonings, beheadings and amputations. In the summer 2014 edition of *Dabiq* there was a 'myth-busting' article clearly designed to appeal to girls and young women; it included a photograph of three laughing, muscular and handsome young men playing with kittens (dogs are *haram*) and helping themselves from an overflowing bowl of chocolate bars. Elsewhere, photographs showed girls and young women in classrooms, and the text emphasised that Islamic State encourages education for girls.

Anecdotal evidence suggests that, compared with their counterparts in Muslim countries, young Muslim women from the West are most likely to respond to the call, and that the most effective recruiters are other Western-raised women who have already migrated to Islamic State. Using social media, women such as Aqsa Mahmood – a twenty-year-old medical student who ran away from Glasgow to marry a Swedish IS fighter she had met online – post pictures and tweets about how happy they are to be part of the state-building project. Mahmood, using the Twitter handle Umm Ubaydah, messages a friend to hurry to Syria for the 'cookies with M&Ms on' that she's saved for her, and posts pictures of her kittens. The official Islamic State Twitter feed posted pictures of a local shop with a huge selection of handbags and a woman in full niqab (cloth hiding the face) browsing the gaudy ranks. In October 2014, Umm Ubaydah told girls on their way to Syria to pack warm clothes as winter set in, as only summer clothes were available in the local shops. Other British girls have posted more gruesome invitations to join Islamic State including one who posted a picture of herself on Instagram holding a severed head.

Umm Ubaydah offered practical help to 'sisters needing help or advice' regarding travel arrangements and put forward a contact person: 'a dear and trustworthy friend of mine... Umm Khattab'.

She sympathises in tweets with 'those afraid of being caught, know Allah is with the sincere and he will grant you a way here, *inshallah* [God willing]'. She confides that she was 'caught and detained in Turkey but *wallah* [I swear to God] I still had *tawakkal* [trust in Allah] and He guided me and granted me a way out again.' The general impression is that, while European women tend to travel together in small groups, young British women tend to travel alone.

For many migration is less about the religious imperative than escaping the prejudice and Islamaphobia associated with cultural assertiveness – in the West, women wearing the niqab are more likely to be racially attacked than Muslim men. Tweeting from Canada, and preparing for *hijra* herself, Umm Khattab Kanadiya moans, 'Can someone inject Arabic into my brain?' She also muses, 'They call this a free country when they want us to dress, walk, talk, do everything a way that pleases them.' This particular female jihadist has many pictures of guns and knives and daggers on her feed and tweets that she wants 'an AK-47, a Steyr AUG and jadgdokommando [sic] tri dagger blade knife' on arrival in the Islamic State.

In mid 2014, a Twitter feed was established called Jihad Matchmaker on which those 'seeking marriage in Jihad (Syria) should direct message info on your background, status and location'. Applicants are then put in touch with potential partners via anonymous platforms such as Ask.fm or Kik to make arrangements. Others arrive single in *Dawla* (Islamic State), where they are housed with other young unmarried people of the same sex; if they wish to marry, they are matched by older women. If the match is successful, bewildered parents back home receive a call from an unknown male asking for their daughter's hand in marriage.

Via Ask.fm, our researchers talked to several Muslim girls who have migrated from the West about their motives for doing so. Several said they viewed their new life as 'freedom' and referred to a desire to escape restrictive home lives with overprotective, conservative parents; others were fleeing an arranged marriage to a stranger. There is clearly a romantic and sexual appeal and, in online chat, girls who are considering running away describe jihadists as 'knights'. Some girls are very forward in their approaches to potential mates met on Facebook, to the extent that some young jihadists have chided their 'sisters' with conducting themselves in a manner that is *haram*. They are seeking marriage and commitment but with a big dose of adventure thrown in; in addition there is an undeniable bravery (and in some cases, naivety) in taking such a huge, life-changing step, producing a feeling of liberation which may, perhaps, be challenged on arrival. One questioner on Ask. fm enquired whether women were 'allowed to leave the house' in the Islamic State and received the answer, 'That depends on your husband.'

If their jihadist husband is killed, young women can anticipate the adulation accorded a 'martyr's widow'. This status has seen Samantha Lewthwaite, for example, the so-called 'white widow', become an iconic figure in the extremist world. This extraordinary cultural pressure sees young women celebrating their husband's martyrdom on Twitter while others lament their partner's safe return from battle, since his martyrdom will now have to wait. For girls saddled with young men who express reluctance to join the fight, Umm Ubaydah suggests they 'make jihad as a condition of the marriage... many sister[s] who eventually came [to Syria] with their husbands did this.' For jihadists couples who are experiencing marital problems, an agony aunt is at hand – Umm Saifullah has 50,000 followers.

Research suggests that the average age for Western girls travelling to Syria is nineteen to twenty,[35] although some are as young as fourteen.[36] Women constitute 10 per cent of those travelling from the West to join the caliphate; a conservative guess would put their number, then, at around 2,500.

The largest cohort is from France – around 25 per cent. Bernard Cazeneuve, the French Interior Minister, told reporters in September 2014 that French police had broken up a ring in central France that was recruiting young French women for Islamic State and facilitating their travel with all expenses paid. The next largest group comes from the UK, where at least fifty female 'migrants' have been identified.[37] It seems that Germans also find the idea of the caliphate alluring, with forty 'jihadi brides' running away from home and ending up in Syria. *Rheinische Post* reported that a group of four underage girls had met some jihadists online and had managed to fund and arrange their flight to Syria. The youngest was just thirteen.

Austria has experienced a similar phenomenon. While only fourteen girls are known to have left the country for Syria, Austrian authorities fear there may be many more whose families have not reported them missing – possibly for cultural reasons, in that the girls have brought 'shame' on the family. The same may well apply to other countries' statistics. The US has refused to divulge how many of its nationals have left for Islamic State. Austrian 'migrants' included fifteen- and sixteen-year-old friends Samra Kesinovic and Sabina Selimovic, whose families originally came from Bosnia. The former had been openly advocating for 'jihad' at school and had written 'I love al-Qa'ida' on the school's walls. When the pretty blonde pair arrived in Syria, they became poster girls for Islamic State online propaganda and recruitment campaigns. They left a note for their parents saying, 'Don't come looking for us. We will serve Allah and we will die for Him.'

Judging by the posts one can easily find on the internet on platforms such as Twitter, JustPaste.it, Ask.fm and Instagram, life as a jihadi bride is much like that of any housewife, revolving round housework, cooking and childcare. Many extol the 'pleasures' of jihad but in reality few women jihadists get to fight and their only prospect of training is if their husband undertakes to teach them how to use a gun. Nevertheless, in their gravatars ('globally recognised avatar'; this is an image that follows the user from site to site appearing beside their name when they comment or post on a blog) many seemingly enjoy posing with machine guns and hand-guns, black-gloved index fingers of the right hand pointing heavenwards in the Islamic State salute. One female Malaysian medic tweeted, 'Stethoscope round my neck and kalash on my shoulder. Martyrdom is my highest dream.'

The dream life girls imagine they will find in the caliphate is not always borne out by reality. The system of temporary marriages – *al-Nikha* – is allowed in the jihadist community and reduces a woman agreeing to it to the status of 'concubine'; some fighters avail themselves of the opportunity to have several such arrangements. A woman who marries a particularly extreme extremist may find herself locked in the house. However, at the other end of the scale, the more liberal husbands allow their wives to drive.

The two Austrian girls we discussed above, Kesinovic and Selimovic, contacted their parents in October 2014 saying they wanted to come home. They had married Chechen fighters and the parents inferred they might be pregnant. Even if they were able to leave Islamic State – which is highly unlikely for obvious security reasons – Austrian law forbids the re-entry of those who have migrated for jihad.

Western governments' response

European governments were taken by surprise by the rapid rise of Islamic State and the rush of their nationals to join it. By and large, they have been slow to act.

Britain led the way with a particularly hardline decision to seize passports at the border from anyone police suspected of travelling to join extremist groups. In October 2014, the Conservative government under David Cameron proposed charging jihadists with High Treason under a law dating back to 1351 – a crime that carried the death penalty until 1998.[38] Home Secretary Theresa May also expressed a hope to pass new legislation that would prevent people 'suspected of radicalism' from using the internet. She said at the 2014 Tory party conference that a future Tory government would ban all extremist groups. There are several government and non-governmental organisations that aim to counter radicalisation; hotlines aimed at parents and siblings encourage calls from anyone worried about 'signs of radicalisation' in a loved one.

In October 2014 France, Britain and Turkey began to develop methods to collaborate on identifying returning fighters who might pose a risk at home, using the European Border Control's computer system. The problem is compounded, however, by the Schengen Agreement, which allows free passage through Europe for nationals of member countries. European nationals can travel through Europe to Turkey, and thence to Syria. Entry into Turkey is possible on an easily obtained tourist visa that can be bought at the point of entry.

Australian Premier Tony Abbott oversaw legislation enabling authorities to cancel the passports of Australian nationals who have joined the conflict. He has toughened up border security which has, in the past, allowed convicted criminals to escape the country using false passports. Abbott has also suggested allowing the country's intelligence agencies greater access to monitoring internet traffic but, as with all Western governments, he is mindful of the human rights aspect of doing so. When he tried to introduce a similar scheme called the 'mobile data surveillance plan' in 2012 there were violent demonstrations against it.

The US has yet to pass any legislation to prevent fighters returning from Syria or Iraq. President Obama made the rather gung-ho comment that he would rather destroy Islamic State.

Experts on radicalisation believe that, far from being excluded or prosecuted on their return, fighters should be encouraged to go home where they can be rehabilitated and share their experiences with others who may be dissuaded from going to jihad themselves.[39] Richard Barrett, the former director of M16's counter-terrorism department, also noted that they are a potential source of valuable information.[40] On the other hand, Denmark's more liberal approach favours community support and counselling for returning fighters. Rather than closing the radical Grimhojvej mosque that allegedly acts as a conduit for fighters travelling to Syria, the Danish government engages it in dialogue.[41] The policy did not prevent the deadly 15 February 2015 attacks in Copenhagen

Nevertheless, all national governments greatly fear 'blowback', whereby returning nationals or sleeper cells under instruction from Islamic State or its allies carry out terrorist acts at home. According to the International Centre for the Study of Radicalisation and Political Violence (ICSR – an international think tank based in London), 250 Britons have returned home already, as have seventy Belgians and 100 Germans.[42] ICSR statistical analysis also suggests that the presence of at least one battle-hardened 'veteran' in a terror cell increases by 40 per cent the chance of it launching a successful attack.

Issue four of *Dabiq* called on Western followers to attack in the West. Almost immediately, in May 2014, twenty-nine-year-old Mehdi Nemmouche opened fire on visitors to the Jewish museum in Brussels, Belgium, killing three; Nemmouche had recently returned from Syria where he had been fighting with ISIS. In September 2014, a man beheaded a female colleague in Oklahoma; again, he was known for his radical Islamist views and had been proselytising at work. As Canada sent its first fighter jets to bomb Islamic State positions in Syria, on 20 October 2014 recent Muslim convert Martin Rouleau-Couture drove his car into two Canadian soldiers in Quebec, killing one of them. Rouleau had praised Islamic State on his Facebook page and commended its violence. He was shot dead by police. Another attack followed on 22 October when a lone gunman, Michael Zehaf-Bibeau, went on the rampage in Ottowa, Canada, first killing a soldier guarding the war memorial, then storming the capital's parliament building where he was killed by police. In January 2015, after the murders in Paris, Amedy Coulibaly left a video that posthumously announced he had been under the supervision of the Islamic State.

These are, thankfully, relatively isolated incidents. But, as the allied bombing campaign gains momentum and the possibility of 'boots on the ground' becomes more likely, we should expect more of this kind of attack in the West.

TEN

A DANGEROUS GAME: THE WEST'S ATTEMPTS TO EXPLOIT RADICAL ISLAM

Since 1980 the US has intervened in the affairs of fourteen Muslim countries, at worst invading or bombing them. They are (in chronological order): Iran, Libya, Lebanon, Kuwait, Iraq, Somalia, Bosnia, Saudi Arabia, Afghanistan, Sudan, Kosovo, Yemen, Pakistan and now Syria. Latterly these efforts have been in the name of the 'War on Terror' and the attempt to curb Islamic extremism.

Yet for centuries Western countries have sought to harness the power of radical Islam to serve the interests of their own foreign policy. In the case of Britain, this dates back to the days of the Ottoman Empire; in more recent times the US/UK alliance first courted, then turned against, Islamists in Afghanistan, Iraq, Libya and Syria. In my view the policies of the US and Britain – which see them supporting and arming a variety of groups for short-term military, political or diplomatic advantage – have directly contributed to the rise of IS.

Supporting the caliphate

The Turkish Ottoman Empire was, for centuries, the largest Muslim political entity the world has ever known, encompassing much of North Africa, south-eastern Europe and the Middle East. From the sixteenth century onwards, Britain not only championed the Ottoman Empire, but also supported and endorsed the institution of the caliphate and the Sultan's claim to be the caliph and leader of the *ummah* (the Muslim world).

Britain's support for the Ottoman Caliph – a policy known as 'The Eastern Question'[1] – was entirely motivated by self-interest. Initially this was so the Ottoman lands would act as a buffer against its regional imperial rivals, France and Russia; subsequently, following the colonisation of India, the Ottoman territories acted to protect Britain's eastward trade routes. This support was not merely diplomatic; it translated into military action. In the Crimean War (1854–56), Britain fought with the Ottoman Empire against Russia and won.

It was only with the onset of the First World War, in 1914, that this 400-year-old regional paradigm unravelled. When Mehmed V sided with the Germans, Britain was reluctantly excluded from dealing with the caliphate's catchment of over 15 million Muslims, reasoning that 'whoever controlled the person of the Caliph, controlled Sunni Islam.'[2] London decided that an Arab uprising to unseat Mehmed would enable them to reassign the role of caliph to a trusted and more malleable ally: Hussein bin Ali Hussein, the Sherif of Mecca and a direct descendant, it is claimed, of the Prophet Muhammad. The British employed racism to garner support for the uprising, appealing to the Arabs' sense of ownership over Islam, which had originated in Mecca and Medina, not among the Turks of Constantinople. A 1914 British proclamation declared that, 'There is no nation among the Muslims which is now capable of upholding the Islamic Caliphate except the Arab nation.'[3] A letter was dispatched to Sherif Hussein, fomenting his ambition and suggesting that, 'It may be that an Arab of true race will assume the Caliphate at Mecca or Medina' (Medina being the seat of the First Caliphate after the death of the Prophet). Again, the British were prepared to defend the caliphate with the sword, promising to 'guarantee the Holy Places against all external aggression'. It is a strange thought that, just 100 years ago, the prosecutors of today's 'War on Terror' were promising to restore the Islamic caliphate to the Arab world, and defend it militarily.

The Arab Revolt against the Ottoman Empire, fomented by the British, got underway in 1916, the same year that the infamous Sykes-Picot agreement was made in secret, carving up between the British and French the very lands Sherif Hussein had been promised. Betrayal, manipulation and self-interest were, and remain, the name of the game when it comes to Western meddling in the Middle East. The revolt would last two years and was a major factor in the fall of the Ottoman Empire. At the same time, the British Army and allied forces, including the 'Arab Irregulars', were fighting the Ottomans on the battlefields of the First World War. A key figure in these battles was T. E. Lawrence, who became known as 'Lawrence of Arabia' because of the loyalty he engendered in the hearts of Sherif Hussein and his son, Emir Faisal. He was given the status of honorary son by the former, and fought under the command of the latter in many battles, later becoming Faisal's advisor. When the Ottomans put a £15,000 reward on Lawrence's head, no Arab was tempted to betray him.

Sadly this honourable behaviour and respect were not reciprocated. In a memo to British intelligence in 1916, Lawrence described the hidden agenda behind the Arab Uprising: 'The Arabs are even less stable than the Turks. If properly handled they would remain in a state of political mosaic, a tissue of small, jealous, principalities, incapable of cohesion... incapable of co-ordinated action against us.' In a subsequent missive he explained, 'When war broke out, an urgent need to divide Islam was added... Hussein was ultimately chosen because of the rift he would create in Islam. In other words, divide and rule.'[4]

Oil security and Western foreign policy

Let us fast-forward to the 1950s and '60s, by which time oil had become a major factor in the West's foreign policy agenda. Again, the principle of 'divide and rule' was put to work: a 1958 British cabinet memo noted, 'Our interest lies... in keeping the four principal oil-producing areas [Saudi Arabia, Kuwait, Iran and Iraq] under separate political control.' The results of this policy saw the West arming both sides in the Iran-Iraq war – which brought both powers to the brink of total destruction in the 1980s – and then intervening militarily with a force of almost 700,000 men[5] in the First Gulf War (to prevent Iraq annexing Kuwait) in 1990–91.

The US, UK and European powers were also deeply troubled by the cohesive potential of Arab Nationalism, a hugely popular movement led by Egypt's Gamal Abdel Nasser and his (at that time) mighty allies in Iraq and Syria. The idea of these three huge, left-leaning regional powers becoming politically and militarily united was unacceptable in the Cold War context and remained so after the fall of the Soviet Empire, because of the regional threat to Israel. To counteract the rise of pan-Arabism, the West began to support Islamist tendencies within each country – mostly branches of the Muslim Brotherhood – and also worked hard in the diplomatic field to create strong and binding relationships with Islamic, pro-Western monarchies in Saudi Arabia, the Gulf States and Jordan. These relationships endure to this day.

The most extreme manifestation of radical Sunni Islam was Saudi Arabia's Wahhabism, which it had started to disseminate via a string of international organisations and its self-designated 'Global Islamic Mission'. In 1962, Saudi Arabia oversaw the establishment of 'The Muslim World League', which was largely staffed by exiled members of the Egyptian Muslim Brotherhood. The West's (and the Gulf Monarchies') relationship with the Muslim Brotherhood has always been inconsistent and entirely selfish. In the run-up to, during, and after, the 2011 'Arab Spring' revolution against Hosni Mubarak, the US and UK were actively supporting the Muslim Brotherhood as the most credible (or only) experienced political entity. In 2014 both countries came under pressure from the Saudis to declare the Muslim Brotherhood a 'terror group': though neither has yet gone that far, the UK duly launched an official investigation into the group, headed by UK Ambassador to Saudi Arabia, Sir John Jenkins,[6] while in the US a bill was introduced in Congress, the 'Muslim Brotherhood Terrorist Designation Act' of 2014.[7]

The House of Saud itself feared an 'Arab Spring' revolution and encouraged and applauded the June 2013 coup that deposed the Brotherhood's legitimately elected President Morsi; Saudi King Abdullah phoned coup leader al-Sisi (now the Egyptian President) within hours to congratulate him on his success. Egypt under al-Sisi would prove a better friend to Israel and, like Saudi Arabia, would brutally extinguish any new uprisings, giving the kingdom moral support in its own battle for survival. Saudi political pragmatism (or, as some might frame it, hypocrisy) has been progressively informed by its close relationship with the US and UK – and is now one of the most significant drivers of the Middle East's present chaos, including the emergence of ISIS.

Communism: the first Public Enemy Number One

From the 1950s on, the Muslim Brotherhood was supported and funded by the CIA.[8] When Nasser decided to stamp out the movement in Egypt, the CIA helped its leaders migrate to Saudi Arabia, where they were assimilated into the Wahhabi kingdom's own particular brand of fundamentalism, many rising to positions of great influence. While Saudi Arabia actively prevented the formation of a home-grown branch of the Muslim Brotherhood, it encouraged and financed the movement abroad in other Arab countries. One of the most prominent leaders of the Western-backed Afghan Jihad (1979–89) was a Cairo-educated Muslim Brotherhood member: Burhanuddin Rabbani, head of Jamaat-i-Islami (JI).

America and, to a lesser extent, Britain fretted about the rise of communism, which was perceived and portrayed as the 'enemy of freedom' – a term that would later be applied to the Islamic extremists. In geopolitical terms, by the end of the Second World War the Soviet Union comprised one-sixth of the world's land mass and was a superpower capable of mounting a devastating challenge to the US. The White House was also concerned about the future alignment of China, where the Chinese Communist Party had seized power in 1949. Communism was enthusiastically embraced by millions of idealistic post-war Americans and Europeans, posing a perceived domestic political threat. Meanwhile the West observed with horror the increasing popularity of communism and socialism in the Middle East; revolutionary, pro-Soviet, Arab regimes would create an enormous strategic disadvantage and threaten oil security.

For the West, radical Islam represented the best way to counter the encroachment of Arab nationalism communism.

Following the Six-Day War in 1967, US and UK governmental planners noted with satisfaction that Arab unity and sense of a shared cause were finding expression in a revival of Islamic fundamentalism and widespread calls for the implementation of Sharia law. This revival continued through the 1970s and, by the end of the decade, produced the pan-Arab mujahideen that would battle the Soviet armies in Afghanistan for the next ten years.

As in Syria and Iraq, the Sunni jihadists were not alone in the insurgency. There were seven major Sunni groups,[9] armed and funded (to the tune of $6 billion) by the US and Saudi Arabia, as well as the UK, Pakistan and China. Abdullah Azzam's Maktab al-Khidamat (the Services Office), which included bin Laden and from which al-Qa'ida would emerge, was at this point only a sub-group of one of these, the Gulbuddin faction (founded in 1977 by Gulbuddin Hekmatyar). Often overlooked in retelling the story of this particular Afghan war is the fact that the insurgency was pan-Islamic: there were eight Shi'i groups,[10] trained and funded by Iran.

Of the Sunni entities it was backing, the CIA preferred the Afghan-Arabs (as the foreign fighters from Arab countries came to be known) because they found them 'easier to read' than their indigenous counterparts.[11] In 2003, Australian-British journalist John Pilger's research confirmed that, 'More than 100,000 Islamic militants were trained in Pakistan between 1986 and 1992, in camps overseen by the CIA and MI6, with the SAS training future al-Qaeda and Taliban fighters in bomb-making and other black arts. Their leaders were trained at a CIA camp in Virginia.'[12] That Western interference in Afghanistan actually precedes the Soviet invasion by several months is rarely acknowledged. In the context of this book it is worth tracing the motives and methods employed by foreign powers to further their own ends in that territory, as these have been repeated and modified in Iraq and Syria.

Afghanistan's location and long borders with Iran and Pakistan make it a strategic prize, and rival powers have often fought to control it. A coup in 1978 (the third in five years) brought the pro-Soviet Muhammad Taraki to power, setting off alarm bells in Islamabad, Washington, London and Riyadh. The Pakistani ISI first tried to foment an Islamist uprising, but this failed owing to lack of popular support. Next, five months before the Soviet invasion, US President Jimmy Carter sent covert aid to Islamist opposition groups with the help of Pakistan and Saudi Arabia. Carter's National Security Advisor, Zbigniew Brzezinski, wrote in a memo to his boss that if the Islamists rose up it would 'induce a Soviet military intervention, likely to fail, and give the USSR its own Vietnam'.[13] Another coup in September 1979 brought Deputy Prime Minister Hafizullah Amin to power; Moscow invaded in the December, killing Amin and replacing him with its own man, Babrak Karmal. Now Brzezinski sent Carter a memo outlining his advised strategy: 'We should concert with Islamic countries both a propaganda campaign and a covert action campaign to help the rebels.'

British Prime Minister Margaret Thatcher enthusiastically endorsed Washington's approach at an 18 December 1979 meeting of the Foreign Policy Association in New York, even praising the Iranian Revolution and concluding, 'The Middle East is an area where we have much at stake... it is in our own interest that they build on their own deep, religious traditions. We do not wish to see them succumb to the fraudulent appeal of imported Marxism.'
Just as IS is a product of Western interference in Iraq and

Syria, so none of the powers that backed the Afghan mujahideen anticipated the emergence of al-Qa'ida, with its vehemently anti-Western agenda, and ambition to re-establish the caliphate. Pakistan's President Pervez Musharraf wrote in his autobiography that, 'Neither Pakistan nor the US realized what Osama bin Laden would do with the organization we had all allowed him to establish.'[14]

Defining extremism: the Western dilemma

In the course of the 1990s, radical political Islam became more extremist – a shift that was encouraged and funded by Saudi Arabia. The star of the Muslim Brotherhood began to wane as its leaders were castigated for being too 'moderate' and for participating in the democratic process in Egypt; standing as 'independents' (since the Muslim Brotherhood was banned) its candidates fared well, becoming the main opposition force to President Hosni Mubarak. There was another reason for the Muslim Brotherhood falling out of favour with Riyadh – it had supported Saddam Hussein's 1990 invasion of Kuwait. The House of Saud now linked its survival with the rise of the Salafi-jihadist tendency, which chimed with its own bespoke Wahhabi ideology.

The West viewed this shift into a more radical gear with some alarm as the Salafists' battle became international: Arab jihadists travelled to Eastern Europe to fight with the Bosnian Muslims from 1992; New York's World Trade Centre was first bombed by radical Islamists in 1993; and in 1995 North African jihadists from the al-Qa'ida-linked GIA (Armed Islamic Group, Algeria) planted bombs on the Paris Metro, killing eight and injuring more than 100.

The US and UK adopted a remarkably laid-back approach to this new wave of radical Islam. The UK government and security services did not consider that the extremists presented a real danger, allowing the establishment of what the media labelled 'Londonistan' through the 1990s. It could be argued that this was a successful arrangement in that, in return for being allowed to live in the British capital and go about their business unmolested, the jihadists did not commit any act of violence on British streets. The Syrian jihadist Abu Musab al-Suri (aka Setmariam Nasar) was a leading light among the 'Londonistan' jihadist community, which also included Osama bin Laden's 'ambassador' to London, Khalid al-Fawwaz. Al-Suri confirmed to me that a tacit covenant was in place between M16 and the extremists.

Saudi entities and individuals funded al-Qa'ida and other violent Salafist groups to the tune of $300 million through the 1990s, and the US and UK remained stalwartly on-side. A year after Margaret Thatcher left parliament for good, she told a 1993 meeting of the Chatham House international affairs think tank that, 'The Kingdom of Saudi Arabia is a strong force for moderation and stability on the world stage.'[15] When challenged on Riyadh's appalling human rights record – which included (and still includes) public executions, floggings and stonings, oppression of women, as well as the incarceration of peaceful dissidents and violent dispersal of any kind of demonstration[16] – she retorted, 'I have no intention of meddling in its internal affairs.' Later, Tony Blair would talk of the Middle East's 'Axis of Moderation', meaning Saudi Arabia, the Gulf States, Turkey, the Palestinian Authority and Israel.

The First Gulf War brought two changes into play. The first was that Saudi Arabia now became completely dependent, militarily, on the US for its survival. The second was that, in an attempt to weaken Saddam Hussein, the CIA encouraged Shi'i groups in Southern Iraq to rebel, resulting in thousands of Shi'i being slaughtered by regime helicopter fire. George Bush senior spent $40 million on clandestine operations in Iraq, flying Shi'i and Kurdish leaders to Saudi Arabia for training, and creating and funding two opposition groups: the Iraqi National Accord was led by Iyad Alawi, who would collaborate in a failed coup plotted by the CIA's Iraq Operations Group in 1996;[17] the Iraqi National Congress, meanwhile, was led by Ahmad Chalabi, who was close to US Defence Secretary Dick Cheney. And yet, for the next twelve years, Saddam Hussein remained in power despite the punitive sanctions regime.

Washington and London continued to believe that an alliance with 'moderate' Islam was key to defeating the extremists. A 2004 Whitehall paper by former UK Ambassador to Damascus Basil Eastwood, and Richard Murphy, who had been US assistant Secretary of State under Reagan, noted: 'In the Arab Middle East, the awkward truth is that the most significant movements which enjoy popular support are those associated with political Islam.' For the first time, they identified two distinct groups within the political Islamists: those 'who seek change but do not advocate violence to overthrow regimes, and the Jihadists... who do'.[18]

This new paradigm gained traction. In 2006 Tony Blair made it clear that the coming fight in the Middle East would be between the 'moderate' Islamists and the 'extremists'. The West, he told an audience in the World Affairs Council in Los Angeles, should seek to 'empower' the moderates. 'We want moderate, mainstream Islam to triumph over reactionary Islam.' Blair enlarged on the economic benefits this would accrue to the large transnational enterprises and organisations he championed: 'A victory for the moderates means an Islam that is open: open to globalisation.'[19]

The West continues to behave as if Saudi Arabia can deliver the world from the menace of extremism. Yet the kingdom has spent $50 billion promoting Wahhabism around the world, and most of the funding for al-Qa'ida – amounting to billions of dollars – still comes from private individuals and organisations in Saudi Arabia. The so-called Sinjar Records (documents captured in Iraq by Coalition forces in 2007) provided a clear picture of where foreign jihadists were coming from: Saudi nationals accounted for 45 per cent of foreign fighters in Iraq. They swell the ranks of IS today.

The Arab revolutions muddied the waters even more, particularly in Libya and Syria, making it almost impossible to distinguish between 'moderates' and 'extremists'. In Libya the West's intervention strengthened the radicals and liberated stockpiles of Gaddafi's sophisticated weapons, which were immediately spirited away by the truckload to jihadist strongholds. In the light of that

error, US President Obama dithered in Syria, much to the fury
of his Saudi allies, allowing the most radical of the extremists to
prevail: Islamic State.

ELEVEN

SAUDI ARABIA, WAHHABISM AND ISLAMIC STATE

The usually restrained and conservative UK newspaper *Financial Times* carried a blistering attack on Saudi Arabia on 8 August 2014, blaming the whole advent of Islamic State on the House of Saud, its wholesale export of Wahhabism and jihadist fighters and its funding of extremist groups. Arguing that the kingdom has lost its claim to lead the Sunni world, the *FT* described the modern jihadist as 'a Wahhabi on steroids'.[1]

In question and answer sessions on radical Islam, I am frequently asked about the complex and perplexing relationship between Saudi Arabia and violent, extremist Islamist groups such as al-Qa'ida and, latterly, Islamic State. This is closely followed by questions about the incongruous closeness between Washington, London and Riyadh. Questioners rightly surmise that these matters are central to the region's politics and security. Saudi Arabia, the seat of Islam's two most holy sites – Mecca and Medina – is the self-proclaimed leader of the Muslim world. It has worked hard to maintain that status, which has gone largely unchallenged – until now.

Such labels as the *FT*'s 'Wahhabi on steroids' capture attention. They appear to offer a temptingly simple picture of a logical path that leads from Saudi Arabia's promulgation and funding of an ultra-conservative brand of Islam – Wahhabism – to the emergence of al-Qa'ida, and then the founding of Islamic State. Of course the narrative is more complicated than that. However, the story of Saudi Arabia, its embrace of Islamic fundamentalism on the one hand and its dealings with Western capitalism on the other, is intricately involved with the narrative we have so far traced in this book. To grasp it properly it has to be told separately – but there is no doubt it unlocks important truths that have to be taken into account if we are to approach a full understanding of how IS has come to power.

Both the House of Saud and Islamic State claim to follow the 'true path' of Islam as outlined by the eighteenth-century scholar Muhammad ibn Abd al-Wahhab, and each considers the other apostate. This could all be dismissed as hot air were it not that 92 per cent of Saudi citizens interviewed in an online opinion poll in July 2014 believed that IS 'conforms to the values of Islam and Islamic law'.[2] Islamic State has mounted a vigorous challenge to the Saudi claim to lead the Muslim world, highlighting the royal family's love of luxury and acceptance of corruption which, it claims, renders its members ideologically and morally unfit for the task. The kingdom's citizens, it seems, agree; Saudi commentator Jamal Khashoggi has warned of Islamic State's many supporters in Saudi Arabia who 'watch from the shadows'.[3]

What is Wahhabism?

Muhammad ibn Abd al-Wahhab (1703–1792), the founder of Wahhabism, was a Sunni scholar in the Najd area of what would later become the Kingdom of Saudi Arabia. Wahhab was greatly influenced by the writings of the fourteenth-century scholar Taqi al-Din ibn Taymiyyah (1262–1328) who is revered as one of the greatest Muslim thinkers of all time by those of the Salafist (meaning forefathers or pioneers) persuasion. Taymiyyah believed that only the first three generations of Muslims followed the correct path of the religion; this is based on the Prophet Muhammad's saying, reported in a *hadith* (recorded saying) that, 'The best of people is my generation, then those that come after them, then those that come after them.'[4]

Taymiyyah urged his contemporaries to revert to the origins of the faith: the Qur'an and the Sunnah. He established the narrow definition of the 'true faith' that would later be enshrined in Wahhab's teachings and established the principles of *takfir* (denouncing fellow Muslims as apostates) and *jihad* against the *kafir* (infidels) – these terms are frequently referenced in Islamic State's online material.

Abd al-Wahhab's resurrection of such austere views nearly 400 years later came partly in response to historical circumstances. The influence of Islam on the world stage was declining as European expansionism got under way and, again, deviation from the 'true path' of Islam was blamed. Wahhab became a wandering teacher until 1741, when he found himself under the protection of tribal leader Muhammad Ibn Saud, who was based in Diriyah, then a desert oasis. Ibn Saud was devout – and ambitious. He could see how Wahhab's teaching might challenge contemporary Arab values and culture and become an instrument of power, particularly as it entailed jihad against those who would not submit to its central requirements.

Central Wahhabi tenets hold that only Allah should be worshipped and considered holy – reverence for saints, 'holy' objects or images, places, shrines or graves is considered heresy. Shaving, alcohol, smoking and swearing are forbidden. Musical instruments are *haram*, although close-harmony singing is allowed and is very popular among today's jihadists. Wahhab also insisted that women should not take leadership roles.

This ideology is at the heart of the Salafist tradition, which finds its most recent expression in Islamic State. Wahhab emphasised the necessity for a 'ruler of all the Muslims' to whom all true believers would give their *bayat*: a caliph or, in a historical gap when there was no caliph, the recognised *emir*. Wahhab clarified the doctrine of 'the three pillars': 'One ruler, one authority, one mosque'. From the perspective of Muhammad Ibn Saud and his descendants, for 'one ruler', read king.

The House of Saud/Wahhabi connection

Muhammad Ibn Saud (died 1765) is regarded as the founder of the Saudi state and dynasty. The *emir* of Diriyah, then an agricultural settlement near present-day Riyadh, he was skilled in desert warfare. In 1745 Wahhab and Ibn Saud swore an oath that, together, they would conquer the Arabian Peninsula (then part of the Ottoman Empire) and establish a kingdom based on Wahhabi tenets. By 1803, the Saud family controlled the area, including Mecca and Medina. The two cities surrendered almost immediately in panic, owing to the fearsome reputation of the Wahhabi warriors. The first Saudi state made the rule of the king a religious imperative.

But it was not to last long; by 1812, the Ottomans decided the rapid expansion overseen by the third Saudi king, Saud bin Abdul-Aziz, represented a real threat to their power, and they invaded. By 1818 they controlled all the major cities and Diriyah, the Wahhabi capital. Nothing was heard of the Wahhabis for almost a century. But their fortunes were improved by the First World War, which resulted in the implosion of the Ottoman Empire. The Al-Saud, under Abdulaziz bin Abdul-Rahman al-Saud, forcibly united religiously diverse tribes, fighting fifty-two battles in the process. Thus today's Kingdom of Saudi Arabia was established, by the sword, in 1932.

The discovery and exploitation of oil were to create tensions between the Wahhabi vision and the ambitions of the king – tensions that have continued to challenge the security of the Saudi state, creating a duality within the nation's identity. With the discovery of oil came the temptations of the West, whose leaders and businessmen flocked to court the Saudi monarch (at the same time as they were promising Sherif Hussein that he would be the ruler of a greater Arabia). Civil conflict ensued when the hardliners refused to compromise their beliefs. King Abdulaziz eventually prevailed by virtue of the machine gun.

Wahhabism was now cynically transformed and harnessed, with great political shrewdness, as an instrument of the state. The hardline, uncompromising, value system was institutionalised to uphold the king's absolute power. When I met Osama bin Laden in 1996, he remarked that the Kingdom of Saudi Arabia was established 'not for Islamic law but for Abdulaziz's family'.

Wealth and corruption

In 1933, King Abdulaziz signed a deal with the American Standard Oil Company, giving it full exploration and exploitation rights. By 1938 the company – and the Saudi royals – realised they were sitting on a liquid gold mine.

When Abdulaziz died in 1953, four of his sons in succession ruled a kingdom with no written constitution, no elected parliament, no judicial system, no political parties and very few civil rights. The situation remains the same today and the kingdom has 6,000 *umara* (princes) who receive a salary from birth. The lifestyles of the princes and their 24,000 relatives and offspring are characterised by ostentatious displays of wealth, which many believe are partly funded by corruption. In a statement at odds with the strict morality supposedly at the heart of the Saudi system, Prince Bandar bin Sultan, the former ambassador to Washington, told a television interviewer that corruption was 'human nature... if you tell me that in building this country and in spending $350 billion out of $400 billion that we misused or got corrupted with $50 billion, I'll tell you, "Yes", I'll take that any time."'[5]

With the nation's oil revenues at nearly $250 billion in 2013, every Saudi should enjoy a comfortable standard of living; yet in 2013 a quarter of the population lived below the poverty line.[6] As in the 'Arab Spring' countries, the potential for dissent is obvious, especially when youth unemployment stands at 30 per cent. The state education system focuses largely on Wahhabism, with the result that youths are not really qualified for anything, except perhaps for recruitment to jihad.

Absolute authority

The entire Saudi state apparatus was constructed on the tenets of Wahhabism, so that the only authority the royal family requires in the execution of its constitutional duties is the approval of the religious establishment. There is dissent, but it is dealt with abruptly and violently. In 1979, radical Wahhabi clerics led more than 200 protestors to occupy the Grand Mosque in Mecca, accusing the royal family of betraying the religion with their decadence and corruption. The House of Saud called on the French government for help; they obliged by sending riot police to dislodge the protestors who gave up after eleven days of extreme violence. Sixty-three were publicly beheaded as a warning to anyone else who felt like speaking up.

More recently, the Saudis feared the domino effect of the Arab Spring and rooted out potential trouble-makers early on. The Facebook organiser of a planned 11 March 2011 'Day of Rage' – Faisal Ahmed Abdul-Ahad – was allegedly killed by Saudi security forces on 2 March after his page had attracted 26,000 followers.[7] Religious instruction teacher Khaled al-Johani found himself the sole participant (apart from the world's media) at a demonstration he organised in Riyadh; he later became known online as 'the only brave man in Saudi Arabia'. He was imprisoned without charge for one year. The regime banned demonstrations and tried to discourage dissent by handing out $127 billion in benefits to its citizens. Sporadic protests were met with gunfire and seventeen people had been killed by early 2013.

A marriage of convenience with the West

The safe and secure exploitation of Saudi Arabia's oil by Western companies requires a stable, friendly and compliant regime. While the US has flown the banner of 'democracy and freedom' over most of its adventures in the Middle East (including the invasions of Afghanistan and Iraq, and more recent interventions in Libya and Syria), it consistently turns a blind eye to the absence of these prerogatives in Saudi Arabia. It steadfastly ignores the backwardness, corruption and routine human rights abuses that keep its desert friends in power. The same week that British newspapers carried a horrific account of Saudi police holding down a woman in the streets of Mecca and beheading her with a sword, the Union Jack flew at half mast over the Houses of Parliament and Buckingham Palace as a mark of respect for the newly deceased King Abdullah. Indeed, in the twenty-one months between US journalist James Foley's capture in November 2012, and his subsequent beheading by ISIS's grim, British executioner known as 'Jihadi John' (now believed to be Londoner Mohammed Emwazi) on 19 August 2014, Saudi Arabia had publicly beheaded 113 people.

The 1979 seizing of the Grand Mosque in Mecca by Wahhabi fundamentalists was the kingdom's first experience of open rebellion. Although this uprising was put down, the flames might easily have been rekindled had it not been for the Soviet invasion of Afghanistan on 25 December. The calls for jihad, eagerly promoted by the royal family, prompted an exodus of hardliners and acted as a pressure valve on the escalating crisis inside the kingdom. Saudi Arabia was immediately brought into the crisis by the US, and the Saudis were keen to do Washington's bidding. They had seen what befell the Shah of Iran earlier the same year when the US abandoned its erstwhile ally and the Islamic Revolution sent him fleeing into exile. Most of the so-called Afghan-Arabs (Arab jihadists) were from Saudi Arabia, establishing a precedent and producing 'core al-Qa'ida' which would be led by Saudi Arabia's most famous son: Osama bin Laden.

The wholesale, worldwide export of Wahhabism began in response to Iran's attempts to export the Shi'i radicalism of its 1979 revolution, but it would also further America's regional aims. A symbiotic relationship developed, whereby Saudi Arabian influence, via its domination of the Sunni bloc, was used to further the American agenda. This agenda included (over time) protecting its oil sources; gaining lucrative arms and development contracts; and countering socialism, Ba'athism, pan-Arabism and the burgeoning influence of Russia and latterly China. The West's gaze was fixed on Saudi Arabia's immense wealth and it simply chose to ignore the skewed Wahhabi extremism that maintained the kingdom's exalted position at the top of the Sunni world.

The Taliban takeover of Afghanistan in 1996 greatly tested the relationship between Riyadh and Washington. Al-Qa'ida was ensconced in Kandahar and was openly protected and supported by the Taliban; but Riyadh joined Pakistan and the UAE in recognising the Taliban's right to rule.

In 2001 al-Qa'ida's 9/11 attack on the Twin Towers in New York was led by a Saudi national, and fifteen out of the total nineteen hijackers that day were Saudis. The Saudis removed their recognition from the Taliban in November 2001, and agreed to back the US bombardment on al-Qa'ida's main hideout in the Tora Bora mountains. Under immense pressure from Washington, they froze the assets of suspected individuals and organisations and shut down Islamic charities that had been channelling funds to extremist groups. Washington demanded that the Saudi education system should no longer include radical teaching on the necessity of jihad and that 1,000 imams who had publicly criticised the West and US policies in the Middle East should be dismissed. Unfortunately, the 'success' of 9/11 saw popular support for al-Qa'ida reach an all-time high. The FBI started to train the interior ministry's secret police, the Mabahith – but Saudi sources told me that 80 per cent of its staff actually sympathised with bin Laden. Meanwhile, Saudi jihadis, fleeing American bombardment in Afghanistan, were returning home, where they would regroup, creating an internal threat to the security of Saudi Arabia.

America meanwhile became embroiled in the Saudi-Iran regional stand-off, imposing sanctions and making warlike noises about Tehran's nuclear ambitions. Paradoxically, the US now became increasingly unpopular with the region's Sunnis: first because it dismantled Saddam Hussein's Sunni regime in Iraq and allowed pro-Tehran Shi'is to dominate the new government; and later because of its failure to intervene militarily on behalf of the majority Sunni's rebellion in Syria.

It seems that, shortly before the 'Arab Spring' revolutions erupted, the US had begun to develop a robust and webbed-up military infrastructure centred on the Gulf. In 2010 it concluded the biggest arms deal in history – valued at $60.5 billion – with Saudi Arabia. The provision of the most sophisticated weapons to such a repressive and backward regime was justified on the grounds of 'inter-operability', suggesting that the US intended to act in tandem with the Saudis at some point in the near future.

Dawaa – spreading the Wahhabi seed

As we have seen, the Saudi regime is predicated on, and protected by, the assumption that the king is the leader of all the Muslims. It is a measure of how desperately the Saudi royals need the legitimacy of religion that in 1996 they begged Osama bin Laden to make a public declaration that the king was a 'true Muslim', offering to double the $200 million they had frozen in his bank accounts if he would agree.

In order to consolidate and preserve the Saudi king's position as leader of the world's Muslims, the kingdom began aggressively exporting the 'official' brand of Wahhabism throughout the world, including to Western Muslim communities. *Dawaa*, or proselytising, has always been a key feature of Wahhabism. It was instrumental in securing the territories that now constitute Saudi Arabia and bringing the restive Bedouin tribes under the control of the House of Saud. Inside the kingdom, religious teaching has increasingly been dictated by the political needs of the royal family rather than by the Qur'an, focusing on the requirement for obedience to the king. Every Saudi school child is required to study

Kitab al-Tawhid (The Oneness of Allah) by Muhammad ibn Abd
al-Wahhab, considered by many to be the source of militant Islam,
in which jihad is normalised, becoming part of the vocabulary of
everyday life. This education system produces young people who
are already radicalised, making recruitment and funding for jihad
easy for extremist groups.

With its enormous oil wealth, the kingdom had no shortage of
funds for a worldwide mission, which began in earnest in the 1970s
under King Fahd and continues to this day. Wahhabi-sponsored
schools, colleges and universities proliferated, often in countries
where there is no state-funded education, making Saudi-funded
madrassas (religious schools) the only available source of literacy.
Their curriculum is almost entirely devoted to the strict Wahhabi
interpretation of Islam, with its attendant sectarianism, its call to
'fight the non-believers' and its unharnessed condemnation of the
depravity of the West. King Fahd gained a reputation as a playboy
and a gambler, yet during his reign $87 billion of government
funding was spent on 210 Islamic centres, 1,500 mosques, 202
colleges and 2,000 madrassas in countries as diverse as Pakistan,
Nigeria, Bosnia, Chechnya, Canada, USA and Britain, among
many others.

Under King Abdullah, *dawaa* was pursued with equal vigour: in
2013, Indian newspapers reported that the kingdom had launched
a $35 billion programme for mosques and madrassas across
the whole of South Asia – the region is home to 1 billion of the
world's 1.6 billion Muslims. The Saudi aim, with this 'soft power'
bombardment, is to 'wahhabise Islam', eliminate diversity within it,
and make of the *ummah* one family – with the Saudi royals at the
head through 'divine right'.

Fuelling and funding jihad

It is well known that when the USSR invaded Afghanistan in 1979,
the West and the Gulf States funded and trained the mujahideen, and

that these jihadists eventually prevailed after ten years of exhausting battles. Osama bin Laden was the public face of jihad through the 1980s; he participated in documentary films and the Saudi regime held him up as a shining example as they encouraged young men to go to Afghanistan and fight. The Saudi media and mosques all over the country launched a huge effort to recruit volunteers. An estimated 35,000 to 45,000 Saudis left the country to join the mujahideen in the late 1980s. The Saudis also contributed large sums of money to the coffers of fighting battalions, some of which would later morph into al-Qa'ida. Although the Saudi government has, in recent years, introduced some anti-terror legislation and rehabilitation for the jihadists it jails, its citizens remain the most numerous among recruits. Those wealthy souls who do not commit their bodies to jihad offer their funds instead.

Saudi Arabia's ongoing support and funding for the most radical extremist groups is well known to Western governments. In 2009, Hillary Clinton signed off a secret briefing memo destined for top US diplomats in which she noted, in the calmest possible terms, that the kingdom's donors are the world's largest source of funds for al-Qa'ida, the Taliban and Lashkar-e-Taiba (Army of the Righteous, based in Pakistan). She also described the 'ongoing challenge to persuade Saudi officials to treat terrorist funds emanating from Saudi Arabia as a strategic priority' and commented that these funds are often used to fund attacks.[8]

The briefing was later released by WikiLeaks, the organisation that publishes secret and classified information. Other WikiLeaks cables revealed that jihadis seeking funding enter Saudi Arabia for *Hajj* (pilgrimage) and then establish so-called 'front' companies to launder money; pilgrims travelling for *Hajj* often carry large sums in cash and consider donations for jihad a worthy cause. Extremist groups also arrange to process funding from government-approved Islamic charities through the front companies. The Pakistani group LeT, which carried out the horrific Mumbai massacre in 2008, had established a front company in Saudi Arabia in 2005.[9] Through its 'charity' wing, Jamaat-ud-Dawa, LeT also sought funding from wealthy Saudi donors for madrassas in Pakistan, but it is likely a proportion of this money was siphoned off to fund training, weapons and attacks. Washington is critical of the Saudi refusal to ban three charities classified as terrorist entities in the US.

The cables reflect a reluctance on the part of Western diplomats to publicly criticise their wealthy friends, owing to the high level of business co-operation with Saudi Arabia. The UK alone has more than 200 joint ventures in the kingdom. WikiLeaks also revealed that the US Embassy staff in Riyadh were less concerned with the fact that Saudi donors were funding al-Qa'ida than the worry that the group might attack the kingdom's oil fields.

When jihadists began to appear among the armed opposition ranks in the Syrian uprising from 2011, Saudi Arabia and other Gulf countries clearly thought that the mujahideen would swiftly accomplish Syrian President Bashar al-Assad's downfall. Saudi Arabia's extremist Wahhabi television clerics, such as Salman al-Ouda, Mohsen al-Awaji and Sheikh Muhammad al-Arifi, declared a jihad in Syria to 'rip Bashar and his dictatorship from the lands' as al-Arifi phrased it.[10] In passionate, tearful speeches these very influential clerics, the stars of Saudi satellite television, actively recruited for fighters and urged people to give those waging jihad in Syria money and arms. Al-Arifi also visited Britain several times to recruit for jihad in Syria, with British newspapers much exercised by his success in doing so. He preached at Cardiff's Al-Manar Centre where two young Britons, Nasser Muthana and Reyaad Khan, worshipped. The pair would later travel to Syria where they appeared in an ISIS recruitment video.[11]

Sir Richard Dearlove, the former head of M16, told veteran Irish journalist Patrick Cockburn that he has no doubt that substantial, ongoing funding from individual Saudi donors, to which the authorities turned a blind eye, 'played a central role in the ISIS surge into Sunni areas of Iraq and Syria'.[12] Cockburn links this unofficial support with the period of tenure of the former Saudi head of General Intelligence Prince Bandar bin Sultan, who was virulently opposed to the Shi'i and urged their destruction while fomenting region-wide sectarianism. The news site *Asrar Arabiya* reported that 'Bandar channelled generous funds to the Islamic State in Iraq and the Levant [ISIS].' As Riyadh realised that it was itself in ISIS's sights, Prince Bandar was sacked in April 2014.

As well as encouraging the jihadists in Syria, the Saudis also believed that the US would launch devastating military strikes on Assad, especially after the latter crossed the 'red line' over chemical weapons; they were deeply shocked and disappointed when a joint Russian-US initiative saw Assad let off the hook in exchange for signing up to the Organisation for the Prohibition of Chemical Weapons (OPCW) in September 2013. In the same month, the House of Saud watched in disbelief as Washington started what looked like rapprochement with Riyadh's regional antagonist, Tehran, and demonstrated its displeasure in uncharacteristically melodramatic fashion: in September 2013 Prince Saud al-Faisal refused to give a scheduled speech at the UN; and in October Saudi Arabia refused to take up a two-year tenure on the UN Security Council. The Saudi's refusal to accept Tehran's presence at the negotiating table ended any chance of a political solution for Syria.

Controlling the media

When Saddam Hussein invaded Kuwait in 1990, the Saudis found themselves on the wrong side of Arab public opinion when they agreed to facilitate the arrival of US troops. The majority of Arabs, it appeared, actually supported Saddam Hussein and had a highly unfavourable view of the Saudi regime. Now King Fahd decided to set about winning over hearts and minds across the Arab world via the media. The first major project, in 1991, was the Middle East Broadcasting Corporation (MBC) established by King Fahd's brother-in-law, Waleed al-Ibrahim. Fittingly for a channel that sounds as though it is linked to the British Broadcasting Corporation (BBC), this was to be based in London. Next, Prince Khalid bin Sultan – who had led the Saudi Army during the Iraq-

Iran War – took control of the London-based *al-Hayat*, a pan-Arab daily newspaper, while the sons of Prince Salman consolidated their grip on the *Asharq al-Awsat* newspaper (also based in London).

In 1994, Prince Khalid bin 'Abdullah bin 'Abd al-Rahman's al-Mawarid group set up Orbit, an entertainment network; and the Arab Radio and Television entertainment network (ART) was established the same year. When Qatar launched Al Jazeera in 1996, the new, cutting-edge, radical satellite channel broke new ground, challenged the Saudi grip on the market... and woke up the viewers. The Saudi attempt at a counterbalance, Al Arabiya (which is part of the MBC network), lost any credibility it might have garnered when, in 2004, George W. Bush refused to speak to Al Jazeera but gave Al Arabiya a lengthy interview, in an attempt to pour oil on the region's troubled waters after allegations of abuse and torture in Iraq's US-run prisons came to light. Interestingly, despite the significant levels of support and funding for the most extremist jihadist groups by Saudi individuals, and the tacit approval of the regime, Al Arabiya refused to broadcast video messages by Osama bin Laden and Ayman al-Zawahiri. Coverage of extremism tended to focus on the threat posed by such groups inside the kingdom which, as we have seen, is now the main challenge for Riyadh. Al Jazeera, on the other hand, showed al-Qa'ida videos and was open to discussing its ideology and history.

The Saudi media recently launched an extensive campaign against Islamic State, conflating it with the Muslim Brotherhood. The London-based Saudi press has carried opinion articles – often purporting to be written by members of the royal family – describing the Muslim Brotherhood's 'treacherous' plans to take over in the Gulf and its 'extended overlap with the Taliban, al-Qa'ida and ISIS'. In December 2014, King Abdullah appointed new cabinet members to ensure that clerics in mosques and Islamic universities do not promulgate extremist ideology.[13] Saudi Prince Mamdouh bin-Abdulaziz al-Saud wrote of 'preachers at the gates of hell' in June 2013. *Asharq al-Awsat* columnist Mashari al-Dhaydi declared Islamic State to be Saudi Arabia's number one enemy and said, 'fighting ISIS is a mission linked to the essence of Saudi Arabia's existence'.[14]

The Saudi regime, rightly, feels that the declaration of the caliphate, and the overt criticism levelled at the House of Saud by the extremists, constitute a very real threat to its existence. That the challenge is mounted within the unique framework of the House of Saud's own construct – Wahhabism – makes it all the more potent.

CONCLUSION

Islamic State is not going to go away – not in the short term at least. Born of a perfect storm of historical circumstances, it has put down roots that will not easily be torn up. These roots are geographical, ideological and political. The 'State' has established itself in large areas across Iraq and Syria, and has significant, allied geopolitical satellites. In addition, a large number of extremist groups, formerly part of the al-Qa'ida network, have shifted their allegiance to Baghdadi.

The jihadists have been honing their strategy and battle techniques for more than three decades; unsurprisingly, this latest extremist entity is more powerful, more effective, more ruthless and more worrying than anything that has gone before. Unlike other jihadist groups, Islamic State is well resourced and has no need of external funding. It is well armed, having seized the contents of military warehouses in Iraq and Syria, and has hundreds of professional Iraqi officers and soldiers in its ranks who have shared their expertise and helped train recruits. Islamic State also benefits from the intelligence expertise of security personnel who honed their craft under Saddam Hussein. To all intents and purposes, it is a state with an army.

Islamic State's achievements on the ground lend it unprecedented credibility. After all, it succeeded in dissolving the Sykes-Picot imposed border between Iraq and Syria, something the sloganeering partisans of Marxism, Ba'athism or pan-Arabism were unable to achieve in the intervening century.

Neighbouring Arab countries and the US-led Alliance that is

grouped against IS have so far shown little appetite for sending in ground troops, which most military experts agree would be necessary if it is to be effectively dismantled. The ongoing aerial bombardment, while destructive, is too imprecise to have a lasting impact on the designated enemy. In addition, this demonstration of superior air power risks losing the sympathy of local people caught up in the devastation; they may turn, instead, to the extremists. The drone campaign in Yemen succeeded in killing numerous al-Qaʿida leaders, but AQAP (Al-Qaʿida in the Arabian Peninsula) has not been destroyed. In fact it appears to be resurgent and is gaining support among the Sunni tribes as the civil conflict with the (Shiʿi) Houthis escalates.

The Islamic State brigades are unlikely to present themselves as willing targets in a situation where they are being outgunned. The jihadists long ago developed the technique of melting away from battles they cannot win only to reappear elsewhere where they can prevail. Islamic State has already adopted the same, effective strategy, dispersing from heavily targeted areas while expanding into new ones – most recently, Libya. Like al-Qaʿida, it seeks out the chaos in which it can thrive. In today's turbulent, war-torn Middle East there are many such opportunities.

Just as it seized territory at lightning speed, Islamic State has been able to consolidate its ideological catchment with unprecedented stealth and efficiency. The internet has given Islamic State opportunities that its predecessors neither fully exploited nor understood. By clever use of social media and digital film making, it has eclipsed the counterweight mainstream media to broadcast its bloody deeds, its triumphs and its caliphate. By using every tool the internet puts at their disposal, the tech-savvy cyber jihadists have been able to attract frustrated, marginalised and vulnerable young people to its ranks and to convince them of its world vision, predicated on reviving the golden age of Islamic conquest, resisting American hegemony and pitting the 'believers' against the 'infidels' and 'crusaders'.

The West's own actions continue to feed into this narrative.

Islamophobia is rampant, particularly in the aftermath of the recent attacks on Europeans in Paris, Copenhagen and Sousse. Little mention is made, either, of the hundreds of attacks on Muslims and Islamic locations in the West or the growing sense of insecurity that Europe's Muslims experience as a result.

The regimes the US and Britain court above all others in the Middle East are among its most unpopular and corrupt – especially Saudi Arabia. And the failure of the Arab-Israeli Peace Process feeds into the ideological pull of Islamic State and endorses the notion that the West does not, in fact, stand for fairness.

There are strong indications that Islamic State cells are already in existence in Rafah, Gaza and Hebron in the West Bank. In the course of researching this book, I spoke to someone very close to the Islamic State leadership (who cannot be named for security reasons). I asked him about the group's policy on Palestine and why they had not targeted Israel. He replied that it was a 'question of priorities' and that Islamic State is currently focusing on 'empowerment', after which 'liberation' will become the priority. At that point, he threatened, Islamic State will 'fight the Zionists and destroy them and their state'. He pointed to the historical precedent of the second Caliph Umar Ibn Al-Khattab, who first took Persia and Mesopotamia and after that Palestine and the Levant.

What next?

In September 2012, with remarkable prescience, the former UN secretary general Kofi Annan told BBC radio's *Today* programme that in his judgement the conflict in Syria will not 'implode' as it did in Libya, but would 'in all likelihood explode... over the borders'. So it did – into Iraq, and sources confirm that Islamic State is intent on expansion into other countries. There are two main ways it can achieve this: by sending its own fighters into neighbouring countries and overrunning territory, as it has done in Iraq and Syria; and by exploiting the existing network of well-established hardline jihadist groups and sleeper cells.

Islamic State has many neighbours: first and foremost the region's two major, opposing powers, Saudi Arabia and Iran; plus Lebanon, Jordan, Israel, Turkey and Kuwait. Kuwait is the smallest and potentially the most vulnerable to incursion. The tiny Gulf State is oil-rich but has just 15,000 soldiers in its army. Islamic State's army of 100,000 not only vastly outnumbers it, but Arab and US military experts warn that one IS soldier equals ten regular soldiers because they are prepared to die for their cause and are well-trained, vicious fighters, particularly in an urban guerrilla environment.[1] Kuwait has been on a state of high alert since June 2014 and has been directly threatened with invasion by IS.[2]

Libya has long been home to militant jihadists and has produced some of al-Qa'ida's main leaders, as well one of the Islamists' most inspirational twentieth-century icons, the leader of the insurgency against the Italian occupation of Libya from 1912–1931, Omar al-Mukhtar. (During the Libyan Arab Spring revolution, the rebels called themselves the 'grandsons of Omar al-Mukhtar'.) The Libyan Islamists rapidly dominated the revolution, and stockpiles of sophisticated weapons looted from Muammar al-Gaddafi's warehouses found their way to emboldened and strengthened jihadists across North Africa and into Iraq and Syria. In October 2014 Libya's most deadly jihadist group, Ansar al-Sharia, declared an 'Islamic Emirate' in Derna where they paraded with Islamic State flags and pledged allegiance to Baghdadi. (In keeping with the 'digital caliphate', when allegiances are pledged *en masse* it is often by a video posted online.)

By the beginning of 2015, each of two rival 'governments' was contesting the other's right to rule. The internationally recognised administration was forced to flee Tripoli (and re-establish itself in Benghazi) while Libya Dawn, a coalition of militias and Islamist and jihadist groups, set up a rival government in Tripoli. In the resulting chaos, IS was able to establish a robust presence in Libya, seizing control of two cities in addition to Derna – Sirte and Nofaliya – as well as parts of Benghazi, which has long been home to radical Islamist groups.

In February 2015, IS surprised everyone by revealing just how strong its presence in Libya had become. First, a group going by the name of 'the Cyrenica Province of Islamic State' beheaded twenty-one Egyptian Coptic Christians on Libya's Mediterranean shore, disseminating a video of the atrocity in which the commentator warned 'we are south of Rome.'[3] When Egyptian fighter planes bombed IS targets in eastern Libya in retaliation, the group killed forty-two people in three devastating suicide car bombings in Qubba, near the Tobruk seat of the internationally recognised government.[4] Next, IS paraded a fleet of brand new Toyota Landcruiser police cars through the streets of Benghazi, where they were greeted by cheering crowds making the IS salute.[5] The parade was filmed and the video was uploaded and disseminated by Ansar al-Sharia, indicating that it is now either part of, or closely allied to, IS. IS intends to make Libya its African hub.

By early March 2015, IS controlled four major cities in Libya, causing southern European countries on the other side of the Mediterranean justifiable panic. Islamic State spokesmen have threatened to send thousands of migrants to Italy's shores if it intervenes militarily in Libya – a peculiar form of revenge first practised by Gaddafi in 2011, when he sent hundreds of ships carrying migrants across the Mediterranean as 'human bombs' against Italy after it joined the NATO campaign to depose him.[6] Europe also worries that extremists may infiltrate these migrations.

Lebanon is a prime target for the jihadists, not only for its proximity and the long border it shares with Syria, but also because the Shi'i militant group and political party Hezbollah have been fighting on the side of the Assad regime in Syria, adding fuel to the already-raging sectarian fire. IS overran the border town of Arsal in August 2014, taking thirty Lebanese police and soldiers hostage. The border with Syria down the country's eastern flank is constantly being tested by IS brigades, as is Tripoli, a large, mainly Sunni, city on the coast in the north of the country. The Lebanese Army has managed to hold on to Tripoli, after three attempts to date to take it, but reporters say that 'hearts and minds are lost' and that the Islamic State flag still flies freely throughout the city.[7]

Turkey is in the unenviable position of having allowed fighters and arms safe passage through its porous 560-mile border with Syria for much of the civil war. Most of those fighters are now part of Islamic State, and there are at least 2,000 Turkish jihadists fighting in Syria who present a potential threat to their homeland if they return. Islamic State has captured many towns and cities along the Turkish border. In July 2015, an IS suicide bomber struck inside Turkish territory in Suruç. A month later, Turkey joined the war on IS and allowed US F-16 fighter jets to use its Incirlik airbase to launch attacks on targets in Syria and Iraq. In response, IS has threatened to attack Turkey's tourist industry, which is worth around $20 billion per annum.[8]

While neighbouring Iran is an unlikely target, given its military might and prowess, Tehran is clearly rattled by this new menace in its backyard. It seeks to join the debate about how to confront IS as well as the military alliance against it. In November three elderly phantom jets belonging to the Iranian Air Force struck Islamic State targets inside Iraq, presumably with the tacit permission of the US. Saudi Arabia, however, is obstinately opposed to its regional nemesis, Tehran, becoming involved.

Israel, another neighbour, is firmly in Islamic State's sights, if only in theory, given Tel Aviv's own military strength and the fact that it is defended by the US. Small, regular attacks aimed at undermining the Hebrew State's security are likely, however, and a deadly new IS governate in the Sinai has carried out a string of attacks, sending shock waves to Tel Aviv.[9]

Jordan is a gatekeeper not only for Israel but also for Saudi Arabia. In June 2014 Baghdadi threatened to invade the tiny kingdom and 'slaughter King Abdullah'.[10] The country was drawn into the bloody mire when IS burned alive Jordanian pilot Moaz al-Kasasbeh; the Jordanian king declared war on IS, threatening an 'earth-shaking' response and launching bombardments on its territories in Iraq and Syria.[11] But the biggest danger for Jordan is the presence of large numbers of sympathisers and sleeper cells, particularly in the east of the country where the kingdom has borders with both Syria and Iraq. Israel has indicated that it would confront Islamic State if it enters Jordan.[12]

Islam's most sacred places – Mecca and Medina – are in Saudi Arabia, and its ruling family, the House of Saud, claim leadership of the Islamic world that Baghdadi has now asserted is his. Many reliable sources reported to me that Saudi Arabia is an imminent target for Islamic State, which is waiting for the most opportune circumstances to be put in place. Saudi Arabia is in double danger because this kingdom, too, is home to many jihadists, sleeper cells and supporters, including members of the royal family and clerics; in addition it has a well-established and virulent 'branch' of al-Qa'ida at its southern border in Yemen, al-Qa'ida in the Arabian Peninsula (AQAP).

In northern Nigeria, the exceptionally bloodthirsty al-Qa'ida affiliate Boko Haram has declared its own 'Islamic State', which comprised some 20,000 square miles in January 2015,[13] and it has been testing the border with Cameroon. Boko Haram flies the IS flag and pledged allegiance to Baghdadi in July 2014.[14] Boko Haram seeks to overthrow the Nigerian government and restore the Sokoto Islamic Caliphate that existed in Northern Niger, southern Cameroon and Nigeria before the British took over in 1903. With thousands of miles between the two 'Islamic States', however, any prospect of contiguity is a long way off, but this is an alarming development nonetheless.

Al-Qa'ida in the Islamic Maghreb (AQIM – Mahgreb signifies northwest Africa) is an umbrella group formed in 2007. It is dominated by members of the Algerian Salafist Group for Preaching and Combat (GSPC) and includes elements from the Libyan Islamic Fighting Group (LIFG) as well as the Moroccan Islamic Combatant Group (MICG) and Tunisian jihadists. AQIM has benefitted from the Arab Spring in two main ways: it has taken advantage of the security vacuum – particularly in the Sahara and Sahel – to expand its area of influence, and it was able to procure vast quantities of sophisticated weaponry from abandoned or unguarded stockpiles in Libya during the revolution. AQIM is now active throughout Algeria and in parts of Mauritania, Mali, Chad and Niger.

Western security agencies are greatly concerned about the increasing 'Africanisation' of al-Qa'ida, and the Arab Spring has seen that process move forward. AQIM is increasingly webbed-up with other al-Qa'ida affiliates; in November 2011, AQIM sent a delegation to 'al-Qa'ida leaders in Pakistan' to begin operational collaborations with them.[15] In May 2012, Timbuktu mayor Hallé Ousman told the US-sponsored online news service *Magharebia* that groups of Pakistani jihadists had entered northern Mali to help AQIM and rebel Islamist Tuaregs consolidate the so-called Azawad 'emirate'. In September 2014, AQIM took the unprecedented step of issuing a joint statement with AQAP, pledging support for Islamic State,[16] implying that unity between the world's Salafi-jihadist groups is synonymous with the expansion of the caliphate.

The Houthi revolution in Yemen, which saw the Shi'i minority seize control in Sanaa, has opened new possibilities for Islamic State. AQAP, which has already pledged allegiance to Baghdadi, is emerging as the dominant force in the Sunni response, and a full-blown civil war seems likely. America's five-year drone campaign against AQAP targets in Yemen has seen the group attract increasing levels of support among the all-important Sunni tribes.[17]

Indeed, sectarian conflict is now the main driver for Islamic State's expansion, fomented by the Sunni extremists and sustained by Shi'i Iran on one hand and Sunni Saudi Arabia on the other. The consequences are global, as major powers and tiny countries alike align themselves along the sectarian fault line that was exposed by the Syrian conflict. Russia and China are firmly in the Shi'i bloc, while the major Western powers favour the Sunni side. With the additional powder keg of Ukraine, where the West is pitting itself against Moscow, and the Russian military build-up inside Syria itself, I doubt I am the only commentator who fears escalation into a global conflict.

Islamic State conflates radical Islam with the Muslim identity and the worldwide *ummah*. Declaring that 'migration to the lands of jihad' is a sacred duty, Baghdadi has ensured that thousands of impressionable youngsters have answered his call. Those who do not travel are urged to attack at home – in the first two months of 2015 alone, first France and then Denmark felt the brunt of this edict. The *Charlie Hebdo* massacre and the attack on the kosher supermarket in the French capital were mirrored in Copenhagen, where a gunman attacked an event championing freedom of speech attended by Lars Vilks, a Swedish artist who had exhibited sketches of the Prophet Muhammad. The gunman then moved on to a synagogue where he shot Jewish worshippers. Summer 2015 saw a deadly attack on tourists in Sousse by a lone IS-inspired gunman.

Unlike al-Qa'ida under bin Laden, Islamic State is not sending fighters to the West to carry out these attacks but is encouraging home-grown terror under its banner – a strategy first suggested and then pioneered by AQAP's Anwar al-Awlaki. Its aim, as in the battlefield, is to spread and maximise its psychological power by the 'management of savagery' and by inspiring dread – the purpose, of course, of 'terrorism'.

What can be done?

To date the US-led anti-Islamic State Alliance has maintained its membership of at least sixty nation states, having fared better than the 'Friends of Syria' who dwindled from 114 to just eleven in the course of 2012. Any successful military intervention would require ground troops but, as we have seen, not one of these sixty nations has committed to boots on the ground.

While Islamic State may be militarily weaker than many of the states that oppose it (having no naval presence, air power, air defence weapons or long-range missiles), it is unrivalled in its aggression, ferocity and its soldiers' willingness to die. I do not believe that Baghdadi is bluffing when, like bin Laden before him, he challenges the US to send soldiers to Iraq and Syria so that 'we can kill them'. The US has to date sent just 320 military personnel to Iraq where they are training Iraqi soldiers in their Ayn al-Asad air base; in February 2015 Islamic State fighters overran the neighbouring town of al-Baghdadi (where they burned alive forty-five members of the security forces) and sent suicide attackers to the base. Only superior air power saved the base itself from being overrun on that occasion – something the Pentagon has been keen to downplay.[18]

At the beginning of March 2015 Iraq began a military operation to recapture Saddam Hussein's hometown of Tikrit, which had been taken by Islamic State in June 2014. According to a recent conversation I had with Saleh al-Mutlaq, the Iraqi Deputy Prime Minister, the international community is mobilising to aid Iraq in an all-out assault to regain Mosul this summer (2015). The plan may well succeed in liberating Mosul, but the problem is a perennial one in the West's approach: it is a localised, short-term fix with no plans for what happens afterwards. Those of the Islamic State's fighters and families who survive the attack will simply relocate to a safer stronghold, while the circumstances that allowed the extremists to flourish in Iraq remain unchanged – a weak, Shi'i-dominated, sectarian, pro-Tehran government in Baghdad provoking resentment and frustration among the Sunnis. Islamic State would have to withstand a psychological blow, certainly, and morale might suffer temporarily; but this would not be enough to wipe the group out when it holds so much territory elsewhere. Al-Qa'ida, which did not have any claim to statehood, managed not only to survive but also to expand and flourish – opening branches all over the Muslim world – during America's fourteen-year war against it.

The US-led 'War on Terror', which began after the attacks of 11 September 2001, failed miserably; it arguably precipitated the economic collapse of 2008, since it has cost the US Treasury around $3 trillion and 6,000 US troops lost their lives.[19] No wonder President Obama appears deeply reluctant to commit thousands of American troops to a second military phase of the 'War on Terror'.

To effectively counter Islamic State militarily would require international unity, with every country, especially its neighbours, determinedly assaulting its strongholds. Powerful, influential countries like Russia and Iran could not be excluded from any such plan; but given the polarisation regarding Syria and the Ukraine this does not appear likely for the present, at least. In addition, the UN Security Council would have to pass a unanimous resolution sanctioning military force. Although such a resolution was drafted in August 2014, it has yet to go to a vote.[20]

The failure of the regional actors to act in concert is largely due to their own, numerous squabbles. There is the Muslim Brotherhood (MB) question, for example, which has become extremely divisive since the military coup in Egypt which overthrew the MB-linked elected President Morsi: the Saudis supported and applauded the coup, joining Egypt and the UAE in declaring the MB a 'terror group'; Qatar and regional heavyweight Turkey, however, condemned it – President Erdogan's Justice and Development Party is closely affiliated with the MB.

Any effective ideological counterbalance to Islamic State and radical Islam in general would have to be rallied behind another powerful Islamic figure or popular movement. In the 1940s, during the sectarian violence that tore India apart, the so-called 'Islamic Peace Warrior', Badshah Khan, gathered around him a 'Peace Army' of 100,000 men and worked with Mahatma Gandhi to challenge violence. Khan became an iconic figure and was admirably brave in his passivity, enduring torture by the British and lengthy jail sentences. By contrast, Western organisations aiming to prevent radicalisation lack credibility among the youths that are Islamic State's targets for recruitment.

Meanwhile, the West will look to increase its own countries' security with even more restrictions at airports, greater intrusion into the private lives of citizens and more widespread policing of the internet. Paradoxically, these measures also diminish the very freedoms on which it prides itself and that it so vigorously recommends to others.

Would the death or assassination of Baghdadi precipitate the demise of Islamic State? Unlikely. While the Caliph is well protected, the presumption is always there that he may be killed. His death would undoubtedly rock IS momentarily, and there is potential for factionalism and discord in the matter of his successor. However, al-Qa'ida was not destroyed by the death of bin Laden – indeed, one might say it became stronger, since it gave rise to Islamic State. As we have seen, the organisational structure of such groups delegates responsibility and decision-making; each significant member of the leadership has at least two deputies so that the group's survival does not depend on one person.

The potential for conflict between the remnants of al-Qa'ida, under Ayman al-Zawahiri, and Islamic State now seems less likely. In February 2015 Islamic State clarified its stance on al-Qa'ida, declaring (in a *Dabiq* article) that 'al-Zawahiri abandoned the pure heritage left by Sheikh Osama [bin Laden].' This implies that the only matter separating al-Qa'ida members and Islamic State is the person of Zawahiri. This might be interpreted as a call for Zawahiri's assassination. Clearly a merger between these two major jihadist entities would be a highly dangerous development. The response of the Afghan Taliban to such a circumstance is unlikely to be hostile; Islamic State already has thousands of supporters in the country and recently announced a new 'province' across the Afghanistan-Pakistan border. The Taliban became allies of al-Qa'ida and offered bin Laden's group protection and a safe haven throughout the late 1990s. The late al-Qa'ida leader swore his personal *bayat* to the late Taliban commander Mullah Omar – the relationship is deep, long-standing and loyal.

In geopolitical terms, the West and its regional allies may look towards a federal paradigm or partition as a means of neutralising the sectarian antagonisms that are oxygen to Islamic State and like-minded groups. In 1947, this solution was applied in India, and the early 1990s saw the former Yugoslavia divided along ethnic lines. Libya, Syria, Iraq and Yemen have exactly the sectarian and ethnic fault lines that would facilitate this solution, but it is for the people to decide on these matters, not outside powers.

The international community has already put measures in place to weaken Islamic State financially; at the end of January 2015, the UN Security Council unanimously adopted a Russian-drafted resolution banning all trade in antiquities from Syria, threatening sanctions on anyone buying oil from the group and urging states to stop paying kidnap ransoms. The problem is that the black market opportunities IS exploits are clearly beyond UN control or international policing. With its recent entry into Libya, for example, IS is well placed to take over the lucrative market trafficking migrants from northern Libya to Italy; some even fear the arrival of a Somali-pirate-style problem in the Mediterranean.[21]

On the brink

To date a major accidental beneficiary of the rise of the Islamic State is Syria's President Bashar al-Assad. He has remained in power against all the odds since the international community, and his own internal opposition, turned their attentions to the greater threat posed by the jihadists. Any serious attempt to quash Baghdadi's group will require the co-operation of the Syrian state and army; Assad is already informed of, and tacitly approves, Alliance airstrikes within Syria.[22] As long as the rogue state persists on Syrian territory, it is highly unlikely those opposing it will want to see Assad fall, with the last precarious remnants of Syria's administrative infrastructure collapsing with him.

Turkey has been greatly damaged by the Syrian crisis. It facilitated the flow of jihadists and arms into northern Syria and its leader, Recep Tayyip Erdogan, was the most vociferous and unguarded among world leaders in denouncing Assad. Erdogan hoped that moderate Islamists along the lines of his own, Muslim-Brotherhood linked, Justice and Development Party would take control in Damascus, through democratic means. Now, Erdogan faces an extremely hostile and powerful southern neighbour if

Assad survives. He has at the same time compromised his country's status within NATO and jeopardised its chances of joining the EU.

As for Islamic State's own future agenda, we can be sure that it will be seeking to take new territories and expand its alliances. It is unlikely that any former al-Qa'ida affiliates will fail to shift allegiance. Over the coming months and years we can expect these groups to shift focus from local terrorism to seizing and consolidating territory, with a view to multiplying the areas under the flag of Islamic State and, eventually, merging them.

There is reason to fear that the group possesses chemical weapons, with several reports through 2015 of mustard gas being used. On 24 January 2015 the US military announced that it had killed Abu Malik, who served as a chemical weapons engineer under former Iraqi President Saddam Hussein, before joining al-Qa'ida in Iraq and then IS. A statement said he had the 'expertise to pursue a chemical weapons capability'.[23] The Syrian, Iraqi and Libyan armies have all been in possession of such weapons and IS may have looted them in the course of raids on numerous army storage facilities. In fact, in March 2015, there were unconfirmed reports that IS had used chlorine gas against Peshmerga forces.[24]

Baghdadi's men would certainly not hesitate to use chemical weapons to eliminate as many 'infidels' and 'apostates' as possible. Attacks in the West are likely to continue, as are the group's atrocities in the Middle East. In order to maintain its bloody grip on public consciousness, Islamic State has to shock and horrify the world on an almost daily basis.

I asked my source close to Islamic State's leadership what its next military objective is. He did not hesitate with his answer: 'The land of the holy places [Saudi Arabia], Mecca and Medina. We are only waiting for the moment to be right.'

There *is* a chance for a more peaceful way forward – to talk to and negotiate with Islamic State. Few are prepared to even countenance this suggestion, but it is not without precedent. The British government negotiated with the IRA in the end, after almost a century of bloodshed and terrorism; the US sat down with the

Vietnamese in Paris in 1973 after nearly twenty years of slaughter; in 2014 the US negotiated a prisoner swap with the Taliban; and, in January 2015, Jordan agreed to trade prisoners with Islamic State – sadly it was too late to save their hostage. If the West persists in blacklisting the very groups whose rigid ideology might be softened somewhat by dialogue, and with whom some compromise might be made, we will remain in the current phase of endless wars.

It is rare for me to agree with an American hawk, but I fear that Leon Panetta, former director of the CIA, is correct when he asserts that Islamic State is here for the duration. 'I think we're looking at kind of a 30-year war,' he told the newspaper *USA Today* in October 2014, 'one that will have to extend beyond Islamic State to include emerging threats in Nigeria, Somalia, Yemen, Libya and elsewhere.'[25]

ACKNOWLEDGEMENTS

First and foremost, thanks to Susan de Muth for her invaluable research, analysis and editorial contribution to this book.

Thanks too to all our sources, correspondents and contacts throughout the region who have shared or corroborated information – you know who you are.

To my family – Basima, Khaled, Nada and Kareem – thank you for your love, support and patience.

Thanks are also due to Maha Burbar at Rai al-Youm, and my publishers André and Lynn Gaspard of Saqi books.

NOTES

Preface

1. http://www.theguardian.com/world/2015/sep/25/iran-nuclear-deal-hassan-rouhani
2. http://news.sky.com/story/1559201/syrian-rebels-hand-equipment-to-al-qaeda-group
3. http://www.reuters.com/article/2015/06/03/us-mideast-crisis-blinken-idUSKBN0OJ0I620150603
4. http://press.ihs.com/press-release/aerospace-defense-security/syrian-government-loses-56th-territory-ihs-says
5. http://www.bbc.co.uk/news/world-middle-east-29052144
6. http://iswresearch.blogspot.co.uk/
7. www.rt.com/news/311741-suicide-bomber-saudi-mosque/
8. http://www.pressreader.com/uk/the-guardian/20150407/281711203163293/TextView

Introduction

9. http://www.gatestoneinstitute.org/documents/baghdadi-caliph.pdf
10. Ibid.
11. http://www.independent.co.uk/news/world/americas/us-central-command-hacked-by-islamic-state-supporters-9973615.html
12. http://edition.cnn.com/2015/06/18/politics/fbi-social-media-attacks
13. *Sunday Times*, 4 January 2015, 'We have To Understand That ISIS is a Country Now', http://www.thesundaytimes.co.uk/sto/news/world_news/Middle_East/article1502983.ece
14. http://iswresearch.blogspot.co.uk
15. http://www.theguardian.com/world/2015/aug/26/mustard-gas-likely-used-in-suspected-islamic-state-attack-in-syria
16. http://www.breitbart.com/national-security/2015/07/01/report-isis-could-have-42-million-supporters-in-the-arab-world

Chapter 1: Masters of the Digital Universe

1. European Union Institute for Security Studies, 'Brief Issue', January 2015, Beatrice Berton and Patryk Pawlak.
2. Ibid.
3. http://www.theguardian.com/world/2015/jan/03/john-cantlie-ISIS-eighth-video
4. http://www.newsweek.com/19000-french-websites-and-counting-hacked-charlie-hebdo-attack-299675
5. European Union Institute for Security Studies, 'Brief Issue', January 2015, Beatrice Berton and Patryk Pawlak.
6. http://www.theguardian.com/world/2014/sep/24/ISIS-twitter-youtube-message-social-media-jihadi
7. https://www.youtube.com/watch?v=oqbwqmb8Poo

Chapter 2: The Origins – Part One: Iraq

1. http://rawstory.com/news/2005/Clinton_bombing_of_Iraq_far_exceeded_Bushs_in_runup_to_war__Bush_spikes_of_activity_que_0705.html
2. http://www.bbc.co.uk/news/uk-politics-10770239
3. This is referenced in *The Secret History of al-Qa'ida* (London: Saqi Books, 2006), p. 87.
4. http://www.hrw.org/legacy/backgrounder/mena/ansarbk020503.htm
5. http://news.bbc.co.uk/1/hi/programmes/breakfast_with_frost/3029904.stm
6. http://edition.cnn.com/2004/WORLD/asiapcf/05/06/bin.laden.message/
7. http://www.pbs.org/wgbh/pages/frontline/shows/truth/etc/script.html
8. http://www.theguardian.com/world/2003/apr/14/iraq.davidleigh
9. http://www.huffingtonpost.com/mark-levine/iraqs-constitution-and-th_b_6471.html
10. http://www.newyorker.com/magazine/2004/05/17/chain-of-command-2?currentPage=all
11. http://www.theguardian.com/us-news/cia-torture-report
12. http://www.pbs.org/newshour/updates/middle_east-jan-june03-fallujah_05-01/
13. http://www.theguardian.com/world/2003/apr/09/iraq.brianwhitaker

14. *The Secret History of al-Qaʻida*, p. 204.

15. http://col127.mail.live.com/

Chapter 3: The Origins – Part Two: The Taliban, al-Qaʻida and IS

1. http://www.telegraph.co.uk/news/worldnews/asia/afghanistan/10962105/Afghan-Taliban-warns-jihadists-to-avoid-Islamic-State-extremism.html

2. Bahri, *Guarding bin Laden: My Life in al-Qaʻida* (London: Thin Man Press, 2013), p. 218.

3. Selected Questions and Answers from Dr Ayman al-Zawahiri – Part 2, 17 April 2008, http://www.nefafoundation.org/miscellaneous/FeaturedDocs/nefazawahiri0508-2.pdf

4. http://www.telegraph.co.uk/news/worldnews/1570232/Taliban-control-half-of-Afghanistan-says-report.html

5. http://tribune.com.pk/story/741083/eid-message-mullah-omar-urges-fighters-to-protect-afghan-borders-not-interfere-in-other-countries/

6. http://www.washingtonpost.com/world/middle_east/al-Qaʻida-disavows-any-ties-with-radical-islamist-ISIS-group-in-syria-iraq/2014/02/03/2c9afc3a-8cef-11e3-98ab-fe5228217bd1_story.html

7. http://www.nefafoundation.org/miscellaneous/FeaturedDocs/nefazawahiri0408-2.pdf

8. http://www.alarabiya.net/articles/2008/05/16/49930.html

9. http://www.bbc.co.uk/news/world-middle-east-13788594

10. *Guarding bin Laden,* p. 219.

11. Ibid., p. 219.

12. http://www.theaustralian.com.au/news/world/barrel-bombs-rain-terror-in-syria/story-fnb640i6-1226817951295

13. Washin.st/104Dlyc 'Sheikh Abu Mohammad al-Adnani al-Shami, 'This is not our manhaj nor will it ever be' al-Furqan Media

14. http://www.yementimes.com/en/1808/news/4216/AQAP-announces-support-for-ISIL.htm

15. http://abualbawi.blogspot.co.uk/2014/03/sheikh-makmun-abdul-hamid-hatim-aqap-commander-announces-ISIS-will-expand-in-to-arabian-peninsula.html

16. http://www.al-monitor.com/pulse/security/2014/11/egypt-ansar-maqdis-sinai.html

17. http://abualbawi.blogspot.co.uk/2014/02/pakistani-taliban-stance-on-ISIS-in-their-war-against-the-sahwa-of-sham.html

18. http://tribune.com.pk/story/771622/
    joining-forces-ttp-declares-allegiance-to-islamic-state/
19. http://www.christianpost.com/news/boko-haram-declares-islamic-
    caliphate-in-captured-christian-town-in-nigeria-125293/
20. http://blog.lefigaro.fr/algerie/2014/08/letat-islamique-gagne-du-
    terrain-au-maghreb.html
21. http://www.longwarjournal.org/archives/2014/05/shabaab_leader_
    calls.php#ixzz3BQKkZtwu

Chapter 4: The Origins – Part Three: Syria

1. http://syriahr.com/en/2014/12/more-that-300000-people-killed-
   since-the-beginning-of-the-syrian-revolution/
2. http://www.al-monitor.com/pulse/politics/2014/07/syria-clans-
   ISIS.html
3. http://sn4hr.org/public_html/wp-content/pdf/english/Syrian%20
   security%20branches%20and%20Persons%20in%20charge.pdf
4. http://www.itv.com/news/2013-09-05/
   maher-al-assad-the-brutal-enforcer-of-the-family-regime/
5. http://www.theatlantic.com/international/archive/2012/01/the-on-
   ly-remaining-online-copy-of-vogues-asma-al-assad-profile/250753/
6. http://thelede.blogs.nytimes.com/2013/08/29/facebook-post-said-
   to-be-by-assads-son-dares-americans-to-attack/?_php=true&_
   type=blogs&_r=1
7. http://middleeastvoices.voanews.com/2012/06/syrias-tadmor-pris-
   on-massacre-reliving-horrors-of-32-years-past-81070/
8. http://www.foreignpolicy.com/articles/2011/08/05/massacre_city
9. Wright, Robin, *Dreams and Shadow: The Future of the Middle East*,
   (London: Penguin, 2009), p. 246.
10. http://www.theguardian.com/world/2006/jan/26/syria.
    rorymccarthy
11. http://www.telegraph.co.uk/news/uknews/
    terrorism-in-the-uk/9061400/Syria-releases-the-77-mastermind.
    html
12. *Guarding bin Laden*, pp. 32, 129 and 139.
13. http://syrianrefugees.eu/
14. http://www.sipri.org/databases/embargoes/eu_arms_embargoes/
    syria_LAS/eu-embargo-on-Syria
15. http://www.bbc.com/news/world-middle-east-22906965
16. How The Free Syrian Army Became A Largely Criminal Enterprise,

Daily Telegraph, 30 November 2013, http://www.telegraph.co.uk/news/worldnews/middleeast/syria/10485970/Syria-dispatch-from-band-of-brothers-to-princes-of-war.html

17. http://www.nytimes.com/2015/01/15/world/middleeast/kerry-backs-syrian-peace-talks-in-russia.html?_r=0

18. http://www.telegraph.co.uk/news/worldnews/middleeast/syria/9219643/Syrian-opposition-undermined-by-splits-and-infighting-emails-show.html

19. http://bikyamasr.com/62200/jordan-cites-rise-in-attempts-to-smuggle-arms-into-syria/

20. http://www.telegraph.co.uk/news/worldnews/middleeast/syria/10485970/Syria-dispatch-from-band-of-brothers-to-princes-of-war.html

21. Ibid.

22. http://www.telegraph.co.uk/news/worldnews/middleeast/syria/10930345/Syrian-rebel-army-sacked-over-corruption-claims.html

23. http://www.reuters.com/article/2013/03/09/us-syria-crisis-peacekeepers-idUSBRE92808H20130309

24. http://therealnews.com/t2/index.php?option=com_content&task=view&id=31&Itemid=74&jumival=12373

Chapter 5: Abu Bakr al-Baghdadi: A Portrait of 'Caliph Ibrahim'

1. http://www.aljazeera.com/news/middleeast/2014/06/fierce-ambition-isil-baghdadi-201461214224218864.html

2. http://www.telegraph.co.uk/news/worldnews/middleeast/iraq/10948846/How-a-talented-footballer-became-worlds-most-wanted-man-Abu-Bakr-al-Baghdadi.html

3. http://www.bbc.co.uk/news/world-middle-east-30330461

4. http://edition.cnn.com/2014/12/03/world/meast/ISIS-baghdadi-family/index.html?hpt=hp_t1

5. http://www.dailymail.co.uk/news/article-2963380/Scheming-Bride-ISIS-idolise-Mesmerising-tale-wife-terror-chief-inspires-girls-join-bloody-ranks.html

6. http://www.telegraph.co.uk/news/worldnews/middleeast/iraq/10948846/How-a-talented-footballer-became-worlds-most-wanted-man-Abu-Bakr-al-Baghdadi.html

7. Ibid.

8. http://www.independent.co.uk/news/world/middle-east/

dress-like-a-jihadist-ISIS-and-terrorrelated-merchandise-flogged-online-and-in-indonesian-stores-9560230.html

Chapter 6: Consolidation and Expansion

1. http://www.aljazeera.com/news/middleeast/2013/07/20137127710849717.html
2. http://www.reuters.com/article/2013/07/22/us-iraq-violence-idUSBRE96L0RM20130722
3. http://www.bbc.co.uk/news/world-middle-east-24403003
4. http://www.newyorker.com/magazine/2014/01/27/going-the-distance-2?currentPage=all
5. http://www.theguardian.com/world/2014/jun/11/mosul-ISIS-gunmen-middle-east-states
6. http://english.alarabiya.net/en/News/middle-east/2014/06/13/Report-ISIS-steals-429mn-in-Mosul-capture.html
7. http://www.telegraph.co.uk/news/worldnews/middleeast/iraq/10913275/ISIS-storms-Saddam-era-chemical-weapons-complex-in-Iraq.html
8. http://www.washingtonpost.com/world/middle_east/islamic-state-militants-allegedly-used-chlorine-gas-against-iraqi-security-forces/2014/10/23/c865c943-1c93-4ac0-a7ed-033218f15cbb_story.html
9. http://www.theguardian.com/world/2014/jun/16/terrifying-rise-of-ISIS-iraq-executions
10. http://www.aljazeera.com/news/middleeast/2014/06/isil-declares-new-islamic-caliphate-201462917326669749.html
11. http://reliefweb.int/report/iraq/un-casualty-figures-july-2014-anbar-province-excluded
12. http://eaworldview.com/2014/11/syria-daily-jabhat-al-nusra-denies-alliance-islamic-state/
13. http://www.independent.co.uk/news/world/middle-east/iraq-crisis-islamic-militants-buried-alive-yazidi-women-and-children-in-attack-that-killed-500-9659695.html
14. http://www.theguardian.com/world/2014/oct/04/turkey-troops-ISIS-siege-kobani-refugees-rape-and-murder
15. http://barnabasfund.org/UK/Syria.html
16. http://www.globalpost.com/dispatch/news/regions/middle-east/syria/140821/text-last-email-islamic-state-sent-foley-familys

17. http://www.dailymail.co.uk/news/article-2746379/Doctor-called-desperately-ill-British-hostage-held-brutal-Jihadi-John-Aid-worker-tortured-Tasers-digestive-problems.html

18. Ibid.

19. Abbottabad letters number 0019, https://www.ctc.usma.edu/posts/letters-from-abbottabad-bin-ladin-sidelined

20. http://www.yementimes.com/en/1808/news/4216/AQAP-announces-support-for-ISIL.htm

21. http://www.shamikh1.info/vb/showthread.php?t=148330

22. http://www.asianews.it/news-en/Indonesia,-jailed-Islamic-extremist-leader-swears-allegiance-ISIS-31802.html

23. http://www.npr.org/2014/10/27/359403462/in-pakistan-islamic-state-draws-in-taliban-commanders

24. http://online.wsj.com/articles/pakistani-taliban-leaders-pledge-allegiance-to-islamic-state-1413283423

Chapter 7: Within Islamic State

1. http://www.islamweb.net/emainpage/articles/167309/al-khansaa-poetess-and-mother-of-martyrs

2. http://www.alaraby.co.uk/english/news/cfcffec9-d966-4f3d-8ffc-aa2ef16f9a5d

3. The Times January 17 2015 'Militants throw gay men to death from building', http://www.thetimes.co.uk/tto/news/world/middleeast/iraq/article4325814.ece

4. http://www.alaraby.co.uk/english/news/cfcffec9-d966-4f3d-8ffc-aa2ef16f9a5d

5. Ibid.

6. http://www.newsweek.com/islamic-state-bans-math-social-studies-evolution-classrooms-271096

7. http://www.alaraby.co.uk/english/news/cfcffec9-d966-4f3d-8ffc-aa2ef16f9a5d

8. http://www.independent.co.uk/news/world/middle-east/ISIS-urges-more-attacks-on-western-disbelievers-9749512.html

9. http://www.telegraph.co.uk/news/worldnews/middleeast/iraq/10956280/Inside-the-leadership-of-Islamic-State-how-the-new-caliphate-is-run.html#sthash.tmvPjtou.dpuf

10. http://www.dailymail.co.uk/news/article-2914358/What-did-expect-Towie-fan-travelled-Syria-infant-son-tells-shock-living-war-zone-jihadists-treatment-women-forced-escape-border.html

11. http://www.theguardian.com/world/2014/oct/27/citizens-mosul-iraq-economic-collapse-repression-ISIS-islamic-state

12. http://www.treasury.gov/press-center/press-releases/Pages/jl2672.aspx

13. http://www.bloomberg.com/news/2014-09-13/islamic-state-bombs-iraq-oil-refinery-tank-catches-fire.html

14. http://www.longwarjournal.org/threat-matrix/archives/2014/09/islamic_state_assaults_baiji_0.php

15. http://www.bbc.co.uk/news/world-middle-east-29370484

16. http://www.cnbc.com/id/102115652#.

17. http://www.businessinsider.com/breakdown-of-the-oil-assets-ISIS-controls-2014-9#ixzz3HSuNAb7C

18. http://www.newyorker.com/tech/elements/ISIS-looting-campaign-iraq-syria

19. Ibid.

20. http://news.usni.org/2014/10/27/ISIS-funds-terror-black-market-antiquities-trade

21. http://www.docdroid.net/j8dr/dabiq-magazine-issue-4.pdf.html

22. Ibid.

23. http://mashable.com/2014/09/16/ISIS-slave-iraq/

24. http://news.yahoo.com/smuggled-oil--sex-slaves--kidnap-pings--crime--inside-the-islamic-state-s-million-dollar-money-stream-214126980.html

25. http://www.cbsnews.com/news/multiple-kidnappings-for-ransom-funding-ISIS-source-says/

26. http://www.independent.co.uk/news/world/middle-east/war-with-ISIS-islamic-militants-have-army-of-200000-claims-kurdish-leader-9863418.html

27. http://edition.cnn.com/2014/09/11/world/meast/ISIS-syria-iraq/index.html

28. http://www.numbeo.com/cost-of-living/country_result.jsp?country=Iraq

29. http://www.academia.edu/7632564/ISIS_MILITARY_STRATEGY

30. http://www.independent.co.uk/news/world/middle-east/ISIS-and-alqaida-agree-to-end-fighting-and-join-against-their-opponents-9859999.html

31. http://news.nationalpost.com/2014/11/11/moderate-syrian-rebels-defecting-to-ISIS-blaming-lack-of-u-s-support-and-weapons/

32. *The Times* 17 January 2015 'ISIS doubles caliphate in Syria as allies

bomb Iraq' Catherine Philip, http://www.thetimes.co.uk/tto/news/
world/middleeast/article4325819.ece

33. http://www.academia.edu/7632564/
ISIS_MILITARY_STRATEGY

Chapter 8: The Management of Savagery

1. http://www.theguardian.com/world/2014/oct/04/
turkey-troops-ISIS-siege-kobani-refugees-rape-and-murder

2. http://rt.com/news/222319-ISIS-boy-execution-hostages/

3. Donald G. Dutton, *The Psychology of Genocide, Massacres and
Extreme Violence* (Greenwood, 2007), p. X.

4. http://www.chathamhouse.org/expert/comment/16541?g-
clid=CjoKEQiAuf2lBRDW07y3z6f96awBEiQA-
oIngJllgwkbWqoyLB8peP7CUVLkwwU2SyF3nf_
R8VQUVEuMaAjoi8P8HAQ

5. R. J. Rummel, 'Death By Government', http://www.hawaii.edu/
powerkills/NOTE1.HTM

6. *The Psychology of Genocide, Massacres and Extreme Violence*, p. 5.

7. Iris Chang, *The Rape of Nanking*, http://bit.ly/1BopIIa, p. 59.

8. http://www.dailymail.co.uk/news/article-1340207/I-didnt-think-
Iraqis-humans-says-U-S-soldier-raped-14-year-old-girl-killing-her-
family.html]

9. suite.io/michael-streich/252q2nv

10. http://middleeast.about.com/od/terrorism/a/bin-laden-jihad.htm

11. http://www.historynet.com/muhammad-the-warrior-prophet.htm

12. *The Secret History of al-Qa'ida*, p. 221.

Chapter 9: The Caliph's Foreign Fighters

1. http://belfercenter.ksg.harvard.edu/files/The_Rise_of_Muslim_
Foreign_Fighters.pdf

2. http://www.globalsecurity.org/military/library/news/2005/09/
mil-050911-rferl03.htm

3. http://www.cbsnews.com/8301-502684_162-4524075-502684.html

4. http://www.dailymail.co.uk/news/article-2742630/There-don-t-
know-Hagel-says-100-US-citizens-fighting-alongside-ISIS-Middle-
East.html

5. http://www.washingtoninstitute.org/policy-analysis/view/
who-are-the-foreign-fighters-in-syria

6. http://www.thetimes.co.uk/tto/news/world/middleeast/

article4209768.ece

7. http://www.nytimes.com/2014/10/01/world/europe/ISIS-europe-muslim-radicalization.html

8. http://www.washingtoninstitute.org/policy-analysis/view/convoy-of-martyrs-in-the-levant

9. *Paris Match,* 24 March 2014, http://www.parismatch.com/Actu/International/Les-escadrons-francais-du-Djihad-555918

10. http://www.dailymail.co.uk/news/article-2742630/There-don-t-know-Hagel-says-100-US-citizens-fighting-alongside-ISIS-Middle-East.html

11. *Toronto Star* 23 August 2013

12. http://www.jamestown.org/fileadmin/Recent_Reports/Trans_amd_Speaker_NCC09142006/Al-Shishani-14Sep06.pdf

13. Evan Kohlmann, *Al-Qaida's Jihad in Europe* (New York: Berg, 2004), p. 174.

14. http://www.jamestown.org/programs/nca/single/?tx_ttnews[tt_news]=1773&tx_ttnews[backPid]=185&no_cache=1

15. http://www.kavkaz.org.uk/eng/content/2011/08/30/15062.shtml [interview with emir Dokku Umarov 30 August 2011]

16. *The Diplomat,* Tokyo 1 February 2014. http://thediplomat.com/2014/02/indonesian-extremists-drawn-to-syrian-conflict/

17. www.cfr.org/publication/12717/alqaeda_in_the_islamic_maghreb_aka_salafist_group_for_preaching_and_combat

18. 'Die hard in Derna' cable wikileaks website, http://www.telegraph.co.uk/news/wikileaks-files/libya-wikileaks/8294818/DIE-HARD-IN-DERNA.html

19. http://www.theguardian.com/world/2015/jan/29/libya-peace-talks-urgency-after-ISIS-attack-tripoli-hotel

20. http://edition.cnn.com/2012/07/28/world/meast/syria-libya-fighters/index.html?iid=article_sidebar

21. http://www.independent.co.uk/news/world/asia/british-muslims-have-become-a-mainstay-of-the-global-jihad-1040232.html

22. https://www.opendemocracy.net/article/conflicts/global_security/the-thirty-year-war-revisited

23. http://www.telegraph.co.uk/news/worldnews/asia/pakistan/6226935/Pakistan-discovers-village-of-white-German-al-Qa'ida-insurgents.html

24. Researcher Professor Kamaldeep Bhui from London University has found, through extensive interviews and surveys, that women are just as likely to espouse the radical views of the extremists

as men, http://www.theguardian.com/world/2014/oct/15/
female-british-muslims-vulnerable-radicalisation-men

25. http://www.theguardian.com/world/2014/sep/06/
british-women-married-to-jihad-ISIS-syria

26. 'Western Foreign Fighters' Institute for Strategic Dialogue,
December 2014. Briggs & Silverman. http://www.strategicdialogue.
org/ISDJ2784_Western_foreign_fighters_V7_WEB.pdf

27. http://www.express.co.uk/news/uk/525715/
Express-Debate-British-jihadists-return-UK

28. http://www.thedailybeast.com/articles/2015/01/25/after-charlie-
hebdo-attacks-french-muslims-face-increased-threats.html

29. http://www.mirror.co.uk/news/uk-news/
terror-group-islamic-state-talent-5039268

30. http://www.newstatesman.com/religion/2014/08/what-
jihadists-who-bought-islam-dummies-amazon-tell-us-about-
radicalisation

31. 'We can't stop jihadists going to Syria admits Turkish PM' Roger
Boyes, *The Times*, 22 January 2015, http://www.thetimes.co.uk/tto/
news/world/middleeast/article4330184.ece

32. http://www.standard.co.uk/news/crime/exclusive-suicide-bomber-
brit-worked-as-driver-for-hate-cleric-omar-bakri-9125787.html

33. http://www.huffingtonpost.com/2014/10/17/ISIS-
kids_n_6002828.html?utm_hp_ref=politics&ir=Politics

34. http://www.theguardian.com/world/2014/sep/29/
schoolgirl-jihadis-female-islamists-leaving-home-join-ISIS-iraq-syria

35. http://www.theguardian.com/world/2014/sep/06/
british-women-married-to-jihad-ISIS-syria

36. Schoolgirl jihadists, *Guardian*, 29 September 2014,
http://www.theguardian.com/world/2014/sep/29/
schoolgirl-jihadis-female-islamists-leaving-home-join-ISIS-iraq-syria

37. Ibid.

38. http://www.dailymail.co.uk/news/article-2795771/british-terror-
ists-fighting-ISIS-iraq-syria-tried-high-treason-reveals-foreign-secre-
tary-philip-hammond.html

39. http://www.mirror.co.uk/news/uk-news/
ISIS-defectors-coming-home-should-4173302

40. http://www.theguardian.com/world/2014/sep/06/
richard-barrett-mi6-ISIS-counter-terrorism

41. http://www.ft.com/cms/s/0/ce2db704-b52f-11e4-b186-00144fe-
ab7de.html#slide0

42. http://news.yahoo.com/uk-grapples-delicate-issue-returning-jihadists-062207574.html

Chapter 10: A Dangerous Game: The West's Attempts to Exploit Radical Islam

1. Mark Curtis, *Secret Affairs: Britain's Collusion with Radical Islam*, (Serpents Tail, London, 2010), p. 6.
2. Ibid.
3. http://www.academia.edu/8640525/Arab_Religious_Nationalism_Rashid_Rida_and_the_Caliphate
4. http://www.telstudies.org/writings/works/articles_essays/181104_reconstruction%20of%20arabia.shtml
5. https://web.archive.org/web/20131105011128/http://www.nationmaster.com/graph/mil_gul_war_coa_for-military-gulf-war-coalition-forces
6. http://www.alaraby.co.uk/english/news/37241d2e-ba35-41dd-be0c-d6bb910195d0
7. https://www.congress.gov/bill/113th-congress/house-bill/5194
8. http://www.newenglishreview.org/Jerry_Gordon/How_the_CIA_Helped_The_Muslim_Brotherhood_Infiltrate_the_West/
9. These were IRM, Gulbuddin faction, Ittehad-i-Islami, Jamiat-i-islami, NLF and NIFA.
10. These were Harakat-i-Islami, the Afghan branch of Hezbollah, Nasr Party, COIRGA, Shura Party, IRM, UOIF and the Raad Party.
11. MSNBC, 8/24/1998, http://www.nbcnews.com/id/3340101
12. *Guardian,* 20 September 2003, http://www.theguardian.com/world/2003/sep/20/afghanistan.weekend7
13. *Secret Affairs*, p. 135.
14. Pervez Musharraf, *In the Line of fire: A Memoir,* Simon & Schuster, New York, 2006, p. 208.
15. http://www.margaretthatcher.org/document/108323
16. http://www.hrw.org/middle-eastn-africa/saudi-arabia
17. http://www.theguardian.com/world/2005/sep/28/iraq.military
18. *Secret Affairs*, p. 303.
19. http://news.bbc.co.uk/1/hi/uk/5236896.stm

Chapter 11: Saudi Arabia, Wahhabism and Islamic State

1. 'Saudis have lost the right to take Sunni leadership', David Gardner, *Financial Times* 7 August 2014, http://www.ft.com/cms/s/0/

ab1b61c4-1cb6-11e4-b4c7-00144feabdc0.html#axzz3TLVTeFRf

2. http://www.globalsecurity.org/military/world/para/isil-2.htm
3. http://www.huffingtonpost.com/alastair-crooke/ISIS-aim-saudi-arabia_b_5748744.html
4. http://www.missionislam.com/knowledge/companions.htm
5. http://www.pbs.org/wgbh/pages/frontline/shows/terrorism/interviews/bandar.html
6. http://www.theguardian.com/world/2013/jan/01/saudi-arabia-riyadh-poverty-inequality
7. http://eu-digest.blogspot.co.uk/2011/03/faisal-ahmed-abdul-ahadwas-saudi.html
8. Ibid.
9. http://www.theguardian.com/world/2010/dec/05/wikileaks-cables-saudi-terrorist-funding
10. https://www.youtube.com/watch?v=mxou-JayUeE
11. http://www.dailymail.co.uk/news/article-2665307/Did-Saudi-preacher-groom-jihadi-Britons.html
12. 'How Saudi Arabia Helped ISIS Take over the North of Iraq', Patrick Cockburn, Independent 13 July 2014, http://www.independent.co.uk/voices/comment/iraq-crisis-how-saudi-arabia-helped-ISIS-take-over-the-north-of-the-country-9602312.html
13. http://www.breitbart.com/national-security/2014/12/09/saudi-arabia-rounds-up-135-terror-suspects-as-king-appoints-new-officials-to-supervise-radical-clerics/
14. http://www.albawabaeg.com/879

Conclusion

1. http://english.alarabiya.net/en/views/news/middle-east/2014/09/13/ISIS-has-grown-larger-than-Kuwait-s-army-.html
2. http://www.gulf-daily-news.com/NewsDetails.aspx?storyid=383552
3. http://www.theguardian.com/world/2015/feb/15/ISIS-post-video-allegedly-showing-mass-beheading-of-coptic-christian-hostages
4. http://www.reuters.com/article/2015/02/20/us-libya-security-idUSKBN0LO0SS20150220
5. http://www.dailymail.co.uk/news/article-2957344/ISIS-incredible-force-Europe-s-doorstep-Terrorists-Libya-beheaded-21-Egyptian-Christians-parade-fleet-brand-new-police-cars-cheering-children.html

6. http://www.telegraph.co.uk/news/worldnews/europe/8725443/
   Libya-Col-Gaddafi-directed-tens-of-thousands-of-refugees-towards-
   Italy-as-human-bombs.html
7. http://www.independent.co.uk/news/world/middle-east/
   islamic-state-battle-of-tripoli-is-won-but-hearts-and-minds-are-
   lost-9824297.html
8. http://www.traveller.com.au/
   turkeys-20-billion-tourism-industry-under-threat-20fto
9. http://www.bbc.co.uk/news/world-middle-east-25882504
10. http://www.theguardian.com/world/2014/jun/12/
    crisis-in-iraq-insurgents-take-major-cities-live-blog
11. http://uk.reuters.com/article/2015/02/04/
    uk-mideast-crisis-killing-idUKKBN0L71Y720150204
12. http://www.jpost.com/Middle-East/
    Report-Israel-US-prepared-to-help-Jordan-fight-ISIS-360848
13. http://www.telegraph.co.uk/news/worldnews/africaandindian-
    ocean/nigeria/11337722/Boko-Haram-is-now-a-mini-Islamic-State-
    with-its-own-territory.html
14. http://english.alarabiya.net/en/News/africa/2014/07/13/Boko-
    Haram-voices-support-for-ISIS-Baghdadi.html
15. http://www.eurasiareview.
    com/26112011-aqim-emir-laaouar-speaks-out/
16. http://www.ft.com/cms/s/0/d964dcb6-3e82-11e4-adef-00144fe-
    abdc0.html#axzz3HXwwtQPR
17. http://www.reuters.com/article/2015/01/30/
    us-yemen-qaeda-idUSKBN0L31HE20150130
18. http://www.bbc.co.uk/news/world-middle-east-31449976
19. http://edition.cnn.com/2014/08/27/opinion/
    iraq-opinion-united-states-cost-of-war/
20. http://www.un.org/press/en/2014/sc11520.doc.htm
21. http://www.dailymail.co.uk/news/article-2959848/Warning-ISIS-
    pirates-Mediterranean-bring-havoc-European-waters-taking-coastal-
    towns-Libya.html
22. http://www.aljazeera.com/news/2015/02/assad-syria-informed-
    strikes-isil-150210071709375.html
23. http://www.bbc.co.uk/news/world-middle-east-31070249
24. http://www.theguardian.com/world/2015/mar/14/
    islamic-state-isis-used-chemical-weapons-peshmerga-kurds
25. http://www.usatoday.com/story/news/politics/2014/10/06/
    leon-panetta-memoir-worthy-fights/16737615/

INDEX